A CHOICE OF COMIC
AND CURIOUS VERSE

J. M. Cohen, born in London in 1903, is the author of
many Penguin translations, including versions for the
Classics of Cervantes, Rabelais, and Montaigne. He
has also edited the three volumes of *Comic and Curious
Verse*, *Writers in the New Cuba*, and *Latin American
Writing Today*. He has written a good deal of criticism,
broadcasts on a variety of subjects, and has read widely
in several languages. His particular interests are poetry,
and the literature of Spanish America, which he has
visited several times. He now lives in the country and,
though his vision no longer enables him to read, con-
tinues to work and keep up with his favourite subjects.

A CHOICE OF
Comic and
Curious Verse

Edited by J. M. Cohen

Penguin Books

PENGUIN BOOKS

Published by the Penguin Group
27 Wrights Lane, London W8 5TZ, England
Viking Penguin Inc., 40 West 23rd Street, New York, New York 10010, USA
Penguin Books Australia Ltd, Ringwood, Victoria, Australia
Penguin Books Canada Ltd, 2801 John Street, Markham, Ontario, Canada L3R 1B4
Penguin Books (NZ) Ltd, 182–190 Wairau Road, Auckland 10, New Zealand

Penguin Books Ltd, Registered Offices: Harmondsworth, Middlesex, England

Most of the poems in this anthology previously appeared in
The Penguin Book of Comic and Curious Verse, 1952; *More Comic and Curious Verse*, 1956;
and *Yet More Comic and Curious Verse*, 1959

This collection first published 1975
Reprinted 1976, 1978, 1980, 1981, 1983, 1986, 1989

Selection copyright © J. M. Cohen, 1952, 1956, 1959, 1975
All rights reserved

Printed and bound in Great Britain by
Cox & Wyman Ltd, Reading
Set in Monotype Fournier

CONTENTS

ACKNOWLEDGEMENTS

The editor gratefully acknowledges permission to reproduce copyright poems in this book.

W. H. AUDEN: Reprinted from *Collected Shorter Poems 1927–1957* by W. H. Auden by permission of Faber & Faber Ltd. HILAIRE BELLOC: 'Lines to a Don', 'On a General Election', and 'Fatigue' from *Sonnets and Verse;* 'Henry King', 'Matilda', 'Charles Augustus Fortescue', and 'The Python' from *Cautionary Verses*, both published by Gerald Duckworth, reprinted by permission of the publisher and A. D. Peters & Company. ARNOLD BENNETT: By permission of Mrs Cheston Bennett. E. C. BENTLEY: By permission of Mr Nicolas Bentley; NICOLAS BENTLEY: By permission of the author. JOHN BETJEMAN: Reprinted from *Collected Poems* by John Betjeman by permission of John Murray (Publishers) Ltd. MORRIS BISHOP: 'We Have Been Here Before' reprinted by permission of G. P. Putnam's Sons from *Spilt Milk* by Morris Bishop. Copyright 1942 by Morris Bishop. renewed 1969 by Morris Bishop. 'Lines Composed in Fifth Row Centre', 'There's Money in Mother and Father', and 'The Roadside Litterateur' from *A Bowl of Bishop*. Copyright 1954 by Morris Bishop. Used by permission of the publisher. the Dial Press, Inc. First published in the *New Yorker*. J. B. BOOTHROYD: Reproduced from *Punch* magazine. W. BRIDGES ADAMS: Reprinted from *To Charlotte While Shaving*, Barrie Books Ltd, by permission of A. D. Peters & Company. C. W. BRODRIBB: By permission of Mr Conaut Brodribb. HARRY BROWN: Reprinted from *Selected Poems* by Harry Brown by permission of the author and Secker & Warburg Ltd. GERALD BULLET: 'Footnote to Tennyson', first published in *Punch* magazine, reprinted by permission of A. D. Peters & Company. NORMAN CAMERON: Reprinted from *Collected Poems 1905–53* by permission of the Author's Literary Estate and the Hogarth Press. JOHN AND ERNESTINE CARTER: By permission of the authors. G. K. CHESTERTON: Reprinted from *The Collected Poems of G. K. Chesterton* by permission of Miss D. Collins and Methuen & Company. S. J. COHEN: By permission of the author. E. E. CUMMINGS: Reprinted from *Complete Poems* Vol. 1 by permission of MacGibbon & Kee. COLIN CURZON: Reprinted from *Flying Wild* by permission of Hurst &

ACKNOWLEDGEMENTS

Blackett. DAVID DAICHES: By permission of the author. WALTER DE LA MARE: Reprinted from *Collected Rhymes and Verses* and *Peacock Pie*, Faber & Faber Ltd, by permission of the Literary Trustees of Walter de la Mare and The Society of Authors as their representative. PATRIC DICKINSON: By permission of the author. LAWRENCE DURRELL: Reprinted from *Collected Poems* by permission of Faber & Faber Ltd. GAVIN EWART: By permission of the author. J. E. FAULKS: By permission of the authoress. BERNARD FERGUSSON: Reproduced from *Punch* magazine. MICHAEL FLANDERS: By permission of the author. HARRY GRAHAM: 'Poetical Economy' from *Deportmental Ditties* and 'Late Last Night' from *Ruthless Rhymes for Heartless Homes*, reprinted by permission of the Estate of the late Harry Graham. 'Tender Heartedness', 'Misfortunes Never Come Singly', and 'Mr Jones' from *Ruthless Rhymes*; 'Carelessness', 'Compensation', 'Quiet Fun', and 'Indifference' from *More Ruthless Rhymes*, reprinted by permission of Edward Arnold Ltd. ROBERT GRAVES: Reprinted from *Collected Poems*, Cassell & Co. Ltd, by permission of the author. ARTHUR GUITERMAN: Reprinted from *Gaily the Troubador*, E. P. Dutton & Co., Inc., by permission of Mrs V. L. Guiterman. SAMUEL HOFFENSTEIN: Reprinted from *A Treasure of Humorous Verse* by Samuel Hoffenstein by permission of Liveright Publishers, New York. Copyright © 1946 by Liveright Publishing Corporation. A. E. HOUSMAN: Reprinted from Laurence Housman's *A. E. H.* by permission of Jonathan Cape Ltd and The Society of Authors as the literary representative of the Estate of A. E. Housman. P. M. HUBBARD: Reproduced from *Punch* magazine. ALDOUS HUXLEY: Reprinted from *Leda* by permission of Mrs Laura Huxley and Chatto & Windus. PAUL JENNINGS: 'Galoshes' from *Model Oddlies*, 'Garbled Gifts' from *Even Oddlier*, and 'In the Swim' from *Oddly Boddlikins*, reprinted by permission of Max Reinhardt Ltd and the *Observer*. ERICH KÄSTNER: By permission of the translator, Mr Michael Hamburger. E. V. KNOX: Reproduced from *Punch* magazine. ALLAN M. LAING: By permission of Florence Laing. D. H. LAWRENCE: Reprinted from *The Complete Poems of D. H. Lawrence*, William Heinemann Ltd, by permission of Laurence Pollinger Ltd and the Estate of the late Mrs Frieda Lawrence. KENNETH LILLINGTON: Reproduced from *Punch* magazine. J. A. LINDON: By permission of the author. E. V. LUCAS: By permission of Methuen & Co. Ltd. PHYLLIS MCGINLEY: Reprinted from *Times Three*, Secker & Warburg Ltd, by permission of Laurence Pollinger Ltd. WILLIAM MCGONAGALL: Reprinted from *Poetic Gems* by permission of Gerald Duckworth & Co. Ltd. H. S. MACKINTOSH: By permission of the author. F. A. V. MADDEN:

ACKNOWLEDGEMENTS

By permission of the author. DON MARQUIS: Reprinted from *Archy's Life of Mehitabel*, by permission of Faber & Faber Ltd. DONALD MATTAM: Reproduced from *Punch* magazine. HUGHES MEARNS: Reprinted from *Innocent Merriment*, compiled by Franklin Adams, McGraw-Hill Book Company, by permission of Hardee Barovick & Konecky, New York. JAMES MICHIE: By permission of the author. EWART MILNE: Reprinted from *Once More to Tourney* by permission of Centaur Press Ltd. CHRISTOPHER MORLEY: Reprinted from *Streamlines*, by permission of Faber & Faber Ltd. J. E. MORPURGO: By permission of the author. J. B. MORTON: Reprinted by permission of A. D. Peters & Company. OGDEN NASH: 'What's the Use', 'The Turtle', 'England Expects', 'Reflections on Ice Breaking' from *The Face is Familiar*; 'Samson Agonistes', 'Family Court', 'Lather as You Go', 'Song of the Open Road', 'The Firefly', 'No Doctors Today, Thank You', 'The Perfect Husband', 'Reflection on Babies', 'The Parent', 'Polterguest, My Polterguest', 'The Octopus', 'The Ant', 'The Jellyfish' from *Family Reunion*; 'The Japanese', 'A Bas Ben Adhem', 'Requiem', 'Sigmund Freud' from *Many Long Years Ago*; 'Lines on Facing Forty' from *Good Intentions*; 'Stag Night, Palaeolithic' from *Versus*; 'Peekaboo, I Almost See You' from *Private Dining Room*, reprinted by permission of J. M. Dent & Sons Ltd. 'The Dog' from *Everyone but Thee and Me*, and 'Chacun à son Berlitz' from *Collected Verse 1929 On*, reprinted by permission of the Estate of the late Ogden Nash. D. R. PEDDY: By permission of Mrs Pauline A. Peddy. DANIEL PETTIWARD: Reproduced from *Punch* magazine. WILLIAM PLOMER: Reprinted from *Collected Poems*, by permission of the author and Jonathan Cape Ltd. A. G. PRYS-JONES: By permission of the author. A. B. RAMSAY: 'Sui Prodigus' from *Flos Malvae* and 'Epitaph on a Syndic' from *Frondes Salicus*, reprinted by permission of the author and Cambridge University Press. JUSTIN RICHARDSON: Reproduced from *Punch* magazine. E. V. RIEU: By permission of N. Rieu. SIR OWEN SEAMAN: Reproduced from *Punch* magazine. BERNARD SHAW: By permission of The Society of Authors on behalf of the Bernard Shaw Estate. F. SIDGWICK: Reprinted from *Some Verse*, by permission of the author and Sidgwick & Jackson Ltd. ARNOLD SILCOCK: By permission of Winant, Towers Ltd. F. SINCLAIR: Reproduced from *Punch* magazine. EDITH SITWELL: Reprinted from *Façade and Other Poems 1920–1935* by permission of Gerald Duckworth & Co. Ltd. OSBERT SITWELL: Reprinted from *Selected Poems Old and New* by permission of Gerald Duckworth & Co. Ltd. JOHN SKELTON: 'At Elinor Rumming's Ale-House' from *The Complete Poems of John Skelton*, edited by Philip Henderson,

FOREWORD

The three collections of *Comic and Curious Verse* appeared in the fifties and sold by their hundred thousands. They covered the whole tradition of English comic verse from the masters – Hood, Lear, Carroll, and the rest – to anonymous lampoonists of the eighteenth century and hitherto unpublished practitioners of the twentieth. In the late sixties they fell out of print, and we are here reviving a choice of the best in the three books in a single volume.

Is this choice, I wonder, a 'period piece'? Has the idea of comic poetry so changed in twenty years that my fiftyish choices will seem quaint or antiquated? I cannot think that good poetry, serious or comic, decays by growing older. A new generation sees new qualities in it.

But would an anthology of comic verse compiled in the seventies fundamentally differ from this one? I remember a review by Mr Kingsley Amis of the last of my volumes in which he scolded me for excluding verses that circulated in the pubs and the *graffiti* in public lavatories. Here, he suggested, was to be found the true tradition of English comic poetry. I contend, on the contrary, that the true tradition is literary, and if there are any gems on walls of lavatories they were scrawled there by some inglorious and 'unlucky Jim' who once did a course in 'Eng. Lit'. The breaking of the language-taboos in the sixties would enable a contemporary anthology to print 'The Ram of Derbyshire' and 'Esquimaux Nell', which I had to exclude. But when I consider the abuse I received, from a lady in Wimbledon I think, for including 'Hans Carvel', I do not now regret these exclusions.

The choice is submitted for the approval and enjoyment of a new generation in the hope that it will find much here to please.

J. M. C.

Knappswood,
October 1973

At Elinor Rumming's Ale-house

Then Margery Milkduck
Her kirtle she did uptuck
An inch above her knee
Her legs that ye might see;
But they were sturdy and stubbéd,
Mighty pestles and clubbéd,
As fair and as white
As the foot of a kite:
She was somewhat foul,
Crooked-necked like an owl;
And yet she brought her fees,
A cantel of Essex cheese,
Was well a foot thick
Full of maggots quick:
It was huge and great,
And mighty strong meat
For the devil to eat
It was tart and pungete![1]

Another set of sluts:
.Some brought walnuts,
Some apples, some pears,
Some brought their clipping shears,
Some brought this and that,
Some brought I wot n'ere what;
Some brought their husband's hat,
Some puddings and links,
Some tripes that stinks.
But of all this throng
One came them among,
She seemed half a leech,
And began to preach
Of the Tuesday in the week
When the mare doth kick,

1. pungent.

Of the virtue of an unset leek,
Of her husband's breek;
With the feathers of a quail
She could to Bordeaux sail;
And with good ale barme
She could make a charme
To help withal a stitch:
She seemed to be a witch.

Another brought two goslings
That were naughty froslings[1];
She brought them in a wallet,
She was a comely callet[2]:
The goslings were untied,
Elinor began to chide,
'They be wretchocks[3] thou hast brought,
They are sheer shaking nought!'

JOHN SKELTON

On Otho

Three daughters Otho hath, his onely heirs,
But will by no means let them learn to write;
'Cause, after his own humour much he fears,
They'll one day learn, love-letters to indite.
The youngest now's with childe; who taught her then,
Or of her self learn'd she to hold her pen?

ANON.

---

1. worthless frostbitten things.   2. jade.   3. the smallest of the brood.

Sir Hudibras, His Passing Worth

He was in *Logick* a great Critick,
Profoundly skill'd in Analytick.
He could distinguish, and divide
A Hair 'twixt *South* and *South-West* side:
On either which he would dispute,
Confute, change hands, and still confute.
He'd undertake to prove by force
Of Argument, a Man's no Horse.
He'd prove a Buzard is no Fowl,
And that a *Lord* may be an Owl;
A Calf an *Alderman*, a Goose a *Justice*,
And Rooks *Committee-men* and *Trustees*.
He'd run in Debt by Disputation,
And pay with Ratiocination,
All this by Syllogism, true
In Mood and Figure, he would do.

In *Mathematicks* he was greater
Than *Tycho Brahe*, or *Erra Pater*:
For he by *Geometrick* scale
Could take the size of *Pots of Ale;*
Resolve by Signes and Tangents straight,
If *Bread* or *Butter* wanted weight;
And wisely tell what hour o'th day
The Clock does strike, by *Algebra*.

Beside he was a shrewd *Philosopher;*
And had read every Text and gloss over:
What e'er the crabbed'st Author hath
He understood b'implicit Faith,
What ever *Sceptick* could inquere for;
For every *why* he had a *wherefore:*
Knew more then forty of them do,
As far as words and terms could go.
All which he understood by Rote,

And as occasion serv'd, would quote;
No matter whether right or wrong:
They might be either said or sung.
His Notions fitted things so well,
That which was which he could not tell;
But oftentimes mistook the one
For th'other, as Great Clerks have done.
He could reduce all things to Acts
And knew their Natures by Abstracts,
Where Entity and Quiddity
The Ghosts of defunct Bodies flie;
Where Truth in Person does appear,
Like words congeal'd in Northern Air.
He knew *what's what*, and that's as high
As *Metaphysick* wit can fly.
In *School Divinity* as able
As he that hight *Irrefragable;*
Profound in all the Nominal
And real ways beyond them all,
And with as delicate a Hand
Could twist as tough a Rope of Sand,
And weave fine Cobwebs, fit for skull
That's empty when the moon is full;
Such as take Lodgings in a Head
That's to be lett unfurnished.
He could raise Scruples dark and nice,
And after solve 'em in a trice:
As if Divinity had catch'd
The Itch, of purpose to be scratch'd;
Or, like a Mountebank, did wound
And stab herself with doubts profound,
Only to shew with how small pain
The sores of faith are cur'd again;
Although by woful proof we find,
They always leave a Scar behind.
He knew the Seat of Paradise,
Could tell in what degree it lies:
And, as he was dispos'd, could prove it,

Below the Moon, or else above it:
What *Adam* dreamt of when his Bride
Came from her Closet in his side:
Whether the Devil tempted her
By a *High Dutch* Interpreter:
If either of them had a Navel;
Who first made Musick malleable:
Whether the Serpent at the fall
Had cloven Feet, or none at all,
All this without a Gloss or Comment,
He would unriddle in a moment
In proper terms, such as men smatter
When they throw out and miss the matter.

SAMUEL BUTLER

Hypocrisy

Hypocrisy will serve as well
To propagate a church as zeal;
As persecution and promotion
Do equally advance devotion:
So round white stones will serve, they say,
As well as eggs to make hens lay.

SAMUEL BUTLER

Cheltenham Waters

Here lie I and my four daughters,
Killed by drinking Cheltenham waters.
Had we but stuck to Epsom salts,
We wouldn't have been in these here vaults.

ANON.

The White Knight tells his Tale

I'll tell thee everything I can;
  There's little to relate,
I saw an aged aged man,
  A-sitting on a gate.
'Who are you, aged man?' I said.
  'And how is it you live?'
And his answer trickled through my head
  Like water through a sieve.

He said 'I look for butterflies
  That sleep among the wheat:
I make them into mutton-pies,
  And sell them in the street.
I sell them unto men,' he said,
  'Who sail on stormy seas;
And that's the way I get my bread —
  A trifle, if you please.'

But I was thinking of a plan
  To dye one's whiskers green,
And always use so large a fan
  That they could not be seen.
So, having no reply to give
  To what the old man said,
I cried, 'Come, tell me how you live!'
  And thumped him on the head.

His accents mild took up the tale:
  He said 'I go my ways,
And when I find a mountain-rill,
  I set it in a blaze;
And thence they make a stuff they call
  Rowland's Macassar-Oil —
Yet twopence-halfpenny is all
  They give me for my toil.'

But I was thinking of a way
    To feed oneself on batter,
And so go on from day to day
    Getting a little fatter.
I shook him well from side to side,
    Until his face was blue:
'Come, tell me how you live,' I cried,
    'And what it is you do!'

He said 'I hunt for haddocks' eyes
    Among the heather bright,
And work them into waistcoat-buttons
    In the silent night.
And these I do not sell for gold
    Or coin of silvery shine,
But for a copper halfpenny,
    And that will purchase nine.

'I sometimes dig for buttered rolls,
    Or set limed twigs for crabs;
I sometimes search the grassy knolls
    For wheels of Hansom-cabs.
And that's the way' (he gave a wink)
    'By which I get my wealth –
And very gladly will I drink
    Your Honour's noble health.'

I heard him then, for I had just
    Completed my design
To keep the Menai bridge from rust
    By boiling it in wine.
I thanked him much for telling me
    The way he got his wealth,
But chiefly for his wish that he
    Might drink my noble health.

And now, if e'er by chance I put
    My fingers into glue,

Or madly squeeze a right-hand foot
   Into a left-hand shoe,
Or if I drop upon my toe
   A very heavy weight,
I weep, for it reminds me so
Of that old man I used to know –

Whose look was mild, whose speech was slow,
Whose hair was whiter than the snow,
Whose face was very like a crow,
With eyes, like cinders, all aglow,
Who seemed distracted with his woe,
Who rocked his body to and fro,
And muttered mumblingly and low,
As if his mouth were full of dough,
Who snorted like a buffalo –
That summer evening long ago
   A-sitting on a gate.

LEWIS CARROLL

The Pobble who has no Toes

The Pobble who has no toes
   Had once as many as we;
When they said, 'Some day you may lose them all;' –
He replied, – 'Fish fiddle de-dee!'
And his Aunt Jobiska made him drink,
Lavender water tinged with pink,
For she said, 'The World in general knows
There's nothing so good for a Pobble's toes!'
The Pobble who has no toes,
   Swam across the Bristol Channel;
But before he set out he wrapped his nose
   In a piece of scarlet flannel.
For his Aunt Jobiska said, 'No harm
Can come to his toes if his nose is warm;

24

And it's perfectly known that a Pobble's toes
Are safe, – provided he minds his nose.'
The Pobble swam fast and well,
   And when boats or ships came near him
He tinkledy-binkledy-winkled a bell,
   So that all the world could hear him.
And all the Sailors and Admirals cried,
When they saw him nearing the further side, –
'He has gone to fish, for his Aunt Jobiska's
Runcible Cat with crimson whiskers!'
But before he touched the shore,
   The shore of the Bristol Channel,
A sea-green Porpoise carried away
   His wrapper of scarlet flannel.
And when he came to observe his feet,
Formerly garnished with toes so neat,
His face at once became forlorn
On perceiving that all his toes were gone!
And nobody ever knew
   From that dark day to the present,
Whoso had taken the Pobble's toes,
   In a manner so far from pleasant.
Whether the shrimps or crawfish gray,
Or crafty Mermaids stole them away –
Nobody knew; and nobody knows
How the Pobble was robbed of his twice five toes!
The Pobble who has no toes
   Was placed in a friendly Bark,
And they rowed him back, and carried him up,
   To his Aunt Jobiska's Park.
And she made him a feast at his earnest wish
Of eggs and buttercups fried with fish; –
And she said, – 'It's a fact the whole world knows,
That Pobbles are happier without their toes.'

EDWARD LEAR

On a Tired Housewife

Here lies a poor woman who was always tired,
She lived in a house where help wasn't hired:
Her last words on earth were: 'Dear friends, I am going
To where there's no cooking, or washing, or sewing,
For everything there is exact to my wishes,
For where they don't eat there's no washing of dishes.
I'll be where loud anthems will always be ringing,
But having no voice I'll be quit of the singing.
Don't mourn for me now, don't mourn for me never,
I am going to do nothing for ever and ever.'

ANON.

Henry King

WHO CHEWED BITS OF STRING, AND WAS EARLY CUT OFF IN DREADFUL AGONIES

The Chief Defect of Henry King
Was chewing little bits of String.
At last he swallowed some which tied
Itself in ugly Knots inside.
Physicians of the Utmost Fame
Were called at once; but when they came
They answered, as they took their Fees,
'There is no Cure for this Disease.
Henry will very soon be dead.'
His Parents stood about his Bed
Lamenting his Untimely Death,
When Henry, with his Latest Breath,
Cried 'Oh, my Friends, be warned by me,
That Breakfast, Dinner, Lunch, and Tea
Are all the Human Frame requires . . .'
With that, the Wretched Child expires.

HILAIRE BELLOC

Matilda

WHO TOLD LIES, AND WAS BURNED TO DEATH

Matilda told such Dreadful Lies,
It made one Gasp and Stretch one's Eyes;
Her Aunt, who, from her Earliest Youth,
Had kept a Strict Regard for Truth,
Attempted to Believe Matilda:
The effort very nearly killed her,
And would have done so, had not She
Discovered this Infirmity.
For once, towards the Close of Day,
Matilda, growing tired of play,
And finding she was left alone,
Went tiptoe to the Telephone
And summoned the Immediate Aid
Of London's Noble Fire-Brigade.
Within an hour the Gallant Band
Were pouring in on every hand,
From Putney, Hackney Downs, and Bow.
With Courage high and Hearts a-glow,
They galloped, roaring through the Town,
'Matilda's House is Burning Down!'
Inspired by British Cheers and Loud
Proceeding from the Frenzied Crowd,
They ran their ladders through a score
Of windows on the Ball Room Floor;
And took Peculiar Pains to Souse
The Pictures up and down the House,
Until Matilda's Aunt succeeded
In showing them they were not needed;
And even then she had to pay
To get the Men to go away!

It happened that a few Weeks later
Her Aunt was off to the Theatre
To see that Interesting Play

The Second Mrs Tanqueray.
She had refused to take her Niece
To hear this Entertaining Piece:
A Deprivation Just and Wise
To Punish her for Telling Lies.
That Night a Fire *did* break out —
You should have heard Matilda Shout!
You should have heard her Scream and Bawl,
And throw the window up and call
To People passing in the Street —
(The rapidly increasing Heat
Encouraging her to obtain
Their confidence) — but all in vain!
For every time She shouted 'Fire!'
They only answered 'Little Liar!'
And therefore when her Aunt returned,
Matilda, and the House, were Burned.

HILAIRE BELLOC

I Do Like to Be Beside the Seaside

When
                    Don
Pasquito arrived at the seaside
Where the donkey's hide tide brayed, he
Saw the banditto Jo in a black cape
Whose black shape waved like the sea —
Thetis wrote a treatise noting wheat is silver like the sea; the lovely
          cheat is sweet as foam; Erotis notices that she
                    Will
                    Steal
                    The
Wheat-King's luggage, like Babel
Before the League of Nations grew —
So Jo put the luggage and the label
In the pocket of Flo the Kangaroo.

Through trees like rich hotels that bode
Of dreamless ease fled she,
Carrying the load and goading the road
Through the marine scene to the sea.
'Don Pasquito, the road is eloping
With your luggage, though heavy and large;
You must follow and leave your moping
Bride to my guidance and charge!'

When
       Don
Pasquito returned from the road's end,
Where vanilla-coloured ladies ride
From Sevilla, his mantilla'd bride and young friend
Were forgetting their mentor and guide.
For the lady and her friend from Le Touquet
In the very shady trees upon the sand
Were plucking a white satin bouquet
Of foam, while the sand's brassy band
Blared in the wind. Don Pasquito
Hid where the leaves drip with sweet . . .
But a word stung him like a mosquito . . .
For what they hear, they repeat!

EDITH SITWELL

Forgive me, Sire

Forgive me, sire, for cheating your intent,
That I, who should command a regiment,
Do amble amicably here, O God,
One of the neat ones in your awkward squad.

NORMAN CAMERON

Elegy for Mr Goodbeare

Do you remember Mr Goodbeare, the carpenter,
Godfearing and bearded Mr Goodbeare,
Who worked all day
At his carpenter's tray,
Do you remember Mr Goodbeare?
Mr Goodbeare, that Golconda of gleaming fable,
Lived, thin-ground between orchard and stable,
Pressed thus close against Alfred, his rival –
Mr Goodbeare, who had never been away.

Do you remember Mr Goodbeare,
Mr Goodbeare, who never touched a cup?
Do you remember Mr Goodbeare,
Who remembered a lot?

    Mr Goodbeare could remember
      When things were properly kept up:
    Mr Goodbeare could remember
      The christening and the coming-of-age:
    Mr Goodbeare could remember
      The entire and roasted ox:
    Mr Goodbeare could remember
      When the horses filled the stable,
And the port-wine coloured gentry rode after the tawny fox:
    Mr Goodbeare could remember
      The old lady in her eagle rage,
        Which knew no bounds.
    Mr Goodbeare could remember
      When the escaped and hungering tiger
Flickered lithe and fierce through Foxton Wood,
When old Sir Nigel took his red-tongued, clamouring hounds,
And hunted it then and there,
      As a Gentleman should.

Do you remember Mr Goodbeare,
Mr Goodbeare who never forgot?
Do you remember Mr Goodbeare,
That wrinkled and golden apricot,
Dear, bearded, godfearing Mr Goodbeare
Who remembered remembering such a lot?

Oh, do you remember, do you remember,
As *I* remember and deplore,
That day in drear and far-away December
When dear, godfearing, bearded Mr Goodbeare
Could remember
No more!

SIR OSBERT SITWELL

Epigram of Straw

It is easier for a drowning man
   To make bricks on the back of a camel than
For a rich man to know
   Which way the winds blow.
Who'd flirt with Threadneedle Street yet flatter Mt Zion
Has bitten off more of the bed than he can lie on.

GEOFFREY TAYLOR

What's the Use?

Sure, deck your lower limbs in pants;
Yours are the limbs, my sweeting.
You look divine as you advance —
Have you seen yourself retreating?

OGDEN NASH

31

Buttons

There was an old skinflint of Hitching
Had a cook, Mrs Casey, of Cork;
There was nothing but crusts in the kitchen,
    While in parlour was sherry and pork.
So at last Mrs Casey, her pangs to assuage,
Having snipped off his buttons, curried the page;
And now, while that skinflint gulps sherry and pork
    In his parlour adjacent to Hitching,
To the tune blithe and merry of knife and of fork,
    Anthropophagy reigns in the kitchen.

WALTER DE LA MARE

archy the cockroach says

now and then
there is a person born
who is so unlucky
that he runs into accidents
which started out to happen
to somebody else.

i suppose the human race
is doing the best it can
but hells bells thats
only an explanation
it's not an excuse.

germs are very
objectionable to men
but a germ
thinks of a man
as only the swamp

in which
he has to live.

a louse i
used to know
told me that
millionaires and
bums tasted
about alike
to him.

(*A Maxim*)
if you will drink
hair restorer follow
every dram with some
good standard
depilatory
as a chaser.

DON MARQUIS

Horny Hogan

A FEELTHY POME

Critchers! Horny Hogan sayed
& walked his beat — beat his walk
& saw loif larf, loif cree —
Critchers! Horny scorfed, and spart.

Oi arm the cocker here! Moi
brarss poilished & moi gon in order
Oi arm the cocker, mocker, bocker,
jocker of em all.

Bibies, little winch, twinty-foive
pinnies fer a chonk of luv —

lovers, sodgers, shoppers, sharpers,
mogs pinny-woise & por

lil ones so hoi what nid pertixion –
Oi arm the cocker here! Horny
Hogan sayed. Oi'll sive the larsies,
Oi'll kip the fithe!

Didee? Did Horny Hogan kip it?
Did Horny Hogan kip the larsies
sife and sound from ivil? Woulduv,
rilly woulduv but that he loiked to flarndle

Loiked to flup too much, did Horny,
fer a cop, perticted blonduns,
riduns & brunettes, gave em
the long orm of the lar

Overdid it somut, did Cocker
Mocker Horny Hogan – gave full pertixion to
one too miny ridid, one too miny
blornde – did it ifter hours ivin

till the Force foundim daid one
cool sprin mornin, still pertictin, still
kipin the fithe, shot at his post in a

tinth strit room, the horsband disappeared
& the blornde there wippin –
Horny Hogan daid! Horny
Hogan – kipper of the fithe

Horny Hogan, the cocker mocker of em all.

x x x

ROBERT LOWRY

34

The Turtle

The turtle lives 'twixt plated decks
Which practically conceal its sex.
I think it clever of the turtle
In such a fix to be so fertile.

OGDEN NASH

Samson Agonistes

I test my bath before I sit,
And I'm always moved to wonderment
That what chills the finger not a bit
Is so frigid upon the fundament.

OGDEN NASH

A Friend of mine was married to a scold,
To me he came, and all his troubles told.
Said he, 'She's like a woman raving mad.'
'Alas! my friend,' said I, 'that's very bad!'
'No, not so bad,' said he; 'for, with her, true
I had both house and land, and money too.'

    'That was well,' said I;
    'No, not so well,' said he;
    'For I and her own brother
    Went to law with one another;
    I was cast, the suit was lost,
And every penny went to pay the cost.'

    'That was bad,' said I;
    'No, not so bad,' said he:
'For we agreed that he the house should keep,
And give to me four score of Yorkshire sheep
All fat, and fair, and fine, they were to be.'
'Well, then,' said I, 'sure that was well for thee?'

    'No, not so well,' said he;
    'For, when the sheep I got,
    They every one died of the rot.
    'That was bad,' said I;
    'No, not so bad,' said he;
    'For I had thought to scrape the fat
    And keep it in an oaken vat;
Then into tallow melt for winter store.'
'Well, then,' said I, 'that's better than before?'

    ' 'Twas not so well,' said he;
    'For having got a clumsy fellow
    To scrape the fat and melt the tallow;
Into the melting fat the fire catches,
    And, like brimstone matches,
Burnt my house to ashes.'

    'That was bad,' said I;

'No! not so bad,' said he; 'for, what is best,
My scolding wife has gone among the rest.'

ANON.

The Doctor Prescribes

A lady lately, that was fully sped
Of all the pleasures of the marriage-bed
Ask'd a physician, whether were more fit
For Venus' sports, the morning or the night?
The good old man made answer, as 'twas meet,
The morn more wholesome, but the night more sweet.
Nay then, i' faith, quoth she, since we have leisure,
We'll to't each morn for health, each night for pleasure.

ANON.

Bibo

AN EPIGRAM

When BIBO thought fit from the world to retreat,
As full of Champagne as an egg's full of meat,
He wak'd in the boat; and to CHARON he said,
He wou'd be row'd back, for he was not yet dead.
Trim the boat, and sit quiet, stern CHARON reply'd:
You may have forgot, you were drunk when you dy'd.

MATTHEW PRIOR

Misadventures at Margate

(Mr Simpkinson loquitur)

I was in Margate last July, I walk'd upon the pier,
I saw a little vulgar Boy – I said, 'What make you here? –
The gloom upon your youthful cheek speaks any thing but joy';
Again I said, 'What make you here, you little vulgar Boy?'

He frown'd, that little vulgar Boy – he deem'd I meant to scoff:
And when the little heart is big, a little 'sets it off';
He put his finger in his mouth, his little bosom rose, –
He had no little handkerchief to wipe his little nose!

'Hark! don't you hear, my little man? – it's striking nine,' I said,
'An hour when all good little boys and girls should be in bed.
Run home and get your supper, else your Ma' will scold – Oh!
    fie! –
It's very wrong indeed for little boys to stand and cry!'

The tear-drop in his little eye again began to spring,
His bosom throbb'd with agony – he cried like any thing!
I stoop'd, and thus amidst his sobs I heard him murmur – 'Ah
I haven't got no supper! and I haven't got no Ma'!! –

'My father, he is on the seas, – my mother's dead and gone!
And I am here, on this here pier, to roam the world alone;
I have not had, this live-long day, one drop to cheer my heart,
Nor "brown" to buy a bit of bread with, – let alone a tart.

'If there's a soul will give me food, or find me in employ,
By day or night, then blow me tight!' (he was a vulgar Boy);
'And now I'm here, from this here pier it is my fixed intent
To jump, as Mister Levi did from off the Monu-ment!'

'Cheer up! cheer up! my little man – cheer up!' I kindly said.
'You are a naughty boy to take such things into your head:

If you should jump from off the pier, you'd surely break your legs,
Perhaps your neck – then Bogey'd have you, sure as eggs are eggs!

'Come home with me, my little man, come home with me and sup;
My landlady is Mrs Jones – we must not keep her up –
There's roast potatoes on the fire, – enough for me and you –
Come home, you little vulgar Boy – I lodge at Number 2.'

I took him home to Number 2, the house beside 'The Foy'
I bade him wipe his dirty shoes – that little vulgar Boy, –
And then I said to Mistress Jones, the kindest of her sex,
'Pray be so good as go and fetch a pint of double X!'

But Mrs Jones was rather cross, she made a little noise,
She said she 'did not like to wait on little vulgar Boys.'
She with her apron wiped the plates, and, as she rubb'd the delf,
Said I might 'go to Jericho, and fetch my beer myself!'

I did not go to Jericho – I went to Mr Cobb –
I changed a shilling – (which in town the people call 'a Bob') –
It was not so much for myself as for that vulgar child –
And I said, 'A pint of double X, and please to draw it mild!'

When I came back I gazed about – I gazed on stool and chair –
I could not see my little friend – because he was not there!
I peep'd beneath the table-cloth – beneath the sofa too –
I said 'You little vulgar Boy! why what's become of you?'

I could not see my table-spoons – I look'd, but could not see
The little fiddle-pattern'd ones I use when I'm at tea;
– I could not see my sugar-tongs – my silver watch – oh, dear!
I know 'twas on the mantel-piece when I went out for beer.

I could not see my Mackintosh! – it was not to be seen!
Nor yet my best white beaver hat, broad-brimm'd and lined with
    green;
My carpet-bag – my cruet-stand, that holds my sauce and soy, –
My roast potatoes! – all are gone! – and so's that vulgar Boy!

I rang the bell for Mrs Jones, for she was down below,
'– Oh, Mrs Jones! what do you think? – ain't this a pretty go?
– That horrid little vulgar Boy whom I brought here to-night,
– He's stolen my things and run away!!' – Says she, 'And serve you
   right!!'

*

Next morning I was up betimes – I sent the Crier round,
All with his bell and gold-laced hat, to say I'd give a pound
To find that little vulgar Boy, who'd gone and used me so;
But when the Crier cried 'O Yes!' the people cried, 'O No!'

I went to 'Jarvis' Landing-place,' the glory of the town,
There was a common sailor-man a-walking up and down;
I told my tale – he seem'd to think I'd not been treated well,
And called me 'Poor old Buffer!' – what that means I cannot tell.

That sailor-man, he said he'd seen that morning on the shore,
A son of – something – 'twas a name I'd never heard before,
A little 'gallows-looking chap' – dear me; what could he mean?
With a 'carpet-swab' and 'muckingtogs,' and a hat turned up with
   green.

He spoke about his 'precious eyes,' and said he'd seen him 'sheer,'
– It's very odd that sailor-men should talk so very queer –
And then he hitch'd his trousers up, as is, I'm told, their use,
– It's very odd that sailor-men should wear those things so loose.

I did not understand him well, but think he meant to say
He'd seen that little vulgar Boy, that morning swim away
In Captain Large's Royal George about an hour before,
And they were now, as he supposed, 'some*wheres*' about the
   Nore.

A landsman said, 'I *twig* the chap – he's been upon the Mill –
And 'cause he *gammons* so the flats, ve calls him Veeping Bill!'
He said 'he'd done me *wery* brown,' and 'nicely *stow'd* the *swag*.'
– That's French, I fancy, for a hat – or else a carpet-bag.

I went and told the constable my property to track;
He asked me if 'I did not wish that I might get it back!'
I answered, 'To be sure I do! – it's what I come about.'
He smiled and said, 'Sir, does your mother know that you are out?'

Not knowing what to do, I thought I'd hasten back to town,
And beg our own Lord Mayor to catch the Boy who'd 'done me
    brown.'
His Lordship very kindly said he'd try and find him out,
But he 'rather thought that there were several vulgar boys about.'

He sent for Mr Withair then, and I described 'the swag,'
My Mackintosh, my sugar-tongs, my spoons, and carpet-bag;
He promised that the New Police should all their powers employ;
But never to this hour have I beheld that vulgar Boy!

Moral

Remember, then, what when a boy I've heard my Grandma' tell,
'BE WARN'D IN TIME BY OTHERS' HARM, AND YOU SHALL
    DO FULL WELL!'
Don't link yourself with vulgar folks, who've got no fix'd abode,
Tell lies, use naughty words, and say they 'wish they may be
    blow'd!'
Don't take too much of double X! – and don't at night go out
To fetch your beer yourself, but make the pot-boy bring your
    stout!
And when you go to Margate next, just stop and ring the bell,
Give my respects to Mrs Jones, and say I'm pretty well!

R. H. BARHAM

The Sorrows of Werther

Werther had a love for Charlotte
    Such as words could never utter;
Would you know how first he met her?
    She was cutting bread and butter.

Charlotte was a married lady,
    And a moral man was Werther,
And for all the wealth of Indies,
    Would do nothing for to hurt her.

So he sigh'd and pined and ogled,
    And his passion boil'd and bubbled,
Till he blew his silly brains out,
    And no more was by it troubled.

Charlotte, having seen his body
    Borne before her on a shutter,
Like a well-conducted person,
    Went on cutting bread and butter.

W M. THACKERAY

The Heathen Chinee

Which I wish to remark –
    And my language is plain –
That for ways that are dark
    And for tricks that are vain,
The heathen Chinee is peculiar,
    Which the same I would rise to explain.

Ah Sin was his name;
    And I shall not deny

In regard to the same
    What that name might imply;
But his smile was pensive and child-like,
    As I frequent remarked to Bill Nye.

It was August the third;
    And quite soft was the skies.
Which it might be inferred
    That Ah Sin was likewise;
Yet he played it that day upon William
    And me in a way I despise.

Which we had a small game,
    And Ah Sin took a hand:
It was Euchre. The same
    He did not understand;
But he smiled as he sat by the table,
    With the smile that was child-like and bland.

Yet the cards they were stocked
    In a way that I grieve,
And my feelings were shocked
    At the state of Nye's sleeve:
Which was stuffed full of aces and bowers,
    And the same with intent to deceive.

But the hands that were played
    By that heathen Chinee,
And the points that he made,
    Were quite frightful to see, –
Till at last he put down a right bower,
    Which the same Nye had dealt unto me.

Then I looked up at Nye,
    And he gazed upon me;
And he rose with a sigh,
    And said, 'Can this be?
We are ruined by Chinese cheap labour,'
    And he went for that heathen Chinee.

In the scene that ensued
  I did not take a hand,
But the floor it was strewed
  Like the leaves on the strand
With the cards that Ah Sin had been hiding,
  In the game 'he did not understand'.

In his sleeves, which were long,
  He had twenty-four packs, –
Which was coming it strong,
  Yet I state but the facts;
And we found on his nails, which were taper,
  What is frequent in tapers, – that's wax.

Which is why I remark,
  And my language is plain,
That for ways that are dark,
  And for tricks that are vain,
The heathen Chinee is peculiar –
  Which the same I am free to maintain.

BRET HARTE

On Mary Ann

Mary Ann has gone to rest,
Safe at last on Abraham's breast,
Which may be nuts for Mary Ann,
But is certainly rough on Abraham.

ANON.

Muddled Metaphors

Oh, ever thus from childhood's hour
    I've seen my fondest hopes recede!
I never loved a tree or flower
    That didn't trump its partner's lead.

I never nursed a dear gazelle,
    To glad me with its dappled hide,
But when it came to know me well
    It fell upon the buttered side.

I never taught a cockatoo
    To whistle comic songs profound,
But just when 'Jolly Dogs' it knew
    It failed for ninepence in the pound.

I never reared a walrus cub
    In my aquarium to plunge,
But, when it learnt to love its tub,
    It placidly threw up the sponge.

I never strove a metaphor
    To every bosom home to bring,
But – just as it had reached the door –
    It went and cut a pigeon's wing.

THOMAS HOOD, JR.

Shake, Mulleary and Go-ethe

I have a bookcase, which is what
Many much better men have not.
There are no books inside, for books,
I am afraid, might spoil its looks,
But I've three busts, all second-hand,
Upon the top. You understand
I could not put them underneath –
Shake, Mulleary and Go-ethe.

Shake was a dramatist of note;
He lived by writing things to quote,
He long ago put on his shroud:
Some of his works are rather loud.
His bald-spot's dusty, I suppose.
I know there's dust upon his nose.
I'll have to give each nose a sheath –
Shake, Mulleary and Go-ethe.

Mulleary's line was quite the same;
He has more hair, but far less fame.
I would not from that fame retrench –
But he is foreign, being French.
Yet high his haughty head he heaves,
The only one done up in leaves,
They're rather limited on wreath –
Shake, Mulleary and Go-ethe.

Go-ethe wrote in the German tongue:
He must have learned it very young.
His nose is quite a butt for scoff,
Although an inch of it is off.
He did quite nicely for the Dutch;
But here he doesn't count for much.
They all are off their native heath –
Shake, Mulleary and Go-ethe.

They sit there, on their chests, as bland
As if they were not second-hand.
I do not know of what they think,
Nor why they never frown or wink.
But why from smiling they refrain
I think I clearly can explain:
They none of them could show much teeth –
Shake, Mulleary and Go-ethe.

H. C. BUNNER

Hans Breitmann's Barty

Hans Breitmann gife a barty;
   Dey had biano-blayin',
I felled in lofe mit a Merican frau,
   Her name vas Madilda Yane.
She hat haar as prown ash a pretzel,
   Her eyes vas himmel-plue,
Und vhen dey looket indo mine,
   Dey shplit mine heart in dwo.

Hans Breitmann gife a barty,
   I vent dere you'll be pound;
I valtzet mit Madilda Yane,
   Und vent shpinnen' round und round.
De pootiest Fraulein in de house,
   She vayed 'pout dwo hoondred pound,
Und efery dime she gife a shoomp
   She make de vindows sound.

Hans Breitmann gife a barty,
   I dells you it cost him dear;
Dey rolled in more ash sefen keeks
   Of foost-rate lager beer.
Und vhenefer dey knocks de shpicket in
   De Deutschers gifes a cheer;

I dinks dot so vine a barty
  Nefer coom to a het dis year.

Hans Breitmann gife a barty;
  Dere all vas Souse and Brouse,
Vhen de sooper comed in, de gompany
  Did make demselfs to house;
Dey ate das Brot and Gensy broost,
  De Bratwurst and Braten vine,
Und vash der Abendessen down
  Mit four parrels of Neckarwein.

Hans Breitmann gife a barty;
  Ve all cot troonk ash bigs.
I poot mine mout' to a parrel of beer,
  Und emptied it oop mit a schwigs;
Und den I gissed Madilda Yane,
  Und she shlog me on de kop,
Und de gompany vighted mit daple-lecks
  Dill de coonshtable made oos shtop.

Hans Breitmann gife a barty –
  Vhere ish dot barty now?
Vhere ish de lofely golden cloud
  Dot float on de moundain's prow?
Vhere ish de himmelstrahlende Stern –
  De shtar of de shpirit's light?
All goned afay mit de lager beer –
  Afay in de Ewigkeit!

                                        C. G. LELAND

On a Wag in Mauchline

Lament him, Mauchline husbands a',
   He often did assist ye;
For had ye staid whole weeks awa',
   Your wives they ne'er had missed ye.

Ye Mauchline bairns, as on ye pass,
   To school in bands thegither,
Oh, tread ye lightly on his grass,
   Perhaps he was your father.

ROBERT BURNS

The Owl-Critic

'Who stuffed that white owl?' No one spoke in the shop.
The barber was busy, and he couldn't stop;
The customers, waiting their turns, were all reading
The 'Daily,' the 'Herald,' the 'Post,' little heeding
The young man who blurted out such a blunt question;
No one raised a head, or even made a suggestion;
      And the barber kept on shaving.

'Don't you see, Mr Brown,'
Cried the youth, with a frown,
'How wrong the whole thing is,
How preposterous each wing is,
How flattened the head is, how jammed down the neck is –
In short, the whole owl, what an ignorant wreck 't is!
I make no apology;
I've learned owl-eology.

'I've passed days and nights in a hundred collections,
And cannot be blinded to any deflections
Arising from unskilful fingers that fail
To stuff a bird right, from his beak to his tail.

Mister Brown! Mister Brown!
Do take that bird down,
Or you'll soon be the laughing-stock all over town!'
       And the barber kept on shaving.

'I've studied owls,
And other night-fowls,
And I tell you
What I know to be true;
An owl cannot roost
With his limbs so unloosed;
No owl in this world
Ever had his claws curled,
Ever had his legs slanted,
Ever had his bill canted,
Ever had his neck screwed
Into that attitude.
He can't do it, because
'Tis against all bird-laws.

'Anatomy teaches,
Ornithology preaches,
An owl has a toe
That can't turn out so!
I've made the white owl my study for years,
And to see such a job almost moves me to tears!
Mr Brown, I'm amazed
You should be so gone crazed
As to put up a bird
In that posture absurd!
To look at that owl really brings on a dizziness;
The man who stuffed him don't half know his business!'
       And the barber kept on shaving.

'Examine those eyes.
I'm filled with surprise
Taxidermists should pass
Off on you such poor glass;

So unnatural they seem
They'd make Audubon scream,
And John Burroughs laugh
To encounter such chaff.
Do take that bird down;
Have him stuffed again, Brown!'
      And the barber kept on shaving.

'With some sawdust and bark
I could stuff in the dark
An owl better than that.
I could make an old hat
Look more like an owl
Than that horrid fowl,
Stuck up there so stiff like a side of coarse leather.
In fact, about him there's not one natural feather.'

Just then, with a wink and a sly normal lurch,
The owl, very gravely, got down from his perch,
Walked round, and regarded his fault-finding critic
(Who thought he was stuffed) with a glance analytic,
And then fairly hooted, as if he should say:
'Your learning's at fault this time, anyway;
Don't waste it again on a live bird, I pray.
I'm an owl; you're another. Sir Critic, good day!'
      And the barber kept on shaving.

J. T. FIELDS

The Japanese

How courteous is the Japanese;
He always says, 'Excuse it, please.'
He climbs into his neighbour's garden,
And smiles, and says, 'I beg your pardon';
He bows and grins a friendly grin,
And calls his hungry family in;
He grins, and bows a friendly bow;
'So sorry, this my garden now.'

OGDEN NASH

Tender Heartedness

Billy, in one of his nice new sashes,
Fell in the fire and was burnt to ashes;
Now, although the room grows chilly,
I haven't the heart to poke poor Billy.

HARRY GRAHAM

Misfortunes never come Singly

Making toast at the fireside,
Nurse fell in the grate and died;
And what makes it ten times worse,
All the toast was burnt with nurse.

HARRY GRAHAM

Willie's Epitaph

Little Willie from his mirror
   Licked the mercury right off,
Thinking, in his childish error,
   It would cure the whooping cough.
At the funeral his mother
   Smartly said to Mrs Brown:
   ' 'Twas a chilly day for Willie
When the mercury went down.'

ANON.

Miss Twye

Miss Twye was soaping her breasts in her bath
When she heard behind her a meaning laugh
And to her amazement she discovered
A wicked man in the bathroom cupboard.

GAVIN EWART

56

FOR VARIOUS
OCCASIONS

To the Immortal Memory of the Halibut

Where hast thou floated, in what seas pursued
Thy pastime? when wast thou an egg new spawn'd,
Lost in th'immensity of ocean's waste?
Roar as they might, the overbearing winds
That rock'd the deep, thy cradle, thou wast safe —
And in thy minikin and embryo state,
Attach'd to the firm leaf of some salt weed,
Didst outlive tempests, such as wrung and rack'd
The joints of many a stout and gallant bark,
And whelm'd them in the unexplored abyss.
Indebted to no magnet and no chart,
Nor under guidance of the polar fire,
Thou wast a voyager on many coasts,
Grazing at large in meadows submarine,
Where flat Batavia, just emerging, peeps
Above the brine — where Caledonia's rocks
Beat back the surge — and where Hibernia shoots
Her wondrous causeway far into the main.
— Wherever thou hast fed, thou little thought'st,
And I not more, that I should feed on thee.
Peace, therefore, and good health, and much good fish
To him who sent thee! and success, as oft
As it descends into the billowy gulf,
To the same drag that caught thee! — Fare thee well!
Thy lot thy brethren of the slimy fin
Would envy, could they know that thou wast doom'd
To feed a bard, and to be praised in verse.

WILLIAM COWPER

59

Ode to St Swithin

'THE RAIN IT RAINETH EVERY DAY'

The Dawn is overcast, the morning low'rs,
On ev'ry window-frame hang beaded damps
Like rows of small illumination lamps
To celebrate the Jubilee of Show'rs!
A constant sprinkle patters from all leaves,
The very Dryads are not dry, but soppers,
  And from the Houses' eaves
  Tumble eaves-droppers.

The hundred clerks that live along the street,
Bondsmen to mercantile and city schemers,
With squashing, sloshing, and galloshing feet,
Go paddling, paddling, through the wet, like steamers,
Each hurrying to earn the daily stipend –
Umbrellas pass of every shade of green,
And now and then a crimson one is seen
  Like an Umbrella *ripen'd.*

  Over the way a waggon
Stands with six smoking horses, shrinking, blinking,
  While in the George and Dragon
The man is keeping himself dry – and drinking!
The Butcher's boy skulks underneath his tray,
  Hats shine – shoes don't – and down droop collars,
And one blue Parasol cries all the way
  To school, in company with four small scholars!

Unhappy is the man to-day who rides,
Making his journey sloppier, not shorter;
Aye, there they go, a dozen of outsides,
Performing on 'a Stage with real water!'
A dripping Pauper crawls along the way,
  The only real willing out-of-doorer,
  And says, or seems to say,
'Well, I am poor enough – but here's a *pourer*!'

The scene in water colours thus I paint,
Is your own Festival, you Sloppy Saint!
Mother of all the Family of Rainers!
　　Saint of the Soakers!
　　Making all people croakers,
Like frogs in swampy marshes, and complainers!
And why you mizzle forty days together,
Giving the earth your water-soup to sup,
I marvel – Why such wet, mysterious weather?
　　I wish you'd *clear it up*!

　　Why cast such cruel dampers
On pretty Pic Nics, and against all wishes
Set the cold ducks a-swimming in the hampers,
And volunteer, unask'd, to wash the dishes?
Why drive the Nymphs from the selected spot,
　　To cling like lady-birds around a tree –
　　Why spoil a Gipsy party at their tea,
By throwing your cold water upon hot?

Cannot a rural maiden, or a man,
Seek Hornsey-Wood by invitation, sipping
　　Their green with Pan,
But souse you come, and show their Pan all dripping!
Why upon snow-white table-cloths and sheets,
That do not wait, or want a second washing,
　　Come squashing?
Why task yourself to lay the dust in streets,
As if there were no Water-Cart contractors,
No pot-boys spilling beer, no shop-boys ruddy
　　Spooning out puddles muddy,
Milkmaids, and other slopping benefactors!

A Queen you are, raining in your own right,
Yet oh! how little flatter'd by report!
　　Even by those that seek the Court,
Pelted with every term of spleen and spite.
Folks rail and swear at you in every place;

They say you are a creature of no bowel;
They say you're always washing Nature's face,
    And that you then supply her
      With nothing drier
Than some old wringing cloud by way of towel!
The whole town wants you duck'd, just as you duck it,
They wish you on your own mud porridge supper'd,
They hope that you may kick your own big bucket,
Or in your water-butt go souse! heels up'ard!
They are, in short, so weary of your drizzle,
They'd spill the water in your veins to stop it –
Be warn'd! You are too partial to a mizzle –
    Pray *drop* it!

                      THOMAS HOOD

The Old Loony of Lyme

There was an old loony of Lyme,
Whose candour was simply sublime;
    When they asked, 'Are you there?'
    'Yes,' he said, 'but take care,
For I'm never "all there" at a time.'

                      ANON.

Ode to Tobacco

Thou who, when fears attack,
Bidst them avaunt, and Black
Care, at the horseman's back
    Perching, unseatest;
Sweet, when the morn is gray;
Sweet, when they've cleared away
Lunch; and at close of day
    Possibly sweetest:

I have a liking old
For thee, though manifold
Stories, I know, are told,
   Not to thy credit;
How one (or two at most)
Drops make a cat a ghost –
Useless, except to roast –
   Doctors have said it:

How they who use fusees
All grow by slow degrees
Brainless as chimpanzees,
   Meagre as lizards:
Go mad, and beat their wives;
Plunge (after shocking lives)
Razors and carving knives
   Into their gizzards.

Confound such knavish tricks!
Yet know I five or six
Smokers who freely mix
   Still with their neighbours;
Jones – (who, I'm glad to say,
Asked leave of Mrs J.) –
Daily absorbs a clay
   After his labours.

Cats may have had their goose
Cooked by tobacco-juice;
Still why deny its use
   Thoughtfully taken?
We're not as tabbies are:
Smith, take a fresh cigar!
Jones, the tobacco-jar!
   Here's to thee, Bacon!

C. S. CALVERLEY

Lines on Hearing the Organ

Grinder, who serenely grindest
  At my door the Hundredth Psalm,
Till thou ultimately findest
  Pence in thy unwashen palm:

Grinder, jocund-hearted Grinder,
  Near whom Barbary's nimble son,
Poised with skill upon his hinder
  Paws, accepts the proffered bun:

Dearly do I love thy grinding;
  Joy to meet thee on thy road
Where thou prowlest through the blinding
  Dust with that stupendous load,

'Neath the baleful star of Sirius,
  When the postmen slowlier jog,
And the ox becomes delirious,
  And the muzzle decks the dog.

Tell me by what art thou bindest
  On thy feet those ancient shoon:
Tell me, Grinder, if thou grindest
  Always, always out of tune.

Tell me if, as thou art buckling
  On thy straps with eager claws,
Thou forecastest, inly chuckling,
  All the rage that thou wilt cause.

Tell me if at all thou mindest
  When folks flee, as if on wings,
From thee as at ease thou grindest:
  Tell me fifty thousand things.

Grinder, gentle-hearted Grinder!
   Ruffians who lead evil lives,
Soothed by thy sweet strains, are kinder
   To their bullocks and their wives:

Children, when they see thy supple
   Form approach, are out like shots;
Half-a-bar sets several couple
   Waltzing in convenient spots;

Not with clumsy Jacks or Georges:
   Unprofaned by grasp of man
Maidens speed those simple orgies,
   Betsey Jane with Betsey Ann.

As they love thee in St Giles's
   Thou art loved in Grosvenor Square:
None of those engaging smiles is
   Unreciprocated there.

Often, ere yet thou hast hammer'd
   Through thy four delicious airs,
Coins are flung thee by enamour'd
   Housemaids upon area stairs:

E'en the ambrosial-whisker'd flunkey
   Eyes thy boots and thine unkempt
Beard and melancholy monkey
   More in pity than contempt.

Far from England, in the sunny
   South, where Arno leaps in foam,
Thou wast rear'd, till lack of money
   Drew thee from thy vineclad home:

And thy mate, the sinewy Jocko,
   From Brazil or Afric came,
Land of simoom and sirocco –
   And he seems extremely tame.

There he quaff'd the undefilèd
   Spring, or hung with apelike glee
By his teeth or tail or eyelid,
   To the slippery mango-tree:

There he woo'd and won a dusky
   Bride, of instincts like his own;
Talk'd of love till he was husky
   In a tongue to us unknown:

Side by side 'twas theirs to ravage
   The potato ground, or cut
Down the unsuspecting savage
   With the well-aim'd cocoa-nut: –

Till the miscreant Stranger tore him
   Screaming from his blue-faced fair;
And they flung raiment o'er him,
   Raiment which he could not bear:

Sever'd from the pure embraces
   Of his children and his spouse,
He must ride fantastic races
   Mounted on reluctant sows:

But the heart of wistful Jocko
   Still was with his ancient flame
In the nutgroves of Morocco;
   Or if not it's all the same.

Grinder, winsome grinsome Grinder!
   They who see thee and whose soul
Melts not at thy charms, are blinder
   Than a trebly-bandaged mole:

They to whom thy curt (yet clever)
   Talk, thy music and thine ape,
Seem not to be joys for ever,
   Are but brutes in human shape.

'Tis not that thy mien is stately,
   'Tis not that thy tones are soft;
'Tis not that I care so greatly
   For the same thing play'd so oft:

But I've heard mankind abuse thee;
   And perhaps it's rather strange,
But I thought that I would choose thee
   For encomium, as a change.

C. S. CALVERLEY

The Schoolmaster

ABROAD WITH HIS SON

O what harper could worthily harp it,
   Mine Edward! this wide-stretching wold
(Look out *wold*) with its wonderful carpet
   Of emerald, purple, and gold!
Look well at it – also look sharp, it
     Is getting so cold.

The purple is heather (*erica*);
   The yellow, gorse – call'd sometimes 'whin'.
Cruel boys on its prickles might spike a
   Green beetle as if on a pin.
You may roll in it, if you would like a
   Few holes in your skin.

You wouldn't? Then think of how kind you
   Should be to the insects who crave
Your compassion – and then, look behind you
   At yon barley-ears! Don't they look brave
As they undulate (*undulate*, mind you,
   From *unda*, a wave).

The noise of those sheep-bells, how faint it
    Sounds here – (on account of our height)!
And this hillock itself – who could paint it,
    With its changes of shadow and light?
Is it not – (never, Eddy, say 'ain't it') –
      A marvellous sight?

Then yon desolate eerie morasses,
    The haunts of the snipe and the hern –
(I shall question the two upper classes
    On *aquatiles*, when we return) –
Why, I see on them absolute masses
      Of *filix* or fern.

How it interests e'en a beginner
    (Or *tiro*) like dear little Ned!
Is he listening? As I am a sinner
    He's asleep – he is wagging his head,
Wake up! I'll go home to my dinner
      And you to your bed.

The boundless ineffable prairie;
    The splendour of mountain and lake
With their hues that seem ever to vary;
    The mighty pine-forests which shake
In the wind, and in which the unwary
      May tread on a snake;

And this wold with its heathery garment
    Are themes undeniably great.
But – although there is not any harm in't –
    It's perhaps little good to dilate
On their charms to a dull little varmint
      Of seven or eight.

                           C. S. CALVERLEY

A Woice of the Wicious

'Ere, Bill, you listen, while I tell
'Ow I've just done the Mission: well,
The blokes all come, and fust some swell
      As seemed important;

Ses he: – 'Dear lads, what's vicked bin,
We vish to rexcue you from sin
And see you earnin' honest tin,
      If you'll allow us.'

And then some old 'un speaks genteel
And axes 'ow your innuds feel,
And 'ow yer fust was drew to steal,
      And then you blubs.

They called it 'druv', they did, by gum!
I dayn't say 'twarn't, but kept quite mum;
But all their talk's so precious rum,
      A kid must veep or laugh.

In course a vise un veeps – dayn't I?
And then says they: – 'My lad, don't cry –
We'll see to you.' Ses I: – 'O why
      Veren't you my parients?'

That paid, my cockie, just a few,
They stared at me a minute or two,
Then chummed together, and I knew
      I'd took their vind.

My heyes and limbs, what game it is
To stand and pull a Solomon phiz,
And bust to make the blubber rig,
      And come the penitent.

So now I specs to get repweave,
A stunnin' character, and I b'lieve
Not three week more afore I leave
   This Penny Stenchery.

But spose them buffers (oh my vig!)
'Adnt come and I 'adnt played this rig,
Why, I shouldn't get a horse and gig
   If I lived to ninety.

A steady cove is all my heye,
D'ye think I'd go to starve and cry
' 'Ot taters', when i' this-un's I
   Becomes so interestin'

There is some folks as takes it meek
And starve theirselves to 'scape the Beak
While us 'deluded' kids are slick
   As Bottomuppermosts.

Now Bill, my say is this (which I'm
On Fortin's path) recelect this rhyme,
That 'Honesty's the thief of time' –
   You mark my wurds.

         C. P.

The Bards

My aged friend, Miss Wilkinson,
 Whose mother was a Lambe,
Saw Wordsworth once, and Coleridge, too
 One morning in her 'pram'.[1]

1. This was a three wheeled vehicle
 Of iron and of wood;
 It had a leather apron,
  But it hadn't any hood.

Birdlike the bards stooped over her
   Like fledgling in a nest;
And Wordsworth said, 'Thou harmless babe!'
   And Coleridge was impressed.

The pretty thing gazed up and smiled,
   And softly murmured, 'Coo!'
William was then aged sixty-four
   And Samuel sixty-two.

WALTER DE LA MARE

Culture in the Slums

BALLADE

I often does a quiet read
   At Booty Shelly's poetry;
I thinks that Swinburne at a screed
   Is really almost too too fly;
   At Signor Vagna's harmony
I likes a merry little flutter;
   I've had at Pater many a shy;
In fact, my form's the Bloomin' Utter.

My mark's a tidy little feed,
   And 'Enery Irving's gallery,
To see old 'Amlick do a bleed,
   And Ellen Terry on the die,
   Or Frankey's ghostes at hi-spy,
And parties carried on a shutter.
   Them vulgar Coupeaus is my eye!
In fact, my form's the Bloomin' Utter.

The Grosvenor's nuts – it is, indeed!
   I goes for 'Olman 'Unt like pie.
It's equal to a friendly lead
   To see B. Jones's judes go by.

71

Stanhope he make me fit to cry.
Whistler he makes me melt like butter.
Strudwick he makes me flash my cly –
In fact, my form's the Bloomin' Utter.

ENVOY

I'm on for any Art that's 'Igh;
I talks as quiet as I can splutter;
I keeps a Dado on the sly;
In fact, my form's the Bloomin' Utter.

W. E. HENLEY

The Lady with Technique

As I was letting down my hair
I met a guy who didn't care;
He didn't care again to-day –
I *love* 'em when they get that way!

HUGHES MEARNS

Frustrated Male

One night I met when stepping out
A gal who wasn't thereabout;
I said, '*Hel*-lo! And how are *you*!'
She didn't say; so I never knew.

HUGHES MEARNS

72

The Practical Joker

Oh, what a fund of joy jocund lies hid in harmless hoaxes!
　　　　What keen enjoyment springs
　　　　From cheap and simple things!
What deep delight from sources trite inventive humour coaxes,
　　　　That pain and trouble brew
　　　　For every one but you!
Gunpowder placed inside its waist improves a mild Havana,
　　　　Its unexpected flash
　　　　Burns eyebrows and moustache.
When people dine no kind of wine beats ipecacuanha,
　　　　But common sense suggests
　　　　You keep it for your guests –
Then naught annoys the organ boys like throwing red hot coppers.
　　　　And much amusement bides
　　　　In common butter slides;
And stringy snares across the stairs cause unexpected croppers.
　　　　Coal scuttles, recollect,
　　　　Produce the same effect.
　　　　　A man possessed
　　　　　　Of common sense
　　　　　Need not invest
　　　　　　At great expense –
　　　　　It does not call
　　　　　　For pocket deep,
　　　　　These jokes are all
　　　　　　Extremely cheap.
If you commence with eighteenpence – it's all you'll have to pay;
You may command a pleasant and a most instructive day.

A good spring gun breeds endless fun, and makes men jump like
　　rockets –
　　　　And turnip heads on posts
　　　　Make very decent ghosts.
Then hornets sting like anything, when placed in waistcoat
　　pockets –

73

Burnt cork and walnut juice
Are not without their use.
No fun compares with easy chairs whose seats are stuffed with
needles —
Live shrimps their patience tax
When put down people's backs.
Surprising, too, what one can do with a pint of fat black beetles —
And treacle on a chair
Will make a Quaker swear!
Then sharp tin tacks
And pocket squirts —
And cobbler's wax
For ladies' skirts —
And slimy slugs
On bedroom floors —
And water jugs
On open doors —
Prepared with these cheap properties, amusing tricks to play
Upon a friend a man may spend a most delightful day.

SIR W. S. GILBERT

The Young Lady from Wantage

There was a young lady from Wantage
Of whom the town clerk took advantage.
Said the borough surveyor:
'Indeed you must pay 'er.
You've totally altered her frontage.'

ANON.

Wine and Water

Old Noah he had an ostrich farm and fowls on the largest scale,
He ate his egg with a ladle in an egg-cup big as a pail,
And the soup he took was Elephant Soup and the fish he took was Whale,
But they all were small to the cellar he took when he set out to sail,
And Noah he often said to his wife when he sat down to dine,
'I don't care where the water goes if it doesn't get into the wine.'

The cataract of the cliff of heaven fell blinding off the brink
As if it would wash the stars away as suds go down a sink,
The seven heavens came roaring down for the throats of hell to drink,
And Noah he cocked his eye and said, 'It looks like rain, I think.
The water has drowned the Matterhorn as deep as a Mendip mine,
But I don't care where the water goes if it doesn't get into the wine.'

But Noah he sinned, and we have sinned; on tipsy feet we trod,
Till a great big black teetotaller was sent for us for a rod,
And you can't get wine at a P.S.A., or chapel, or Eisteddfod,
For the Curse of Water has come again because of the wrath of God,
And water is on the Bishop's board and the Higher Thinker's shrine,
But I don't care where the water goes if it doesn't get into the wine.

G. K. CHESTERTON

Ballade of Suicide

The gallows in my garden, people say,
Is new and neat and adequately tall.
I tie the noose on in a knowing way
As one that knots his necktie for a ball;
But just as all the neighbours – on the wall –
Are drawing a long breath to shout 'Hurray!'
The strangest whim has seized me ... After all
I think I will not hang myself to-day.

To-morrow is the time I get my pay –
My uncle's sword is hanging in the hall –
I see a little cloud all pink and grey –
Perhaps the rector's mother will not call –
I fancy that I heard from Mr Gall
That mushrooms could be cooked another way –
I never read the works of Juvenal –
I think I will not hang myself to-day.

The world will have another washing day;
The decadents decay; the pedants pall;
And H. G. Wells has found that children play,
And Bernard Shaw discovered that they squall;
Rationalists are growing rational –
And through thick woods one finds a stream astray,
So secret that the very sky seems small –
I think I will not hang myself to-day.

ENVOI

Prince, I can hear the trump of Germinal,
The tumbrils toiling up the terrible way;
Even to-day your royal head may fall –
I think I will not hang myself to-day.

G. K. CHESTERTON

Ballade of Plain Common Sense

The croakers say that Mr Justice Peck
    Was briefless both as junior and K.C.
That nasty business of the altered cheque
    Was never quite hushed up, unhappily,
    But still, it was the Bench or bankruptcy;
Besides, the man was getting on in years,
    And nothing done for him. It had to be.
I simply wag my great, long, furry ears.

They say the Duke of Deal is wont to deck
    His forehead with a huge phylactery;
They say Sir Buckley Boldwood is a Czech,
    And Lord Fitz Waldemar a Portuguee;
    They say Lord Penge began in poverty
Outside Pompeii, selling souvenirs.
    I cannot think of any repartee,
I simply wag my great, long, furry ears.

They speak of England as a moral wreck,
    Stone-blind and deaf to all reality;
Her mind asleep, the usurer on her neck,
    Her God forgotten, and her history.
    They say, 'Shall these things perish utterly,
These that were England through the glorious years –
    Faith and green fields and honour and the sea?'
I simply wag my great, long, furry ears.

ENVOI

Prince, they deride your purse, your pedigree,
Your taste in Art, and wine, and clothes, and peers.
    Such things make no impression upon me;
I simply wag my great, long, furry ears.

E. C. BENTLEY

Ambitionist

I should like to see
Better become best;
I should like to see the savage
Wear both shirt and vest.

I should like to see
The Daily Press
Taking its cues
From the weekly reviews.

GAVIN EWART

The Schoolmaster Abroad

(The Steam Yacht 'Argonaut' was chartered from Messrs Perowne and Lunn by a body of Public School Masters for the purpose of an educative visit to the Levant.)

O 'Isles', as Byron said, 'of Greece!'
    For which the firm of Homer sang,
    Especially that little piece
    Interpreted by Mr Lang;
Where the unblushing Sappho wrote
The hymns we hardly like to quote.

I cannot share his grave regret
    Who found your fame had been and gone;
There seems to be a future yet
    For Tenedos and Marathon,
Fresh glory gilds their deathless sun,
And this is due to Dr Lunn!

What though your harpers twang no more?
    What though your various lyres are dumb?
See where by Cirrha's sacred shore,
    Bold Argonauts, the Ushers come!

And bring their maps, and some their wives,
And at the vision Greece revives!

The Delphic oracles are off,
   But still the site is always there;
The fumes that made the Pythian cough
   Still permeate the conscious air;
Parnassus, of the arduous 'grade',
May still be climbed, with local aid.

Lunching upon the self-same rock
   Whence Xerxes viewed the wine-red frith,
They realize with vivid shock
   The teachings of 'the smaller Smith';
With bated breath they murmur – 'This
Is actually Salamis!'

They visit where Penelope
   Nightly unwove the work of day,
Staving her suitors off till he,
   Ulysses, let the long-bow play,
And in his grave grass-widow's breast
Forgot Calypso and the rest.

In Crete, where Theseus first embraced
   His Ariadne, they explore
(Just now authentically traced)
   The footprints of the minotaur,
And follow, to the maze's source,
The thread of some profound discourse.

That isle where Leto, sick with fright,
   So scandalized her mortal kin,
Where young Apollo, lord of light
   Commenced his progress as a twin –
Fair Delos, they shall get to know,
And Paros, where the marbles grow.

Not theirs the course of crude delight
   On which the common tourist wends;
From faith they move, by way of sight,
   To knowledge meant for noble ends,
'Twill be among their purest joys
To work it off upon the boys.

One hears the travelled teacher call
   Upon the Upper Fifth to note
(Touching the Spartan counter-wall)
   How great the lore of Mr Grote;
And tell them, 'His are just the views
I formed myself – at Syracuse!'

When Jones is at a loss to show
   Where certain islands ought to be,
How well to whack him hard and low,
   And say, 'The pain is worse for me,
To whom the Cyclades are quite
Familiar, like the Isle of Wight.'

And then the lecture after prep!
   The Magic Lantern's lurid slide!
The speaker pictured on the step
   Of some old shrine, with no inside,
Or groping on his reverent knees
For Eleusinian mysteries!

Hellas defunct? O say not so,
   When Public School-boys faint to hear
The tales of antique love or woe,
   Brought home and rendered strangely clear
With instantaneous Kodak shots
Secured by Ushers on the spots!

SIR OWEN SEAMAN

The Crimes of Lizzie Borden

Lizzie Borden with an axe,
Hit her father forty whacks.
When she saw what she had done,
She hit her mother forty-one.

ANON.

Ballade of Soporific Absorption

Ho! Ho! Yes! Yes! It's very all well,
   You may drunk I am think, but I tell you I'm not,
I'm as sound as a fiddle and fit as a bell,
   And stable quite ill to see what's what.
   I under *do* stand you surprise a got
When I headed my smear with gooseberry jam:
   And I've swallowed, I grant, a beer of lot –
But I'm not so think as you drunk I am.

Can I liquor my stand? Why, yes, like hell!
   I care not how many a tossed I've pot
I shall stralk quite weight and not yutter an ell,
   My feech will not spalter the least little jot:
   If you knownly had own! – well, I gave him a dot,
And I said to him, 'Sergeant, I'll come like a lamb –
   The floor it seems like a storm in a yacht,
But I'm not so think as you drunk I am.'

For example, to prove it I'll tale you a tell –
   I once knew a fellow named Apricot –
I'm sorry, I just chair over a fell –
   A trifle – this chap, on a very day hot –
   If I hadn't consumed that last whisky of tot! –
As I said now, this fellow, called Abraham –

81

Ah? One more? Since it's you! Just a do me will spot –
But I'm not so think as you drunk I am.

So, Prince, you suggest I've bolted my shot?
Well, like what you say, and soul your damn!
    I'm an upple litset by the talk you rot –
But I'm not so think as you drunk I am.

SIR J. C. SQUIRE

Family Court

One would be in less danger
From the wiles of the stranger
If one's own kin and kith
Were more fun to be with.

OGDEN NASH

A Bas Ben Adhem

My fellow man I do not care for.
I often ask me, What's he there for?
The only answer I can find
Is, Reproduction of his kind.

OGDEN NASH

Lather as You Go

Beneath this slab
John Brown is stowed.
He watched the ads
And not the road.

OGDEN NASH

82

Pot Pourri from a Surrey Garden

Miles of pram in the wind and Pam in the gorse track,
  Coco-nut smell of the broom and a packet of Weights
Press'd in the sand. The thud of a hoof on a horse track –
A horse-riding horse for a horse-track –
          Conifer county of Surrey approached
Through remarkable wrought-iron gates.

Over your boundary now, I wash my face in a bird-bath,
  Then which path shall I take? That over there by the pram?
Down by the pond? or else, shall I take the slippery third path.
          Trodden away with gymn. shoes,
          Beautiful fir-dry alley that leads
To the bountiful body of Pam?

Pam, I adore you, Pam, you great big mountainous sports girl,
  Whizzing them over the net, full of the strength of five;
That old Malvernian brother, you zephyr and khaki shorts girl,
          Although he's playing for Woking,
Can't stand up to your wonderful backhand drive.

See the strength of her arm, as firm and hairy as Hendren's;
  See the size of her thighs, the pout of her lips as, cross,
And full of a pent-up strength, she swipes at the rhododendrons,
          Lucky the rhododendrons,
          And flings her arrogant love-lock
Back with a petulant toss.

Over the redolent pinewoods, in at the bathroom casement,
  One fine Saturday, Windlesham bells shall call
Up the Butterfield aisle rich with Gothic enlacement,
          Licensed now for embracement,
Pam and I, as the organ
  Thunders over you all.

                                        JOHN BETJEMAN

Song of the Open Road

I think that I shall never see
A billboard lovely as a tree.
Perhaps unless the billboards fall,
I'll never see a tree at all.

OGDEN NASH

Lines on Facing Forty

I have a bone to pick with fate,
Come here and tell me, girlie,
Do you think my mind is maturing late,
Or simply rotted early?

OGDEN NASH

PROTESTS AND
EXPOSTULATIONS

A Curse on the Cat

O cat of churlish kind,
The fiend was in thy mind
When thou my bird untwin'd![1]
I would thou hadst been blind!
The leopards savage,
The lions in their rage
Might catch thee in their paws,
And gnaw thee in their jaws!
The serpents of Libany
Might sting thee venomously!
The dragons with their tongues
Might poison thy liver and lungs!
The manticors[2] of the mountains
Might feed upon thy brains!

JOHN SKELTON

Doctors of the Vintrie

A little rag of rhetoric,
A less lump of logic,
A piece or a patch of philosophy,
Then forthwith by and by
They tumble so in theology,
Drowned in dregs of divinity,
That they judge themselves to be
Doctors of the chair in the Vintrie
At the Three Cranes ...

JOHN SKELTON

1. destroyed.
2. human-headed dragons.

On my Joyful Departure from the City of Cologne

As I am a Rhymer
And now at least a merry one,
Mr Mum's Rudesheimer
And the church of St Geryon
Are the two things alone
That deserve to be known
In the body-and-soul-stinking town of Cologne.

S. T. COLERIDGE

Mrs Frances Harris's Petition, 1699

To their Excellencies the Lords Justices of Ireland,
The humble petition of Frances Harris,
Who must starve and die a maid if it miscarries;
Humbly sheweth that I went to warm myself in Lady Betty's chamber because I was cold;
And I had in a purse seven pounds, four shillings and sixpence, (besides farthings) in money and gold;
So because I had been buying things for my Lady last night,
I was resolved to tell my money, to see if it was right.
For, you must know, because my trunk has a very bad lock,
Therefore all the money I have, which, God knows, is a very small stock,
I keep in my pocket, ty'd about my middle, next my smock.
So when I went to put up my purse, as God would have it, my smock was unript,
And instead of putting it into my pocket, down it slipt;
Then the bell rung, and I went down to put my lady to bed;
And, God knows, I thought my money was as safe as my maidenhead.
So, when I came up again, I found my pocket feel very light;
But when I search'd, and missed my purse, Lord! I thought I should have sunk outright.

'Lord, Madam,' says Mary, 'how d'ye do?' 'Indeed,' says I, 'never worse:

But pray, Mary, can you tell what I have done with my purse?'

'Lord help me,' says Mary, 'I never stirr'd out of this place!'

'Nay,' said I, 'I had it in Lady Betty's chamber, that's a plain case.'

So Mary got me to bed, and cover'd me up warm:

However, she stole away my garters, that I might do myself no harm.

So I tumbled and toss'd all night, as you may very well think.

But hardly ever set my eyes together, or slept a wink

So I was a-dream'd, methought, that I went and search'd the folkes round,

And in a corner of Mrs Dukes's box, ty'd in a rag, the money was found.

So next morning we told Whittle, and he fell a swearing:

Then my dame Wadger came, and she, you know, is thick of hearing.

'Dame,' said I, as loud as I could bawl, 'do you know what a loss I have had?'

'Nay,' says she, 'my Lord Colway's folks are all very sad:

For my Lord Dromedary comes a Tuesday without fail.'

'Pugh,' said I, 'but that's not the business that I ail.'

Says Cary, says he, 'I have been a servant this five and twenty years come spring,

And in all the places I lived I never heard of such a thing.'

'Yes,' says the steward, 'I remember when I was at my Lord Shrewsbury's

Such a thing as this happen'd, just about the time of *gooseberries*.'

So I went to the party suspected, and I found her full of grief:

(Now, you must know, of all things in the world I hate a thief)

However, I was resolved to bring the discourse slyly about:

'Mrs Duke,' said I, 'here's an ugly accident has happened out:

'Tis not that I value the money three ships of a louse:

But the thing I stand upon is the credit of the house.

'Tis true, seven pounds, four shillings and sixpence makes a great hole in my wages:

Besides, as they say, service is no inheritance in these ages.

Now, Mrs Duke, you know, and everybody understands,
That though 'tis hard to judge, yet money can't go without hands.'
'The devil take me!' said she (blessing herself) 'if ever I saw't!'
So she roar'd like a bedlam, as thof I had call'd her all to naught.
So, you know, what could I say to her any more?
I e'en left her, and came away as wise as I was before.
Well; but then they would have had me gone to the cunning man:
'No,' said I, ''tis the same thing, the CHAPLAIN will be here
    anon.'
So the Chaplain came in. Now the servants say he is my sweetheart,
Because he's always in my chamber, and I always take his part.
So, as the *devil* would have it, before I was aware, out I blunder'd,
'*Parson*,' said I, 'can you cast a *nativity*, when a body's plunder'd?'
(Now you must know, he hates to be call'd Parson, like the *devil*!)
'Truly,' says he, 'Mrs Nab, it might become you to be more civil;
If your money be gone, as a learned *Divine* sayd, d'ye see,
You are no text for my handling; so take that from me:
I was never taken for a *Conjurer* before, I'd have you to know.'
'Lord,' said I, 'don't be angry, I am sure I never thought you so;
You know I honour the cloth; I design to be a Parson's wife, –
I never took one in *your coat* for a conjurer in all my life.'
With that he twisted his girdle at me like a rope, as who should say,
'Now you may go hang yourself for me!' and so went away.
Well: I thought I should have swoon'd. 'Lord!' said I, 'what shall
    I do?
I have lost my money, and shall lose my true love too!'
Then my lord call'd me: 'Harry,' said my lord, 'don't cry;
I'll give you something toward thy loss:' 'And,' says my lady, 'so
    will I.'
'Oh! but,' said I, 'what if, after all, the Chaplain won't come to?'
For that, he said (an't please your Excellencies) I must petition
    you.
The premisses tenderly consider'd, I desire your Excellencies'
    protection,
And that I may have a share in next Sunday's collection;
And, over and above, that I may have your Excellencies' letter,
With an order for the Chaplain aforesaid or, instead of him, a
    better:

And then your poor petitioner, both night and day,
Or the Chaplain (for 'tis his trade,) as in duty bound, shall ever
   pray.'

JONATHAN SWIFT

An Expostulation

When late I attempted your pity to move,
   Why seem'd you so deaf to my pray'rs?
Perhaps it was right to dissemble your love –
   But – Why did you kick me downstairs?

ISAAC BICKERSTAFF
(also attributed to J. P. KEMBLE)

On a certain Methodist-teacher being caught in Bed with his Maid

'You a Magistrate chief,' his wife tauntingly said,
'You a Methodist-Teacher! and caught with your Maid!
'A delicate Text this you've chosen to *handle*
'And fine *holding forth*, without Daylight or Candle!'
Quoth Gabriel, 'My Dear, as I hope for Salvation,
'You make in your Anger a wrong Application;
'This evening I taught *how frail our Condition;*
'And the good Maid and I were but at – Repetition.'

ANON.

Rich and Poor; or, Saint and Sinner

The poor man's sins are glaring;
In the face of ghostly warning
  He is caught in the fact
  Of an overt act —
Buying greens on Sunday morning.

The rich man's sins are hidden
In the pomp of wealth and station;
  And escape the sight
  Of the children of light,
Who are wise in their generation.

The rich man has a kitchen,
And cooks to dress his dinner;
  The poor who would roast
  To the baker's must post,
And thus becomes a sinner.

The rich man has a cellar,
And a ready butler by him;
  The poor must steer
  For his pint of beer
Where the Saint can't choose but spy him.

The rich man's painted windows
Hide the concerts of the quality;
  The poor can but share
  A crack'd fiddle in the air,
Which offends all sound morality.

The rich man is invisible
In the crowd of his gay society;
  But the poor man's delight
  Is a sore in the sight,
And a stench in the nose of piety.

T. L. PEACOCK

All Saints

In a church which is furnish'd with mullion and gable,
  With altar and reredos, with gargoyle and groin,
The penitent's dresses are sealskin and sable,
  The odour of sanctity's eau-de-Cologne.
But only could Lucifer, flying from Hades,
  Gaze down on this crowd with its panniers and paints.
He would say, as he looked at the lords and the ladies,
  'Oh, where is ALL SINNERS', if this is ALL SAINTS'?'

EDMUND YATES

On Moll Batchelor

Beneath in the Dust, the mouldy old Crust
Of *Moll Bachelor* lately was shoven,
Who was skill'd in the Arts of Pyes, Custards and Tarts,
And every Device of the Oven.
When she'd liv'd long enough, she made her last Puff,
A Puff by her Husband much prais'd;
And here she doth lie, and makes a Dirt Pye,
In Hopes that her Crust may be rais'd.

ANON.

The Song Against Grocers

God made the wicked Grocer
For a mystery and a sign,
That men might shun the awful shops
And go to inns to dine;
Where the bacon's on the rafter
And the wine is in the wood,
And God that made good laughter
Has seen that they are good.

93

The evil-hearted Grocer
Would call his mother 'Ma'am',
And bow at her and bob at her,
Her aged soul to damn,
And rub his horrid hands and ask
What article was next,
Though *mortis in articulo*
Should be her proper text.

His props are not his children,
But pert lads underpaid,
Who call out 'Cash!' and bang about
To work his wicked trade;
He keeps a lady in a cage
Most cruelly all day,
And makes her count and calls her 'Miss'
Until she fades away.

The righteous minds of innkeepers
Induce them now and then
To crack a bottle with a friend
Or treat unmoneyed men,
But who hath seen the Grocer
Treat housemaids to his teas
Or crack a bottle of fish-sauce
Or stand a man a cheese?

He sells us sands of Araby
As sugar for cash down;
He sweeps his shop and sells the dust
The purest salt in town,
He crams with cans of poisoned meat
Poor subjects of the King,
And when they die by thousands
Why, he laughs like anything.

The wicked Grocer groces
In spirits and in wine,

Not frankly and in fellowship
As men in inns do dine;
But packed with soap and sardines
And carried off by grooms,
For to be snatched by Duchesses
And drunk in dressing-rooms.

The hell-instructed Grocer
Has a temple made of tin,
And the ruin of good innkeepers
Is loudly urged therein;
But now the sands are running out
From sugar of a sort,
The Grocer trembles; for his time,
Just like his weight, is short.

G. K. CHESTERTON

Lines to a Don

Remote and ineffectual Don
That dared attack my Chesterton,
With that poor weapon, half-impelled,
Unlearnt, unsteady, hardly held,
Unworthy for a tilt with men —
Your quavering and corroded pen;
Don poor at Bed and worse at Table,
Don pinched, Don starved, Don miserable;
Don stuttering, Don with roving eyes,
Don nervous, Don of crudities;
Don clerical, Don ordinary,
Don self-absorbed and solitary;
Don here-and-there, Don epileptic;
Don puffed-and empty, Don dyspeptic;
Don middle-class, Don sycophantic,
Don dull, Don brutish, Don pedantic;

Don hypocritical, Don bad,
Don furtive, Don three-quarters mad;
Don (since a man must make an end),
Don that shall never be my friend.

Don different from those regal Dons!
With hearts of gold and lungs of bronze,
Who shout and bang and roar and bawl
The Absolute across the hall,
Or sail in amply bellying gown
Enormous through the Sacred Town,
Bearing from College to their homes
Deep cargoes of gigantic tomes;
Dons admirable! Dons of Might!
Uprising on my inward sight
Compact of ancient tales, and port,
And sleep – and learning of a sort.
Dons English, worthy of the land;
Dons rooted; Dons that understand.
Good Dons perpetual that remain
A landmark, walling in the plain –
The horizon of my memories –
Like large and comfortable trees.

Don very much apart from these,
Thou scapegoat Don, thou Don devoted,
Don to thine own damnation quoted,
Perplexed to find thy trivial name
Reared in my verse to lasting shame.
Don dreadful, rasping Don and wearing,
Repulsive Don – Don past all bearing.
Don of the cold and doubtful breath,
Don despicable, Don of death;
Don nasty, skimpy, silent, level;
Don evil; Don that serves the devil.
Don ugly – that makes fifty lines.
There is a Canon which confines
A Rhymed Octosyllabic Curse

If written in Iambic Verse
To fifty lines. I never cut;
I far prefer to end it – but
Believe me I shall soon return.
My fires are banked, but still they burn
To write some more about the Don
That dared attack my Chesterton.

HILAIRE BELLOC

A Glass of Beer

The lanky hank of a she in the inn over there,
Nearly killed me for asking the loan of a glass of beer;
May the devil grip the whey-faced slut by the hair,
And beat bad manners out of her skin for a year.

That parboiled ape, with the toughest jaw you will see
On virtue's path, and a voice that would rasp the dead,
Came roaring and raging the minute she looked at me,
And threw me out of the house on the back of my head!

If I asked her master he'd give me a cask a day;
But she, with the beer at hand, not a gill would arrange!
May she marry a ghost and bear him a kitten, and may
The High King of Glory permit her to get the mange.

JAMES STEPHENS (*from the Irish*)

Johnny Dow

Wha lies here?
I, Johnny Dow.
Hoo! Johnny is that you?
Ay, man, but a'm dead now.

ANON.

On Miss Arabella Young

Here lies, returned to clay,
Miss Arabella Young,
Who on the first of May
Began to hold her tongue.

ANON.

The Pessimist

Nothing to do but work,
  Nothing to eat but food,
Nothing to wear but clothes,
  To keep one from going nude.

Nothing to breathe but air,
  Quick as a flash 'tis gone;
Nowhere to fall but off,
  Nowhere to stand but on.

Nothing to comb but hair,
  Nowhere to sleep but in bed,
Nothing to weep but tears,
  Nothing to bury but dead.

Nothing to sing but songs,
  Ah, well, alas! alack!
Nowhere to go but out,
  Nowhere to come but back.

Nothing to see but sights,
  Nothing to quench but thirst,
Nothing to have but what we've got.
  Thus through life we are cursed.

Nothing to strike but a gait;
  Everything moves that goes.
Nothing at all but common sense
  Can ever withstand these woes.

B. J. KING

How Beastly the Bourgeois is

How beastly the bourgeois is
especially the male of the species –

Presentable, eminently presentable
Shall I make you a present of him?

Isn't he handsome? isn't he healthy? Isn't he a fine specimen?
doesn't he look the fresh clean englishman, outside?
Isn't it god's own image? tramping his thirty miles a day
after partridges, or a little rubber ball?
wouldn't you like to be like that, well off, and quite the thing?

Oh, but wait!
Let him meet a new emotion, let him be faced with another man's
  need.
Let him come home to a bit of moral difficulty, let life face him with
  a new demand on his understanding
and then watch him go soggy, like a wet meringue.
Watch him turn into a mess, either a fool or a bully.
Just watch the display of him, confronted with a new demand on
  his intelligence,
a new life-demand.

How beastly the bourgeois is
especially the male of the species –

Nicely groomed, like a mushroom
Standing there so sleek and erect and eyeable –

99

and like a fungus, living on the remains of bygone life
sucking his life out of the dead leaves of greater life than his own.
And even so, he's stale, he's been there too long.
Touch him, and you'll find he's all gone inside
just like an old mushroom, all wormy inside, and hollow
under a smooth skin and an upright appearance.

Full of seething, wormy, hollow feelings
rather nasty –
How beastly the bourgeois is!

Standing in their thousands, these appearances, in damp England.
What a pity they can't all be kicked over
like sickening toadstools, and left to melt back, swiftly
into the soil of England.

D. H. LAWRENCE

The Oxford Voice

When you hear it languishing
and hooing and cooing and sidling through the front teeth,
   the oxford voice,
        or worse still
   the would-be oxford voice
you don't even laugh any more, you can't.

For every blooming bird is an Oxford cuckoo nowadays,
you can't sit on a bus or in the tube
but it breathes gently and languishingly in the back of your neck.

And oh, so seductively superior, so seductively
     self effacingly
     deprecatingly
       superior –

We wouldn't insist on it for a moment
    but we are
      we are
  you admit we are
  superior. –

                       D. H. LAWRENCE

A Politician

a politician is an arse upon
which everyone has sat except a man.

                       E. E. CUMMINGS

England Expects

Let us pause to consider the English,
Who when they pause to consider themselves they get all reticently thrilled and tinglish,
Because every Englishman is convinced of one thing, viz:
That to be an Englishman is to belong to the most exclusive club there is:
A club to which benighted bounders of Frenchmen and Germans and Italians et cetera cannot even aspire to belong,
Because they don't even speak English, and the Americans are worst of all because they speak it wrong.
Englishmen are distinguished by their traditions and ceremonials,
And also by their affection for their colonies and their contempt for the colonials.
When foreigners ponder world affairs, why sometimes by doubts they are smitten,
But Englishmen know instinctively that what the world needs most is whatever is best for Great Britain.
They have a splendid navy and they conscientiously admire it,

And every English schoolboy knows that John Paul Jones was only
an unfair American pirate.

English people disclaim sparkle and verve,

But speak without reservations of their Anglo-Saxon reserve.

After listening to little groups of English ladies and gentlemen at
cocktail parties and in hotels and Pullmans, of defining Anglo-
Saxon reserve I despair,

But I think it consists of assuming that nobody else is there,

And I shudder to think where Anglo-Saxon reserve ends when I
consider where it begins,

Which in a few high-pitched statements of what one's income is
and just what foods give one a rash and whether one and one's
husband or wife sleep in a double bed or twins.

All good Englishmen go to Oxford or Cambridge and they all
write and publish books before their graduation,

And I often wondered how they did it until I realized that they have
to do it because their genteel accents are so developed that they
can no longer understand each other's spoken words so the
written word is their only means of intercommunication.

England is the last home of the aristocracy, and the art of protecting
the aristocracy from the encroachments of commerce has been
raised to quite an art.

Because in America a rich butter-and-egg man is only a rich butter-
and-egg man or at most an honorary LLD of some hungry
university, but in England he is Sir Benjamin Buttery, Bart.

Anyhow, I think the English people are sweet,

And we might as well get used to them because when they slip and
fall they always land on their own or somebody else's feet.

OGDEN NASH

Two Footnotes

1

Once for candy cook had stolen
X was punished by Papa;
When he asked where babies came from
He was lied to by Mamma.

Now the city streets are waiting
To mislead him, and he must
Keep an eye on aged beggars
Lest they strike him in disgust.

2

When statesmen gravely say – 'We must be realistic –'
The chances are they're weak and therefore pacifistic:
But when they speak of Principles – look out – perhaps
Their generals are already poring over maps.

W. H. AUDEN

To a Friend

Thou swear'st thou'lt drink no more: kind heav'n, send
Me such a cook or coachman, but no friend.

ANON.

On Cloe

Bright as the day, and as the morning fair,
Such Cloe is – and common as the air.

GEORGE GRANVILLE, LORD LANSDOWNE

Elegy on the Death of a Mad Dog

Good people all, of every sort,
   Give ear unto my song;
And if you find it wond'rous short,
   It cannot hold you long.

In Islington there was a man,
   Of whom the world might say,
That still a godly race he ran,
   When'er he went to pray.

A kind and gentle heart he had,
   To comfort friends and foes;
The naked every day he clad,
   When he put on his clothes.

And in that town a dog was found,
   As many dogs there be,
Both mongrel, puppy, whelp, and hound,
   And curs of low degree.

This dog and man at first were friends;
   But when a pique began,
The dog, to gain some private ends,
   Went mad and bit the man.

Around from all the neighbouring streets
   The wond'ring neighbours ran,
And swore the dog had lost its wits,
   To bite so good a man.

The wound it seem'd both sore and sad
   To every Christian eye;
And while they swore the dog was mad,
   They swore the man would die.

But soon a wonder came to light,
   That showed the rogues they lied:
The man recover'd of the bite,
   The dog it was that died.

OLIVER GOLDSMITH

To a Living Author

Your comedy I've read, my friend,
   And like the half you pilfered best;
Be sure the piece you yet may mend —
   Take courage, man, and steal the rest.

ANON.

The March to Moscow

The Emperor Nap he would set off
On a summer excursion to Moscow;
The fields were green and the sky was blue,
Morbleu! Parbleu!
What a splendid excursion to Moscow!

The Emperor Nap he talk'd so big
That he frighten'd Mr Roscoe.
And Counsellor Brougham was all in a fume
At the thought of the march to Moscow:
The Russians, he said, they were undone,
And the great Fee-Faw-Fum
Would presently come.
With a hop, step, and jump, unto London,
For, as for his conquering Russia,
However some persons might scoff it,
Do it he could, do it he would,
And from doing it nothing would come but good,
And nothing would call him off it.

But the Russians stoutly they turned to
Upon the road to Moscow.
Nap had to fight his way all through;
They could fight, though they could not parlez-vous;
But the fields were green, and the sky was blue,
Morbleu! Parbleu!
But to march back again from Moscow.

The Russians they stuck close to him
All on the road from Moscow –
And Shouvaloff he shovell'd them off,
And Markoff he mark'd them off,
And Krosnoff he cross'd them off,
And Touchkoff he touch'd them off,
And Boroskoff he bored them off,

And Kutousoff he cut them off,
And Parenoff he pared them off,
And Worronzoff he worried them off,
And Doctoroff he doctor'd them off,
And Rodinoff he flogg'd them off.
And, last of all, an Admiral came,
A terrible man with a terrible name,
A name which you all know by sight very well,
But which no one can speak, and no one can spell.

And then came on the frost and snow
All on the road from Moscow.
Worse and worse every day the elements grew,
The fields were so white and the sky was so blue,
Sacrebleu! Ventrebleu!
What a horrible journey from Moscow.

Too cold upon the road was he;
Too hot he had been at Moscow;
But colder and hotter he may be,
For the grave is colder than Muscovy;
And a place there is to be kept in view,
Where the fire is red, and the brimstone blue,
Morbleu! Parbleu!
But there he must stay for a very long day,
For from thence there is no stealing away,
As there was on the road from Moscow.

(abridged)

ROBERT SOUTHEY

Mary's Ghost

A PATHETIC BALLAD

'Twas in the middle of the night,
  To sleep young William tried;
When Mary's ghost came stealing in,
  And stood at his bed-side.

O William dear! O William dear!
  My rest eternal ceases;
Alas! my everlasting peace
  Is broken into pieces.

I thought the last of all my cares
  Would end with my last minute;
But tho' I went to my long home,
  I didn't stay long in it.

The body-snatchers they have come,
  And made a snatch at me;
It's very hard them kind of men
  Won't let a body be!

You thought that I was buried deep,
  Quite decent like and chary,
But from her grave in Mary-bone,
  They've come and boned your Mary.

The arm that used to take your arm
  Is took to Dr Vyse;
And both my legs are gone to walk
  The hospital at Guy's.

I vowed that you should have my hand,
  But fate gives us denial;
You'll find it there, at Dr Bell's,
  In spirits and a phial.

As for my feet, the little feet
  You used to call so pretty,
There's one, I know, in Bedford Row,
  The t'other's in the City.

I can't tell where my head is gone,
  But Doctor Carpue can;
As for my trunk, it's all packed up
  To go by Pickford's van.

I wish you'd go to Mr P.
  And save me such a ride;
I don't half like the outside place,
  They've took for my inside.

The cock it crows – I must be gone!
  My William, we must part!
But I'll be yours in death, altho'
  Sir Astley has my heart.

Don't go to weep upon my grave,
  And think that there I be;
They haven't left an atom there
  Of my anatomie.

THOMAS HOOD

The Young Person of Mullion

There was a young person of Mullion,
Intent upon marrying bullion;
  By some horrible fluke,
  She jilted a duke
And had to elope with a scullion.

SANDYS WASON

Poetical Economy

What hours I spent of precious time,
    What pints of ink I used to waste,
Attempting to secure a rhyme
    To suit the public taste,
Until I found a simple plan
Which makes the lamest lyric scan!

When I've a syllable de trop,
    I cut it off, without apol.:
This verbal sacrifice, I know,
    May irritate the schol.;
But all must praise my dev'lish cunn.
Who realize that Time is Mon.

My sense remains as clear as cryst.,
    My style as pure as any Duch.
Who does not boast a bar sinist.
    Upon her fam. escutch.;
And I can treat with scornful pit.
The sneers of ev'ry captious crit.

I gladly publish to the pop.
    A scheme of which I make no myst.,
And beg my fellow scribes to cop.
    This-labour-saving syst.
I offer it to the consid.
Of ev'ry thoughtful individ.

The author, working like a beav.,
    His readers' pleasure could redoub.
Did he but now and then abbrev.
    The work he gives his pub.
(This view I most partic. suggest
To A. C. Bens. and G. K. Chest.)

If Mr Caine rewrote The Scape.,
 And Miss Correll condensed Barabb.,
What could they save in foolscap pape.
 Did they but cult. the hab.,
Which teaches people to suppress
All syllables that are unnec.!

If playwrights would but thus dimin.
 The length of time each drama takes,
(The Second Mrs Tanq. by Pin.
 Or even Ham., by Shakes.)
We could maintain a watchful att.
When at a Mat. on Wed. or Sat.

Have done, ye bards, with dull monot.!
 Foll. my examp., O, Stephen Phill.,
O, Owen Seam., O, William Wat.,
 O, Ella Wheeler Wil.,
And share with me the grave respons.
Of writing this amazing nons.!

HARRY GRAHAM

Nobody Loses All the Time

nobody loses all the time

i had an uncle named
Sol who was a born failure and
nearly everybody said he should have gone
into vaudeville perhaps because my Uncle Sol could
sing McCann He was A Diver on Xmas Eve like Hell Itself which
may or may not account for the fact that my Uncle

Sol indulged in that possibly most inexcusable
of all to use a highfalootin phrase
luxuries that is or to

wit farming and be
it needlessly
added

my Uncle Sol's farm
failed because the chickens
ate the vegetables so
my Uncle Sol had a
chicken farm till the
skunks ate the chickens when

my Uncle Sol
had a skunk farm but
the skunks caught cold and
died and so
my Uncle Sol imitated the
skunks in a subtle manner

or by drowning himself in the watertank
but somebody who'd given my Uncle Sol a Victor
Victrola and records while he lived presented to
him upon the auspicious occasion of his decease a
scrumptious not to mention splendiferous funeral with
tall boys in black gloves and flowers and everything and

i remember we all cried like the Missouri
when my Uncle Sol's coffin lurched because
somebody pressed a button
(and down went
my Uncle
Sol

and started a worm farm)

                                        E. E. CUMMINGS

Requiem

There was a young belle of old Natchez
Whose garments were always in patchez.
When comment arose
On the state of her clothes,
She drawled, 'When Ah itchez, Ah scratchez.'

OGDEN NASH

We Have Been Here Before

I think I remember this moorland,
  The tower on the tip of the tor;
I feel in the distance another existence;
  I think I have been here before.

And I think you were sitting beside me
  In a fold in the face of the fell;
For Time at its work'll go round in a circle,
  And what is befalling, befell.

'I have been here before!' I asserted,
  In a nook on a neck of the Nile.
I once in a crisis was punished by Isis,
  And you smiled, I remember your smile.

I had the same sense of persistence
  On the site of the seat of the Sioux;
I heard in the tepee the sound of a sleepy
  Pleistocene grunt. It was you.

The past made a promise, before it
  Began to begin to begone.
This limited gamut brings you again. . . . Damn it,
  How long has this got to go on?

MORRIS BISHOP

Note on Intellectuals

To the man-in-the-street, who, I'm sorry to say
    Is a keen observer of life,
The word Intellectual suggests straight away
    A man who's untrue to his wife.

W. H. AUDEN

Mythology

All my favourite characters have been
Out of all pattern and proportion;
Some living in villas by railways,
Some like Katsimbalis heard but seldom seen,
And others in banks whose sunless hands
Moved like great rats on ledgers . . .

Tibble, Gondril, Purvis, the Duke of Puke,
Shatterblossom and Dude Bowdler
Who swelled up in Jaffa and became a tree,
Hollis who had seven wives killed under him like horses
And that man of destiny.

Ramon de something who gave lectures
From an elephant; founded a society
To protect the inanimate against cruelty.
He gave asylum to aged chairs in his home,
Lampposts and crockery, everything that
Seemed to him suffering he took in
Without mockery.

The poetry was in the pity. No judgement
Disturbs people like these in their frames
O men of the Marmion class, sons of the free.

LAWRENCE DURRELL

Reflexions on Ice-Breaking

> Candy
> is dandy
> But liquor
> is quicker.

OGDEN NASH

Arizona Nature Myth

Up in the heavenly saloon
Sheriff sun and rustler moon
Gamble, stuck in the sheriff's mouth
The fag end of an afternoon.

There in the bad town of the sky
Sheriff, nervy, wonders why
He's let himself wander so far West
On his own; he looks with a smoky eye

At the rustler opposite turning white,
Lays down a king for Law, sits tight
Bluffing. On it that crooked moon
Plays an ace and shoots for the light.

Spurs, badge, and uniform red,
(It looks like blood, but he's shamming dead),
Down drops the marshal, and under cover
Crawls out dogwise, ducking his head.

But Law that don't get its man ain't Law.
Next day, faster on the draw,
Sheriff creeping up from the other side,
Blazes his way in through the back door.

118

But moon's not there. He's ridden out on
A galloping phenomenon,
A wonder horse, quick as light.
Moon's left town. Moon's clean gone.

JAMES MICHIE

RIGMAROLES AND
NONSENSE

If All the World were Paper

If all the world were paper,
And all the sea were inke;
And all the trees were bread and cheese,
What should we do for drinke?

If all the world were sand 'o,
Oh, then what should we lack 'o;
If as they say there were no clay,
How should we make tobacco?

If all our vessels ran 'a,
If none but had a crack 'a;
If Spanish apes eat all the grapes,
What should we do for sack 'a?

If fryers had no bald pates,
Nor nuns had no dark cloysters,
If all the seas were beans and pease,
What should we do for oysters?

If there had been no projects,
Nor none that did great wrongs;
If fidlers shall turne players all,
What should we doe for songs?

If all things were eternall,
And nothing their end bringing;
If this should be, then, how should we
Here make an end of singing?

ANON.

Epilogus Incerti Authoris

Like to the mowing tone of unspoke speeches,
Or like two lobsters clad in logick breeches;
Or like the gray fleece of a crimson catt,
Or like the moone-calfe in a slippshod hatt;
Or like the shaddow when the sunne is gone,
Or like a thought, that nev'r was thought upon:
 Even such is man who never was begotten
 Untill his children were both dead and rotten.

Like to the fiery touch-hole of a cabbage,
Or like a crablowse with his bag and baggage;
Or like the guilt reflection of the winde,
Or like the abortive issue borne behind;
Or like the four square circle of a ring,
Or like high downe a ding a ding a ding;
 Even such is man who breathlesse without a doubt
 Spake to small purpose when his tongue was out.

Like the fresh colours of a withered rose,
Or like a running verse that's writ in prose;
Or like the umbles of a tynder box,
Or like a sound man, troubled with the pox;
Or like to hobbnayles coyn'd in single pence,
Lest they should lose their preterperfect tence,
 Even such is man who dyed, and yet did laugh,
 To read these strong lines for his Epitaph.

RICHARD CORBET

The Great Panjandrum

So she went into the garden
to cut a cabbage-leaf
to make an apple-pie;
and at the same time
a great she-bear, coming down the street,
pops its head into the shop.
What! no soap?
             So he died,
and she very imprudently married the Barber:
and there were present
the Picninnies,
        and the Joblillies,
            and the Garyulies,
and the great Panjandrum himself,
with the little round button at top;
and they all fell to playing the game of catch-as-catch-can,
till the gunpowder ran out at the heels of their boots.

SAMUEL FOOTE

In the Dumps

We're all in the dumps,
  For diamonds are trumps;
The kittens are gone to St Paul's!
  The babies are bit,
  The Moon's in a fit,
And the houses are built without walls.

ANON.

125

A Nocturnal Sketch

Even is come; and from the dark Park, hark
The signal of the setting sun – one gun!
And six is sounding from the chime, prime time
To go and see the Drury-Lane Dane slain, –
Or hear Othello's jealous doubt spout out, –
Or Macbeth raving at that shade-made blade,
Denying to his frantic clutch much touch; –
Or else to see Ducrow with wide stride ride
Four horses as no other man can span;
Or in the small Olympic Pit, sit split
Laughing at Liston, while you quiz his phiz.

Anon Night comes, and with her wings brings things
Such as, with his poetic tongue, Young sung;
The gas up-blazes with its bright white light,
And paralytic watchmen prowl, howl, growl,
About the streets and take up Pall-Mall Sal,
Who, hasting to her nightly jobs, robs fobs.

Now thieves to enter for your cash, smash, crash,
Past drowsy Charley, in a deep sleep, creep,
But frightened by Policeman B.3, flee,
And while they're going, whisper low, 'No go!'
Now puss, while folks are in their beds, treads leads.
And sleepers waking, grumble – 'Drat that cat!'
Who in the gutter caterwauls, squalls, mauls
Some feline foe, and screams in shrill ill-will.
Now Bulls of Bashan, of a prize size, rise
In childish dreams, and with a roar gore poor
Georgy, or Charley, or Billy, willy-nilly; –
But Nursemaid, in a nightmare rest, chest-pressed,
Dreameth of one of her old flames, James Games,
And that she hears – what faith is man's! – Ann's banns
And his, from Reverend Mr Rice, twice, thrice:

White ribbons flourish, and a stout shout out,
That upward goes, shows Rose knows those bows' woes!

THOMAS HOOD

Sonnet found in a Deserted Mad-House

Oh that my soul a marrow-bone might seize!
For the old egg of my desire is broken,
Spilled is the pearly white and spilled the yolk, and
As the mild melancholy contents grease
My path the shorn lamb baas like bumblebees.
Time's trashy purse is as a taken token
Or like a thrilling recitation, spoken
By mournful mouths filled full of mirth and cheese.

And yet, why should I clasp the earthful urn?
Or find the frittered fig that felt the fast?
Or choose to chase the cheese around the churn?
Or swallow any pill from out the past?
Ah no, Love, not while your hot kisses burn
Like a potato riding on the blast.

ANON.

Upon St George for England

St George, to save a maid, the dragon slew;
A pretty tale, if all that's said be true;
Some say there was no dragon; and 'tis said,
There was no George; I wish there was a maid.

ANON.

Evidence Read at the Trial of the Knave of Hearts

They told me you had been to her,
    And mentioned me to him:
She gave me a good character,
    But said I could not swim.

He sent them word I had not gone,
    (We know it to be true):
If she should push the matter on,
    What would become of you?

I gave her one, they gave him two,
    You gave us three or more;
They all returned from him to you,
    Though they were mine before.

If I or she should chance to be
    Involved in this affair,
He trusts to you to set them free,
    Exactly as we were.

My notion was that you had been
    (Before she had this fit)
An obstacle that came between
    Him, and ourselves, and it.

Don't let him know she liked them best,
    For this must ever be
A secret, kept from all the rest,
    Between yourself and me.

LEWIS CARROLL

The Voice of the Lobster

' 'Tis the voice of the Lobster; I heard him declare,
"You have baked me too brown, I must sugar my hair."
As a duck with its eyelids, so he with his nose
Trims his belt and his buttons, and turns out his toes.
When the sands are all dry, he is gay as a lark,
And will talk in contemptuous tones of the Shark:
But, when the tide rises and sharks are around,
His voice has a timid and tremulous sound.

'I passed by his garden, and marked, with one eye,
How the Owl and the Panther were sharing a pie:
The Panther took pie-crust, and gravy, and meat,
While the Owl had the dish as its share of the treat.
When the pie was all finished, the Owl, as a boon,
Was kindly permitted to pocket the spoon:
While the Panther received knife and fork with a growl,
And concluded the banquet by –'

LEWIS CARROLL

Lines by a Humanitarian

Be lenient with lobsters, and ever kind to crabs,
And be not disrespectful to cuttle-fish or dabs;
Chase not the Cochin-China, chaff not the ox obese,
And babble not of feather-beds in company with geese.
Be tender with the tadpole, and let the limpet thrive,
Be merciful to mussels, don't skin your eels alive;
When talking to a turtle don't mention calipee –
Be always kind to animals wherever you may be.

ANON.

The Old Man who said 'Hush'

There was an Old Man who said, 'Hush!
I perceive a young bird in this bush!'
 When they said, 'Is it small?'
 He replied, 'Not at all!
It is four times as big as the bush!'

EDWARD LEAR

I Wish I Were

I wish I were a
Elephantiaphus
And could pick off the coconuts with my nose.
But, oh! I am not,
(Alas! I cannot be)
An Elephanti –
Elephantiaphus.
But I'm a cockroach
And I'm a water-bug,
I can crawl around and hide behind the sink.

I wish I were a
Rhinoscerèeacus
And could wear an ivory toothpick in my nose.
But, oh! I am not,
(Alas! I cannot be)
A Rhinoscōri –
Rhinoscerèeacus –
But I'm a beetle
And I'm a pumpkin-bug,
I can buzz and bang my head against the wall.

I wish I were a
Hippopōpotamus

And could swim the Tigris and the broad Gangès.
But, oh! I am not,
(Alas! I cannot be)
A hippopōpo –
Hippopōpotamus –
But I'm a grasshopper
And I'm a katydid,
I can play the fiddle with my left hind-leg.

I wish I were a
Levileviathan
And had seven hundred knuckles in my spine.
But, oh! I am not,
(Alas! I cannot be)
A Levi-ikey –
A Levi-ikey-mo.
But I'm a firefly
And I'm a lightning-bug,
I can light cheroots and gaspers with my tail.

AMERICAN FOLK SONG

Infant Innocence

The Grizzly Bear is huge and wild
He has devoured the infant child.
The infant child is not aware
He has been eaten by the bear.

A. E. HOUSMAN

The Common Cormorant

The common cormorant or shag
Lays eggs inside a paper bag.
The reason you will see no doubt
It is to keep the lightning out.
But what these unobservant birds
Have never noticed is that herds
Of wandering bears may come with buns
And steal the bags to hold the crumbs.

ANON.

Peas

I always eat peas with honey,
I've done it all my life,
They do taste kind of funny,
But it keeps them on the knife.

ANON.

Boston

I come from the city of Boston,
The home of the bean and the cod,
Where the Cabots speak only to Lowells,
And the Lowells speak only to God.

ANON.

Imitation of Chaucer

Women ben full of Ragerie,
Yet swinken not sans secresie
Thilke Moral shall ye understand,
From Schoole-boy's Tale of fayre Irelond:
Which to the Fennes hath him betake,
To filch the gray Ducke fro the Lake.
Right then, there passen by the Way
His Aunt, and eke her Daughters tway.
Ducke in his Trowses hath he hent,
Not to be spied of Ladies gent.
'But ho! our Nephew,' (crieth one)
'Ho,' quoth another, 'Cozen John';
And stoppen, and laugh, and callen out, –
This sely Clerk full low doth lout:
They asken that, and talken this,
'Lo here is Coz, and here is Miss.'
But, as he glozeth with Speeches soote,
The Ducke sore tickleth his Erse-root:
Fore-piece and buttons all-to-brest,
Forth thrust a white neck, and red crest.
'Te-he,' cry'd Ladies; Clerke nought spake:
Miss star'd; and gray Ducke crieth Quake.
'O Moder, Moder' (quoth the daughter)
'Be thilke same thing Maids longen a'ter?
'Bette is to pyne on coals and chalke,
'Then trust on Mon, whose yerde can talke.'

ALEXANDER POPE

135

If You Have Seen

Good reader! if you e'er have seen,
 When Phoebus hastens to his pillow,
The mermaids, with their tresses green,
 Dancing upon the western billow:
If you have seen, at twilight dim,
When the lone spirit's vesper hymn
 Floats wild along the winding shore:
If you have seen, through mist of eve,
The fairy train their ringlets weave,
Glancing along the spangled green; –
 If you have seen all this and more,
God bless me! what a deal you've seen!

THOMAS MOORE

On a Lady's Sporting a Somerset

I saw, I saw, I know not what,
I saw a dash above a dot,
Presenting to my contemplation
A perfect mark of admiration!

L. STERNE (?)

Sincere Flattery of R. B.

Birthdays? yes in a general way;
For the most if not for the best of men:
You were born (I suppose) on a certain day:
So was I: or perhaps in the night: what then?

Only this: or at least, if more,
You must know, not think it, and learn, not speak:
There is truth to be found on the unknown shore,
And many will find where few will seek.

For many are called and few are chosen,
And the few grow many as ages lapse:
But when will the many grow few: what dozen
Is fused into one by Time's hammer-taps?

A bare brown stone in a babbling brook: –
It was wanton to hurl it there, you say:
And the moss, which clung in the sheltered nook
(Yet the stream runs cooler), is washed away.

That begs the question: many a prater
Thinks such a suggestion a sound 'stop thief!'
Which, may I ask, do you think the greater,
Sergeant-at-arms or a Robber Chief?

And if it were not so? Still you doubt?
Ah! Yours is a birthday indeed if so.
That were something to write a poem about,
If one thought a little. I only know

P.S.

There's a Me Society down at Cambridge,
Where my works, *cum notis variorum*,
Are talked about; Well, I require the same bridge
That Euclid took toll of as *Asinorum*.

And, as they have got through several ditties
I thought were as stiff as a brick-built wall,
I've composed the above; and a stiff one *it* is,
A bridge to stop asses at, once for all.

J. K. STEPHEN

Sincere Flattery

OF W. W. (AMERICANUS)

The clear cool note of the cuckoo which has ousted the legitimate nest-holder,

The whistle of the railway guard dispatching the train to the inevitable collision.

The maiden's monosyllabic reply to a polysyllabic proposal,

The fundamental note of the last trump, which is presumably D natural;

All of these are sounds to rejoice in, yea, to let your very ribs re-echo with:

But better than all of them is the absolutely last chord of the apparently inexhaustible pianoforte player.

J. K. STEPHEN

Poem by a Perfectly Furious Academician

I takes and paints,
Hears no complaints,
And sells before I'm dry;
Till savage Ruskin
He sticks his tusk in,
Then nobody will buy.

SHIRLEY BROOKS

On a General Election

The accursed power which stands on Privilege
(And goes with Women, and Champagne and Bridge)
Broke – and Democracy resumed her reign:
(Which goes with Bridge, and Women and Champagne).

HILAIRE BELLOC

The Higher Pantheism in a Nutshell

One, who is not, we see; but one, whom we see not, is;
Surely, this is not that; but that is assuredly this.

What, and wherefore, and whence: for under is over and under;
If thunder could be without lightning, lightning could be without
   thunder.

Doubt is faith in the main; but faith, on the whole, is doubt;
We cannot believe by proof; but could we believe without?

Why, and whither, and how? for barley and rye are not clover;
Neither are straight lines curves; yet over is under and over.

One and two are not one; but one and nothing is two;
Truth can hardly be false, if falsehood cannot be true.

Parall els all things are; yet many of these are askew;
You are certainly I; but certainly I am not you.

One, whom we see not, is; and one, who is not, we see;
Fiddle, we know, is diddle; and diddle, we take it, is dee.

ALGERNON CHARLES SWINBURNE

The Pin

As Nature H — y's Clay was blending,
Uncertain what her work should end in,
Whether in female or in male,
A Pin dropped in, and turned the Scale.

ANON.

139

The Modern Hiawatha

When he killed the Mudjokivis,
Of the skin he made him mittens,
Made them with the fur side inside,
Made them with the skin side outside,
He, to get the warm side inside,
Put the inside skin side outside;
He, to get the cold side outside,
Put the warm side fur side inside.
That's why he put fur side inside,
Why he put the skin side outside,
Why he turned them inside outside.

ANON.

The Young Man of Montrose

There was a young man of Montrose
Who had pockets in none of his clothes.
    When asked by his lass
    Where he carried his brass
He said 'Darling, I pay through the nose.'

ARNOLD BENNETT

The Shropshire Lad's Cousin

(AN EVEN GLOOMIER FELLOW THAN HIS
CELEBRATED RELATIVE)

When I go to the circus,
My heart is full of woe,
For thinking of the people
Who used to see the show,
And now are laid below.

140

They stood beneath the tent-cloth,
And heard the lion roar;
They saw the striped hyena
Revolve upon the floor;
And now they are no more.

I think of all the corpses
Worm-eaten in the shade;
I cannot chew my peanuts
Or drink my lemonade:
Good God, I am afraid!

I see the grave-worms feeding
Upon the tigers' tails;
I see the people quiet
As prisoners in jails,
Because they're dead as nails.

Then what's the good of watching
The horses and trapeze,
The big show and the little,
And the menageries? –
We're all a lot of fleas.

SAMUEL HOFFENSTEIN

A Description of Maidenhead

Have you not in a Chimney seen
A sullen faggot, wet and green,
How coyly it receives the heat
And at both ends does fume and sweat?

So fares it with the harmless Maid
When first upon her Back she's laid;
But the kind experienced Dame
Cracks, and rejoices in the Flame.

JOHN WILMOT, EARL OF ROCHESTER

A RECENT DISCOVERY

(An old bass-viol was lately bought for a few shillings at a farm sale not a
thousand miles from Mellstock. Pasted on the inside of it was the following
poem in a well-known handwriting. w. p.)

A Right-of-Way: 1865

Decades behind me
When courting took more time,
In Tuphampton ewe-leaze I mind me
Two trudging aforetime:
A botanist he, in quest of a sought-after fleabane,
Wheedling his leman with 'Do you love *me*, Jane?'

Yestreen with bowed back
(To hike now is irksome),
Hydroptic and sagging the cloud wrack,
I spied in the murk some
Wayfarer myopic Linnaeus-wise quizzing the quitches
And snooping at simples and worts in the ditches.

Remarked he, 'A path here
I seek to discover,
A right-of-way bang through this garth here,
Where elsewhiles a lover
I prinked with a pocket herbarium, necked I and cuddled:
Now I'm all mud-sprent, bored and be-puddled.

'I'm long past my noon-time.
The Unweeting Planner
Again proffers bale for one's boon-time
By tossing a spanner
Or crowbar into the works without reckoning the cost, sir.
At eighty,' intoned he, 'life is a frost, sir.'

'When erst here I tarried
I knew not my steady
Had coolly, concurrently married
Three husbands already,
Not learnt I till later, what's more, that all three were brothers,
Though sprung they, it seems, of disparate mothers.

'Well, we two inspected
The flora of Wessex;
More specimens had we collected
Had she pandered less sex;
We botanized little that year ... But I must be wending;
My analyst hints at amnesia impending.'

WILLIAM PLOMER

Burlesque of Lope de Vega

If the man who turnips cries,
Cry not when his father dies,
'Tis a proof that he had rather
Have a turnip than his father.

Imitation of the Style of ...

Hermit hoar, in solemn cell
   Wearing out life's evening grey;
Strike thy bosom, Sage, and tell
   What is bliss, and which the way.

Thus I spoke, and speaking sigh'd,
   Scarce repress'd the starting tear,
When the hoary sage, reply'd,
   Come, my lad, and drink some beer.

SAMUEL JOHNSON

Unfortunate Miss Bailey

A captain bold from Halifax who dwelt in country quarters,
Betrayed a maid who hanged herself one morning in her Garters.
His wicked conscience smited him, he lost his Stomach daily,
And took to drinking Ratafia while thinking of Miss Bailey.

One night betimes he went to bed, for he had caught a Fever;
Says he, 'I am a handsome man, but I'm a gay Deceiver.'
His candle just at twelve o'clock began to burn quite palely,
A Ghost stepped up to his bedside and said 'Behold Miss Bailey!'

'Avaunt, Miss Bailey!' then he cries, 'your Face looks white and
   mealy.'
'Dear Captain Smith,' the ghost replied, 'you've used me
   ungenteelly;
The Crowner's 'Quest goes hard with me because I've acted
   frailly,
And Parson Biggs won't bury me though I am dead Miss Bailey.'

'Dear Corpse!' said he, 'since you and I accounts must once for all
   close,
There really is a one pound note in my regimental Small-clothes;
I'll bribe the sexton for your grave.' The ghost then vanished gaily
Crying, 'Bless you, Wicked Captain Smith, Remember poor Miss
   Bailey.'

ANON.

Epigram
INTENDED TO ALLAY PARTY SPIRIT

God bless the King, I mean the faith's defender;
God bless – no harm in blessing – the Pretender;
But who Pretender is, or who is King,
God bless us all – that's quite another thing.

JOHN BYROM

She was poor but she was honest

She was poor, but she was honest,
    Victim of the squire's whim:
First he loved her, then he left her,
    And she lost her honest name.

Then she ran away to London,
    For to hide her grief and shame;
There she met another squire,
    And she lost her name again.

See her riding in her carriage,
    In the Park and all so gay:
All the nibs and nobby persons
    Come to pass the time of day.

See the little old-world village
    Where her aged parents live,
Drinking the champagne she sends them;
    But they never can forgive.

In the rich man's arms she flutters,
    Like a bird with broken wing:
First he loved her, then he left her,
    And she hasn't got a ring.

See him in the splendid mansion,
    Entertaining with the best,
While the girl that he has ruined,
    Entertains a sordid guest.

See him in the House of Commons,
    Making laws to put down crime,
While the victim of his passions
    Trails her way through mud and slime.

Standing on the bridge at midnight,
   She says: 'Farewell, blighted Love.'
There's a scream, a splash – Good Heavens!
   What is she a-doing of?

Then they drag her from the river,
   Water from her clothes they wrang,
For they thought that she was drownded;
   But the corpse got up and sang:

'It's the same the whole world over,
   It's the poor that gets the blame,
It's the rich that gets the pleasure.
   Isn't it a blooming shame?'

ANON.

A True Maid

No, no, for my Virginity,
   When I lose that, says ROSE, I'll dye:
Behind the Elmes, last Night, cry'd DICK,
   ROSE, were you not extremely Sick?

MATTHEW PRIOR

The Man in the Wilderness

The man in the wilderness asked of me,
How many strawberries grow in the sea?
I answered him as I thought good,
As many red herrings as grow in the wood.

ANON.

Epigram

WRITTEN SOON AFTER DR HILL'S FARCE CALLED
'THE ROUT' WAS ACTED

For physic and farces
His equal there scarce is;
His farces are physic,
His physic a farce is.

DAVID GARRICK

Polly Perkins

I am a broken-hearted milkman, in grief I'm arrayed,
Through keeping of the company of a young servant maid,
Who lived on board and wages the house to keep clean
In a gentleman's family near Paddington Green.

Chorus:
She was as beautiful as a butterfly
And as proud as a Queen
Was pretty little Polly Perkins of
Paddington Green.

She'd an ankle like an antelope and a step like a deer,
A voice like a blackbird, so mellow and clear,
Her hair hung in ringlets so beautiful and long,
I thought that she loved me but I found I was wrong.

When I'd rattle in a morning and cry 'milk below',
At the sound of my milk-cans her face she would show
With a smile upon her countenance and a laugh in her eye,
If I thought she'd have loved me, I'd have laid down to die.

When I asked her to marry me she said 'Oh! what stuff',
And told me to 'drop it, for she had quite enough

Of my nonsense' – at the same time I'd been very kind,
But to marry a milkman she didn't feel inclined.

'Oh, the man that has me must have silver and gold,
A chariot to ride in and be handsome and bold,
His hair must be curly as any watch spring,
And his whiskers as big as a brush for clothing.'

The words that she uttered went straight through my heart,
I sobbed and I sighed, and straight did depart;
With a tear on my eyelid as big as a bean,
Bidding good-bye to Polly and Paddington Green.

In six months she married, – this hard-hearted girl, –
But it was not a Wi-count, and it was not a Nearl,
It was not a 'Baronite', but a shade or two wuss,
It was a bow-legged conductor of a twopenny bus.

ANON.

On the Collar of Tiger, Mrs Dingley's Lap-dog

Pray steal me not, I'm Mrs Dingley's
Whose heart in this four-footed thing lies.

JONATHAN SWIFT

A Note on the Latin Gerunds

When Dido found Aeneas would not come,
She mourned in silence, and was Di-do-dum.

RICHARD PORSON

The Firefly

The firefly's flame
Is something for which science has no name.
I can think of nothing eerier
Than flying around with an unidentified red glow on a person's
   posterior.

OGDEN NASH

The Man on the Flying Trapeze

Oh, the girl that I loved she was handsome,
I tried all I knew her to please.
But I couldn't please her a quarter as well
As the man on the flying trapeze.

Chorus:

Oh, he flies through the air with the greatest of ease,
This daring young man on the flying trapeze.
His figure is handsome, all girls he can please,
And my love he purloined her away.

Last night as usual I went to her home.
There sat her old father and mother alone.
I asked for my love and they soon made it known
That she-e had flown away.

She packed up her box and eloped in the night,
To go-o with him at his ease.
He lowered her down from a four-story flight,
By means of his flying trapeze.

He took her to town and he dressed her in tights,
That he-e might live at his ease.
He ordered her up to the tent's awful height,
To appear on the flying trapeze.

Now she flies through the air with the greatest of ease,
This daring young girl on the flying trapeze.
Her figure is handsome, all men she can please,
And my love is purloinèd away.

Once I was happy, but now I'm forlorn,
Like an old coat that is tattered and torn,
Left to this wide world to fret and to mourn,
Betrayed by a maid in her teens.

ANON.

Roman *Wall Blues*

Over the heather the wet wind blows,
I've lice in my tunic and a cold in my nose.

The rain comes pattering out of the sky.
I'm a Wall soldier, I don't know why.

The mist creeps over the hard grey stone.
My girl's in Tungria; I sleep alone.

Aulus goes hanging around her place,
I don't like his manners, I don't like his face.

Piso's a Christian, he worships a fish;
There'd be no kissing if he had his wish.

She gave me a ring but I diced it away;
I want my girl and I want my pay.

When I'm a veteran with only one eye
I shall do nothing but look at the sky.

W. H. AUDEN

Wot Cher!

OR, KNOCKED 'EM IN THE OLD KENT ROAD

Last week down our alley came a toff,
Nice old geezer with a nasty cough,
Sees my Missus, takes 'is topper off
  In a very gentlemanly way!
'Ma'am,' says he, 'I 'ave some news to tell,
Your rich Uncle Tom of Camberwell
Popped off recent, which it ain't a sell,
  Leaving you 'is little Donkey Shay.'

  'Wot cher!' all the neighbours cried,
    'Who're yer goin' to meet, Bill?
    Have yer bought the street, Bill?'
  Laugh! I thought I should 'ave died,
  Knocked 'em in the Old Kent Road!

Some says nasty things about the moke,
One cove thinks 'is leg is really broke,
That's 'is envy, cos we're carriage folk,
  Like the Toffs as rides in Rotten Row!
Straight! it woke the alley up a bit,
Thought our lodger would 'ave 'ad a fit,
When my missus, who's a real wit,
  Says, 'I 'ates a Bus, because it's low!'

  'Wot cher!' all the neighbours cried,
    'Who're yer goin' to meet, Bill?
    Have yer bought the street, Bill?'
  Laugh! I thought I should 'ave died,
  Knocked 'em in the Old Kent Road!

When we starts the blessed donkey stops,
He won't move, so out I quickly 'ops,
Pals start whackin' him when down he drops,
  Someone says he wasn't made to go.

Lor, it might have been a four-in-'and,
My Old Dutch knows 'ow to do the grand,
First she bows, and then she waves 'er 'and,
    Calling out we're goin' for a blow!

    'Wot cher!' all the neighbours cried,
      'Who're yer going to meet, Bill?
      Have yer bought the street, Bill?'
    Laugh! I thought I should 'ave died,
    Knocked 'em in the Old Kent Road!

Ev'ry evenin' on the stroke of five
Me and Missus takes a little drive,
You'd say, 'Wonderful they're still alive,'
    If you saw that little donkey go.
I soon showed him that 'e'd have to do
Just whatever he was wanted to,
Still I shan't forget that rowdy crew,
    'Ollerin', 'Woa! steady! Neddy woa!'

    'Wot cher!' all the neighbours cried,
      'Who're yer going to meet, Bill?
      Have yer bought the street, Bill?'
    Laugh! I thought I should 'ave died,
    Knocked 'em in the Old Kent Road!

ANON.

The Top of the Dixie Lid

Coolness under fire,
Coolness under fire.
Mentioned in despatches
For pinching the Company rations,
Coolness under fire.

Whiter than the whitewash on the wall,
Whiter than the whitewash on the wall.
Wash me in the water
Where you wash your dirty daughter
And I shall be whiter
Than the whitewash on the wall.

Now he's on the peg,
Now he's on the peg.
Mentioned in despatches
For drinking the Company rum.
Now he's on the peg.

Whiter than the top of the dixie-lid,
Whiter than the top of the dixie lid.
Wash me in the water
Where you wash your dirty daughter
And I shall be whiter
Than the top of the dixie-lid.

ANON. (1914–18 War)

ODD VOICES

To Sally, at the Chop-House

Dear Sally, emblem of the chop-house ware,
As broth reviving, and as white bread fair;
As small beer grateful, and as pepper strong,
As beef-steak tender, as fresh pot-herbs young;
Sharp as a knife, and piercing as a fork,
Soft as new butter, white as fairest pork;
Sweet as young mutton, brisk as bottled beer,
Smooth as is oil, juicy as cucumber,
And bright as cruet void of vinegar.
O Sally! could I turn and shift my love
With the same skill that you your steaks can move,
My heart, thus cooked, might prove a chop-house feast,
And you alone should be the welcome guest.
But, dearest Sal, the flames that you impart,
Like chop on gridiron, broil my tender heart!
Which, if thy kindly helping hand be n't nigh,
Must, like an up-turned chop, hiss, brown and fry;
And must at last, thou scorcher of my soul,
Shrink, and become an undistinguished coal.

ANON.

The Twins

In form and feature, face and limb,
    I grew so like my brother
That folks got taking me for him
    And each for one another.
It puzzled all our kith and kin,
    It reach'd an awful pitch;
For one of us was born a twin
    And not a soul knew which.

One day (to make the matter worse),
    Before our names were fix'd,
As we were being washed by nurse,
    We got completely mix'd.
And thus, you see, by Fate's decree,
    (Or rather nurse's whim)
My brother John got christened *me*,
    And I got christened *him*.

This fatal likeness even dogg'd
    My footsteps when at school,
And I was always getting flogg'd –
    For John turn'd out a fool.
I put this question hopelessly
    To everyone I knew –
What *would* you do if you were me,
    To prove that you were *you*?

Our close resemblance turned the tide
    Of my domestic life;
For somehow my intended bride
    Became my brother's wife.
In short, year after year the same
    Absurd mistakes went on;
And when I died – the neighbours came
    And buried brother John!

H. S. LEIGH

On Photographs

She played me false, but that's not why
I haven't quite forgiven Di,
        Although I've tried.
This curl was hers, so brown, so bright,
She gave it me one blissful night,
        And – more beside.

In photo we were grouped together.
She wore the darling hat and feather
    That I adore:
In profile by her side I sat,
Reading my poetry – but that
    She'd heard before.

Why, after all, Di threw me over
I never knew, and can't discover,
    Or even guess:
Maybe Smith's lyrics, she decided,
Were sweeter than the sweetest I did –
    I acquiesce.

A week before their wedding-day
When Smith was called in haste away
    To join the Staff,
Di gave to him, with tearful mien,
Our only photograph. I've seen
    That photograph.

I've seen it in Smith's album-book!
Just think! her hat – her tender look,
    Are now that brute's!
Before she gave it, off she cut
My body, head and lyrics, but
She was obliged, the little slut,
    To leave my boots.

FREDERICK LOCKER LAMPSON

Turtle Soup

Beautiful Soup, so rich and green,
  Waiting in a hot tureen!
Who for such dainties would not stoop?
Soup of the evening, beautiful Soup!
Soup of the evening, beautiful Soup!
  Beau-ootiful Soo-oop!
  Beau-ootiful Soo-oop!
Soo-oop of the e-e-evening,
  Beautiful, beautiful Soup!

Beautiful Soup! Who cares for fish,
Game, or any other dish?
Who would not give all else for two pennyworth
    only of beautiful Soup?
  Beau-ootiful Soup!
  Beau-ootiful Soup!
Soo-oop of the e-e-evening,
  Beautiful, beauti-FUL SOUP!

LEWIS CARROLL

The Played-Out Humorist

Quixotic is his enterprise, and hopeless his adventure is,
  Who seeks for jocularities that haven't yet been said.
The world has joked incessantly for over fifteen centuries,
  And every joke that's possible has long ago been made.
I started as a humorist with lots of mental fizziness,
  But humour is a drug which it's the fashion to abuse;
For my stock-in-trade, my fixtures, and the goodwill of the
    business
  No reasonable offer I am likely to refuse.
      And if anybody choose
      He may circulate the news
  That no reasonable offer I'm likely to refuse.

Oh happy was that humorist – the first that made a pun at all –
    Who when a joke occurred to him, however poor and mean,
Was absolutely certain that it never had been done at all –
    How popular at dinners must that humorist have been!
Oh the days when some stepfather for a query held a handle out,
    The door-mat from the scraper, is it distant very far?
And when no one knew where Moses was when Aaron blew the
        candle out,
      And no one had discovered that a door could be a-jar!
        But your modern hearers are
        In their tastes particular,
    And they sneer if you inform them that a door can be a-jar!

In search of quip and quiddity, I've sat all day, alone, apart –
    And all that I could hit on as a problem was – to find
Analogy between a scrag of mutton and a Bony-part,
    Which offers slight employment to the speculative mind:
For you cannot call it very good, however great your charity –
    It's not the sort of humour that is greeted with a shout –
And I've come to the conclusion that my mine of jocularity,
    In present Anno Domini, is worked completely out!
      Though the notion you may scout,
      I can prove beyond a doubt
    That my mine of jocularity is utterly worked out!

SIR W. S. GILBERT

The Rake's Progress

    Born lorn,
    Dad bad,
    Nurse worse;
    'Drat brat!'
    School – Fool,
    Work – shirk
    Gal pal,
    Splash cash,

Bets – debts,
Pop shop.
Nil – Till!
Boss – loss
Wired 'Fired!'
Scrub pub,
Drink – Brink –
Found Drowned.
'De Se';
Grief brief.

C. W. BRODRIBB

Korf's Clock

Korf's clock is of a novel sort
In which two pairs of hands are used:
One pair points forwards as it ought,
The other backwards *à la Proust*.

When it says eight it's also four,
When it says nine it's also three;
A single glance and you no more
Need fear the ancient Enemy.

For with this wondrous clock you'll find
As, Janus-like, it turns about
(To such an end it was designed)
Time simply cancels itself out.

CHRISTIAN MORGENSTERN
(translated by R. F. C. HULL)

Palmström's Clock

But Palmström's has a 'higher' power,
Balanced as lightly as a flower.

Scorning a set pedestrian pace,
It keeps time with a certain grace

And will, in answer to a prayer,
　Go *en retard, en arrière.*

One hour, two hours, three hours indeed,
Sympathizing with our need!

Though clockwork in its outward part
It hides within – a tender heart.

CHRISTIAN MORGENSTERN
(translated by R. F. C. HULL)

The Official

Korf has been besieged by swarms
Of grim official-looking forms
Adjuring him to make reply
Who he is and what and why.

Where he resides, what his address is
And what profession he professes,
Where he was born (with day and date)
And whether he is celibate.

Why he had come into this town
And if he thought of settling down
And how much money he possessed
And what religion he thought best.

Contrariwise if he declined
To answer with an open mind
He'd be arrested without fail
And promptly taken off to jail!

Korf sent an answer mild and bland:
'Your letter of the 10th to hand.
The undersigned herewith presents
His most obsequious compliments,

But would apprise you of the fact
That, in the strict sense of the Act
As touching personal matters, he
Is a complete nonentity

And that, officially at least,
He much regrets not to exist.'
The High Official gasped – and read
With eyes fair bursting from his head.

CHRISTIAN MORGENSTERN
(translated by R. F. C. HULL)

Palmström Sculptor

Palmström shakes up his bed with so much feeling
That all his room looks like a Sistine ceiling:
Peopled with gods, and giants and splendid women.

He lunges back and forth with wild invective,
Swinging his lantern o'er the mangled linen
To get his visions into true perspective.

And in the changing play of lights and shadows
He sees madonnas, cherubs and mulattos,
Athletes with snakes and Venuses in foam.

And dreams: were this but real and not mere feather,
'Twould shame the Golden Age and altogether
Eclipse the gloried pomps of Greece and Rome!

CHRISTIAN MORGENSTERN
(translated by R. F. C. HULL)

The Impossible Fact

Professor Palmström, it appears,
Already getting on in years,
Stood at a busy terminus
And got run over by a bus.

'How was it,' he exclaimed anon
And resolutely living on,
'Possible that such a fall
Should ever have occurred at all?

Cannot one claim some compensation
For faulty traffic regulation?
Are cars by order of police
Allowed to do just what they please?

Or is it not prohibited
To turn live people into dead?
And finally, in such a crowd,
Should *any* traffic be allowed?'

Enveloped in wet towels at home
He scans a monstrous legal tome
Till all at once the thing is clear:
No cars should use that thoroughfare!

And so he comes to the conclusion:
The whole affair was an illusion.
'For look,' he cries triumphantly,
'What's not permitted CANNOT be!'

CHRISTIAN MORGENSTERN
(translated by R. F. C. HULL)

The Two Bottles

Two bottles stood upon a bin.
The one was fat, the other thin.
Fain would they taste of married bliss,
But who'll give them advice on this?

And with their suffering double-eye
They gaze into the empty sky.
But no one leaves his heavenly station
To grant the poor dears copulation.

CHRISTIAN MORGENSTERN
(translated by R. F. C. HULL)

The Handkerchief Ghost

There is a ghost
That eats handkerchiefs;
It keeps you company
On all your travels, and
Eats your handkerchiefs
Out of your trunk, your
Bed, your washstand,
Like a bird eating
Out of your hand, – not
All of them and not
All at one go. With

Eighteen handkerchiefs
You set out, a proud mariner,
On the seas of the Unknown;
With eight or perhaps
Seven you come back, the
Despair of the housewife.

CHRISTIAN MORGENSTERN
(translated by R. F. C. HULL)

The Fence

There was a fence with spaces you
Could look through if you wanted to.

An architect who saw this thing
Stood there one summer evening,

Took out the spaces with great care
And built a castle in the air.

The fence was utterly dumbfounded:
Each post stood there with nothing round it.

A sight most terrible to see.
(They charged it with indecency.)

The architect then ran away
To Afric- or Americ-ay.

CHRISTIAN MORGENSTERN
(translated by R. F. C. HULL)

The Sandwich Paper

There was a Sandwich paper which
Mysteriously began to itch.

And in its fear, although till now
It had no thought of thinking – how

Could it indeed, having no head
Worth mentioning – now (from fear, I said)

Began, commenced (you'll hardly guess)
To feel the dawn of consciousness,

To think, to cogitate, to be,
Acquire a personality

Which, be it noted, was not sent
By chance out of the firmament,

But rose out of an earthly plane,
The product of an actual brain,

Whose substance (albumen and glue)
Found in the sandwich paper (through

A permutation, or a sort
Of evolutionary 'sport')

In this same sandwich paper found
Form, content, happy breeding-ground.

Taking advantage of this fact
The paper now resolved to act,

To live, to love, to walk, to try
To flutter like a butterfly . . .

To crawl at first and then to rise
On wings before our wondering eyes,

Then back and forth and to and fro
As all such heavenly creatures go

Who with the zephyrs dip and play
High o'er our hapless human clay!

But O my friends, give ear, give heed!
A Sparrow, fat and full of greed

Espies it, and with tooth and nail
(How end this bitter moral tale!)

With tooth and nail and nail and tooth
(But truth will out, the dreadful Truth!)

(My pen shakes and the ink grows pale!)
Gets ready, sharpening tooth and nail ...

Stop, stop! Enough! Fate will not yield!
The Sandwich paper's doom is sealed!

The vile bird in one horrid spasm
Devoured this priceless protoplasm.

CHRISTIAN MORGENSTERN
(translated by R. F. C. HULL)

The Experiment

Once for experiment I bought
A needle of the better sort.

And furthermore a camel, old
Though one must add, extremely bold.

A rich man too was there with me
Together with his L.S.D.

The rich man, I need hardly tell,
Went up to Heaven and rang the bell.

Thereat spake Peter: 'It stands writ
That any camel, strong and fit

Shall pass the needle's eye before
You put a foot across this door!'

Not doubting God's words in the least
I reassured the valiant beast

Holding behind the needle's eye
A toothsome slice of cherry pie!

And on my oath, the beast went through
— Though creaking cruelly, it is true.

The rich man, who could only blink,
Turned round and muttered: 'Strike me pink!'

CHRISTIAN MORGENSTERN
(translated by R. F. C. HULL)

Scotch Rhapsody

'Do not take a bath in Jordan,
                Gordan,
On the holy Sabbath, on the peaceful day!'
Said the huntsman, playing on his old bagpipe,
Boring to death the pheasant and the snipe —
Boring the ptarmigan and grouse for fun —
Boring them worse than a nine-bore gun.
Till the flaxen leaves where the prunes are ripe,

Hear the tartan wind a-droning in the pipe,
And they heard McPherson say:
'Where do the waves go? What hotels
Hide their bustles and their gay ombrelles?
And would there be room? – Would there be *room*?
  Would there be room for me?'
There is a hotel at Ostend
Cold as the wind, without an end,
Haunted by ghostly poor relations
Of Bostonian conversations
(Bagpipes rotting through the walls.)
And there the pearl-ropes fall like shawls
With a noise like marine waterfalls.
And 'Another little drink wouldn't do us any harm'
Pierces through the Sabbatical calm.
And that is the place for me!
So do not take a bath in Jordan, Gordon,
On the holy Sabbath on the peaceful day –
Or you'll never go to heaven, Gordon McPherson,
And speaking purely as a private person
That is the place – *that* is the place – that is the *place* for me!

DAME EDITH SITWELL

No Doctors Today, Thank You

They tell me that euphoria is the feeling of feeling wonderful; well, today I feel euphorian,
Today I have the agility of a Greek God and the appetite of a Victorian,
Yes, today I may even go forth without my galoshes;
Today I am a swashbuckler, would anybody like me to buckle my swashes?
This is my euphorian day.
I will ring welkins and before anybody answers I will run away.
I will tame me a caribou
And bedeck it with marabou.

I will pen me my memoirs.
Ah, youth, youth! What euphorian days them was!
I wasn't much of a hand for the boudoirs,
I was generally to be found where the food was.
Does anybody want any flotsam?
I've gotsam.
Does anybody want any jetsam?
I can getsam.
I can play 'Chopsticks' on the Wurlitzer,
I can speak Portuguese like a Berlitzer.
I can don or doff my shoes without tying or untying the laces
    because I am wearing moccasins,
And I practically know the difference between serums and anti-
    toccasins.
Kind people, don't think me purse-proud, don't set me down as
    vainglorious,
I'm just a little euphorious.

OGDEN NASH

Peekaboo, I almost See You

Middle-aged life is merry, and I love to lead it,
But there comes a day when your eyes are all right, but your arm
    isn't long enough to hold the telephone book where you can
    read it,
And your friends get jocular, so you go to the oculist,
And of all your friends he is the joculist,
So over his facetiousness let us skim,
Only noting that he has been waiting for you ever since you said
    Good Evening to his grandfather clock under the impression
    that it was him.
And you look at his chart and it says SHRDLU QWERTYOP, and
    you say Well, why SHRDNTLU QWERTYOP? and he says one
    set of glasses won't do.
You need two,

174

One for reading Erle Stanley Gardner's Perry Mason and Keats's
'Endymion' with,
And the other for walking around without saying Hallo to strange
wymion with.
So you spend your time taking off your seeing glasses to put on
your reading glasses, and then remembering that your reading
glasses are upstairs or in the car,
And then you can't find your seeing glasses again because without
them you can't see where they are.
Enough of such mishaps, they would try the patience of an ox,
I prefer to forget both pairs of glasses and pass my declining years
saluting strange women and grandfather clocks.

OGDEN NASH

Lament

'I was never chairman of the company, so far as I know' – *Old Bailey Remark*

> I heard a voice complain in Fenchurch Street,
> Very bitterly it grieved, saying:

1

I wish I knew if I was chairman of this company,
It would make a lot of difference at conferences:
Gorgeous conferences we have, simply gorgeous,
Finest in the City, I imagine.
I am always in the top chair, but the boys will never let on if I'm
chairman or not.

2

Sometimes after a jolly fine conference I say: 'Boys, that was a fine
conference, let's have another.'
Then we have another, right on the spot.
I often slip in a word, as if joking, such as 'Looks to me as if I'm
chairman of this company', but nobody ever takes it up.

Often when I'm signing things or shouting into my dictaphone
    (you ought to see my dictaphone) or maybe ringing through to
    main office and firing somebody, I wish one of the boys would
    just say: 'Look at old Fishy – he's chairman, you know.'
Nobody ever does.

3

For Heaven's sake, why can't they be frank with me one way or
    another?
If they'd just say: 'All right, old boy, you're chairman', I could do
    a lot of things I've always wanted to do.
Such as swinging a big merger,
Or correlating overhead with saturation-point,
Or getting a whole lot of people, say twenty or thirty, on the mat
    at once and raking them with merciless eyes and saying: 'You're
    out!'
I'd get a chairman's portion on the *Southern Belle* too.
Dear Heaven, why can't they tell me?

D. B. WYNDHAM LEWIS

Posy

FOR A TALL NOISY GIRL HEARD AT A BOTTLE PARTY, 3.30 A.M.

    Sweetheart, in all your girlish charm you are
    Like laughter at a West End Cinema
    When lightning wisecracks flash and spurt and throng:
    Too loud, my Love; too late; and far too long.

D. B. WYNDHAM LEWIS

There's Money in Mother and Father

    The lamp burns long in the cottage,
      The light shines late in the shop,
    Their beams disclosing the writers composing
      Memories of Mom and Pop.

Oh don't write a book about Father!
　　Don't write a book about Dad!
Better not bother to tell how Father
　　Went so amusingly mad.
Better pass over the evening
　　Father got locked in the zoo –
For your infant son has possibly begun
　　A funny little book about you.

The author broods in his study,
　　The housewife dreams in her flat:
Since Mommer and Popper were most improper,
　　There ought to be a book in that.

But don't write a book about Mother!
　　Don't write a book about Mum!
We all know Mumsy was vague and clumsy,
　　Dithering, drunken and dumb.
There may be money in Mother,
　　And possibly a movie, too –
But some little mite is learning how to write
　　To write a little book about you.

MORRIS BISHOP

Diplomatic Catechism

Q. Who engineered the Trans-Ugandian Disruption?
Who deposited the cobras in the Minister's bed?
Was it you who arranged the advantageous exit
From the Bulgarian Mint? Come, was it you?
And if not, who?

A. O, really, gentlemen,
I did none of these things, not one; when each one happened
I was somewhere else; yes, once with a red-haired dancer,
Once chasing boars in the tall Carpathian Mountains,
And once I was immersed in my model trains.

Q. *Someone* removed that agent from his head,
Someone used the syringe on those poisoned grapes,
Someone endeavoured to retire with the map-maker's wife,
Someone has laboured, laboured. Come, was it you?
And if not, who?

A. Well, really, gentlemen,
I could speak to my confrères, who must here be nameless,
I could look into my records, or even look over my diary.
Have you read my little book on my Kurdish exploits?
The clue may well be there. My memory's rather musty.

Q. Who slew the wicker-works chap and provoked a scandal?
Who derailed the Trans-Time Express and stole the Queen?
Who put up the anti-aircraft on the Acropolis
And shot down Icarus? Come, was it you,
And if not, who?

A. O, dear, O, dear,
Really, you know, gentlemen, O, yes, really, you know,
You can't accuse me without substantiation.
I'm a peaceful, home-keeping man, I work in my garden,
Love my good wife, like pie, look well for my age,
Keep a strict vegetable diet, smoke no pipe.
If I have, shall we say, a quiet passion for intrigue,
It's merely a whim, and hardly of prime importance.
That which you see there bleeding is my heart.
That which you smell there burning is my zeal.
Good day, good day, good day.

HARRY BROWN

Problem Child

How *shall* I deal with Roger,
                Mrs Prodger?
I've never yet been able
To sit him at a table
And make him paint a label
For the salmon in the kindergarten shop.
    But he's full of animation
    When I mention a dictation,
    And he never wants a spelling-test to stop.
I've encouraged self-expression
And intentional digression
But I think I'll have to let the system drop.
    For the normal child, like Roger,
    Is a *do*-er, not a dodger,
And your methods, Mrs Prodger, are a flop.

How *shall* I deal with Roger,
                Mrs Prodger?
I've had projects on the fairies,
On markets, shops and dairies;
I've had projects on the *prairies*,
But the little fellow doesn't want to play:
    Instead he has a yearning
    For unreasonable learning,
    And wants to do Arithmetic all day.
He shows a strong proclivity
For purposeless activity,
And doesn't want experience in clay.
    So I rather think that Roger
    Is a *do*-er, not a dodger,
And how *would* you deal with Roger, can you say?

J. E. FAULKS

On the Twelfth Day of Christmas I Screamed

(A LETTER FROM HIS GIRL TO A G.I. IN TOKYO)

Now April's here, what ever can I do
With those fantastic gifts I got from you?
Spring's in the air, but, honey, life is hard:
The three French hens are picking in the yard,
And the turtledove, the turtledove
(One of them died) –
Ah, love, my own true love, you have denied
Me nothing the mails or the express could bring.
But look: we're into spring;
The calling birds are calling, calling;
The pear tree's leaves are slowly falling;
I sit here with those cackling geese
And never know a moment's peace.
My memories are mixed and hazy,
The drumming drummers drive me crazy,
The milking maids enjoy canasta,
The lords are leaping ever faster,
The pipers – God in Heaven knows
I've more than had enough of those.

My love, you do such wondrous things
(Who else would think of *five* gold rings?)
I know you send me all you can
Of spoils of occupied Japan,
But you remain on alien shore
And waiting here is such a bore.
My love, the lively lords are leaping:
Some things will not improve with keeping.

Now April's here, the weary days go by;
I watch that wretched dove attempt to fly;
The partridge smells; the geese are getting hoarse;
My diction's growing positively coarse.
You must forgive my gestures of rejection –

I'm crazed with all your tokens of affection.
Enough's enough; next time be less romantic
And don't send gifts that drive a lady frantic.
Send me a postcard with a pretty view
And I shall look at it and think of you.

DAVID DAICHES

Ballade to my Psycho-Analyst

I am concerned because my mind
   Contains no subterranean lair;
Nothing abysmal lurks behind
   My neatly brushed and parted hair;
   No hidden conflict anywhere,
And no neurosis worth the name:
   This has reduced me to despair:
I go about in guilt and shame.

My dreams are the pedestrian kind,
   And come with symbols sparse and bare,
As unexcited and refined
   As ever faced a censor's stare.
   They stand before the censor's chair
And giggle as he calls their name,
   'But we have nothing to declare'.
I go about in guilt and shame.

My deep unconscious was designed
   To function with conditioned air,
And when you lift the lid you find
   No evil brew fermenting there;
   Plenty of good plain wholesome fare –
Sardines in tins and potted game –
   But nothing high and nothing rare.
I go about in guilt and shame.

ENVOI

Prince, you descend my spiral stair:
   No shadows flee your candle flame:
Where is the foetal matter? Where?
   I go about in guilt and shame.

KENNETH LILLINGTON

To the Inevitable Optimist

These days I feel like a man on a cold dawn deck,
   With Mr Masefield's wind like a whetted knife
Sliding between my muffler and my neck
   And cutting short my expectation of life.
At night in bed, I feel a trifle stronger –
Don't tell me that the days are getting longer.

DONALD MATTAM

DOUBTFUL TALES

Hon. Mr Sucklethumbkin's Story

THE EXECUTION
A Sporting Anecdote

My Lord Tomnoddy got up one day;
   It was half after two, He had nothing to do,
So his Lordship rang for his cabriolet.

   Tiger Tim Was clean of limb,
His boots were polish'd, his jacket was trim;
With a very smart tie in his smart cravat,
And a smart cockade on the top of his hat;
Tallest of boys, or shortest of men,
He stood in his stockings just four foot ten;
And he ask'd, as he held the door on the swing,
'Pray, did your Lordship please to ring?'

My Lord Tomnoddy he raised his head,
And thus to Tiger Tim he said,
   'Malibran's dead, Duvernay's fled,
Taglioni has not yet arrived in her stead;
Tiger Tim, come tell me true,
What may a Nobleman find to do? –'

Tim look'd up, and Tim look'd down,
He paused, and he put on a thoughtful frown,
And he held up his hat, and he peep'd in the crown;
He bit his lip, and he scratch'd his head,
He let go the handle, and thus he said,
As the door, released, behind him bang'd:
'An't please you, my Lord, there's a man to be hang'd.'

My Lord Tomnoddy jump'd up at the news,
   'Run to M'Fuze, And Lieutenant Tregooze,
And run to Sir Carnaby Jenks, of the Blues.
   Rope-dancers a score I've seen before –

Madame Sacchi, Antonio, and Master Black-more;
  But to see a man swing At the end of a string,
With his neck in a noose, will be quite a new thing!'

My Lord Tomnoddy stept into his cab –
Dark rifle green, with a lining of drab;
  Through street and through square,
  His high-trotting mare,
Like one of Ducrow's, goes pawing the air,
Adown Piccadilly and Waterloo Place
Went the high-trotting mare at a very quick pace;
  She produced some alarm. But did no great harm,
Save frightening a nurse with a child on her arm,
  Spattering with clay Two urchins at play,
Knocking down – very much to the sweeper's dismay –
An old woman who wouldn't get out of the way,
  And upsetting a stall Near Exeter Hall,
Which made all the pious Church-Mission folks squall.
  But eastward afar Through Temple Bar,

My Lord Tomnoddy directs his car;
  Never heeding their squalls,
  Or their calls, or their bawls,
He passes by Waithman's Emporium for shawls,
And, merely just catching a glimpse of St Paul's,
  Turns down the Old Bailey,
  Where in front of the gaol, he
Pulls up at the door of the gin-shop, and gaily
Cries, 'What must I fork out to-night, my trump,
For the whole first-floor of the Magpie and Stump?'

*

The clock strikes Twelve – it is dark midnight –
Yet the Magpie and Stump is one blaze of light,
  The parties are met; The tables are set;
There is 'punch', 'cold without', 'hot with', 'heavy wet,'
  Ale-glasses and jugs, And rummers and mugs,
And sand on the floor, without carpets or rugs,

Cold fowl and cigars, Pickled onions in jars,
Welsh rabbits and kidneys — rare work for the jaws: —
And very large lobsters, with very large claws;
And there is M'Fuze, And Lieutenant Tregooze;
And there is Sir Carnaby Jenks, of the Blues,
All come to see a man 'die in his shoes!'

The clock strikes One! Supper is done,
And Sir Carnaby Jenks is full of his fun,
Singing 'Jolly companions every one!'
My Lord Tomnoddy Is drinking gin-toddy,
And laughing at ev'ry thing, and ev'ry body. —

The clock strikes Two! and the clock strikes Three!
— 'Who so merry, so merry as we?'
Save Captain M'Fuze, Who is taking a snooze,
While Sir Carnaby Jenks is busy at work,
Blacking his nose with a piece of burnt cork.

The clock strikes Four! — Round the debtors' door
Are gather'd a couple of thousand or more;
As many await At the press-yard gate,
Till slowly its folding doors open, and straight
The mob divides, and between their ranks
A wagon comes loaded with posts and with planks.

The clock strikes Five! The Sheriffs arrive,
And the crowd is so great that the street seems alive;
But Sir Carnaby Jenks Blinks, and winks,
A candle burns down in the socket, and stinks.
Lieutenant Tregooze Is dreaming of Jews,
And acceptances all the bill-brokers refuse;
My Lord Tomnoddy Has drunk all his toddy,
And just as the dawn is beginning to peep,
The whole of the party are fast asleep.

Sweetly, oh! sweetly, the morning breaks,
   With roseate streaks,

Like the first faint blush on a maiden's cheeks;
Seem'd as that mild and clear blue sky
Smiled upon all things far and high,
On all – save the wretch condemn'd to die!
Alack! that ever so fair a Sun,
As that which its course has now begun,
Should rise on such a scene of misery! –
Should gild with rays so light and free
That dismal, dark-frowning Gallows-tree!

And hark! – a sound comes, big with fate;
The clock from St Sepulchre's tower strikes – Eight! –
List to that low funeral bell:
It is tolling, alas! a living man's knell! –
And see! – from forth that opening door
They come – He steps that threshold o'er
Who never shall tread upon threshold more!

– God! 'tis a fearsome thing to see
That pale wan man's mute agony, –
The glare of that wild, despairing eye,
Now bent on the crowd, now turn'd to the sky
As though 'twere scanning, in doubt and in fear,
The path of the Spirit's unknown career;
Those pinion'd arms, those hands that ne'er
Shall be lifted again, – not even in prayer;
That heaving chest! Enough – 'tis done!
The bolt has fallen! – the spirit is gone –
For weal or for woe is known but to One! –
– Oh! 'twas a fearsome sight! Ah me!
A deed to shudder at, – not to see.

Again that clock! 'tis time, 'tis time!
The hour is past: with its earliest chime
The cord is severed, the lifeless clay
By 'dungeon villains' is borne away:
Nine! 'twas the last concluding stroke!
And then – my Lord Tomnoddy awoke!

And Tregooze and Sir Carnaby Jenks arose,
And Captain M'Fuze, with the black on his nose:
And they stared at each other, as much as to say
   'Hollo! Hollo! Here's a rum Go!
Why, Captain! – my Lord! – Here's the devil to pay!
The fellow's been cut down and taken away!
   What's to be done? We've miss'd all the fun! –
Why, they'll laugh at and quiz us all over the town
We are all of us done so uncommonly brown!'

What was to be done? – 'twas perfectly plain
That they could not well hang the man over again:
What was to be done? – The man was dead!
Nought could be done – nought could be said;
So – my Lord Tomnoddy went home to bed!

R. H. BARHAM

The Lamentable Ballad of the Foundling of Shoreditch

Come all ye Christian people, and listen to my tail
  It is all about a doctor was travelling by the rail,
    By the Heastern Counties Railway (vich the shares I don't
    desire,)
From Ixworth town in Suffolk, vich his name did not transpire.

A travelling from Bury this Doctor was employed
With a gentleman, a friend of his, vich his name was Captain
    Lloyd,
And on reaching Marks Tey Station, that is next beyond Colchester,
    a lady entered in to them most elegantly dressed.

She entered into the Carriage all with a tottering step,
And a pooty little Bayby upon her bussum slep;
The gentlemen received her with kindness and siwillaty,
Pitying this lady for her illness and debillaty.

189

She had a fust-class ticket, this lovely lady said;
Because it was so lonesome she took a secknd instead.
Better to travel by secknd class, than sit alone in the fust,
And the pooty little Baby upon her breast she nust.

A seein of her cryin, and shiverin and pail,
To her spoke this surging, the Ero of my tail;
Saysee 'You look unwell, ma'am: I'll elp you if I can,
And you may tell your case to me, for I'm a meddicle man.'

'Thank you, sir,' the lady said, 'I only look so pale,
Because I ain't accustom'd to travelling on the Rale;
I shall be better presnly, when I've ad some rest:'
And that pooty little Baby she squeeged it to her breast.

So in conversation the journey they beguiied,
Capting Loyd and the meddicle man, and the lady and the child,
Till the warious stations along the line was passed,
For even the Heastern Counties' trains must come in at last.

When at Shoreditch tumminus at length stopped the train,
This kind meddicle gentleman proposed his aid again.
'Thank you, sir,' the lady said, 'for your kyindness dear;
My carridge and my osses is probibbly come here.

'Will you old this baby, please, vilst I step and see?'
The Doctor was a family man: 'That I will,' says he.
Then the little child she kist, kist it very gently,
Vich was sucking his little fist, sleeping innocently.

With a sigh from her art, as though she would have bust it,
Then she gave the Doctor the child – wery kind he nust it:
Hup then the lady jumped hoff the bench she sat from,
Tumbled down the carridge steps and ran along the platform.

Vile hall the other passengers vent upon their vays,
The Capting and the Doctor sat there in a maze;
Some vent in a Homminibus, some vent in a Cabby,
The Capting and the Doctor vaited vith the babby.

There they sat looking queer, for an hour or more,
But their feller passinger neather on 'em sore:
Never, never back again did that lady come
To that pooty sleeping Hinfnt a suckin' of his Thum!

What could this pore Doctor do, bein' treated thus,
When the darling Baby woke, cryin' for its nuss?
Off he drove to a female friend, vich she was both kind and mild,
And igsplained to her the circumstance of this year little child.

That kind lady took the child instantly in her lap,
And made it very comfortable by giving it some pap;
And when she took its close off, what d'you think she found?
A couple of ten pun notes sewn up in its little gownd!

Also in its little close, was a note which did conwey,
That this little baby's parents lived in a handsome way
And for its Headucation they reglarly would pay,
And sirtingly like gentlefolks would claim the child one day,
If the Christian people who'd charge of it would say,
Per adwertisement in *The Times*, where the baby lay.

Pity of this bayby many people took,
It had such pooty ways and such a pooty look;
And there came a lady forrard (I wish that I could see
Any kind lady as would do as much for me;

And I wish with all my art, some night in my night gownd,
I could find a note stitched for ten or twenty pound) –
There came a lady forrard, that most honorable did say,
She'd adopt this little baby, which her parents cast away.

While the Doctor pondered on this hoffer fair,
Comes a letter from Devonshire, from a party there,
Hordering the Doctor, at its Mar's desire,
To send the little Infant back to Devonshire.

Lost in apoplexity, this pore meddicle man,
Like a sensable gentleman, to the Justice ran,
Which his name was Mr Hammill, a honorable beak,
That takes his seat in Worship Street four times a week.

'O Justice!' says the Doctor, 'instrugt me what to do.
I've come up from the country, to throw myself on you;
My patients have no doctor to tend them in their ills
(There they are in Suffolk without their draffts and pills!).

'I've come up from the country, to know how I'll dispose
Of this pore little baby, and the twenty pun note, and the close,
And I want to go back to Suffolk, dear Justice, if you please,
And my patients wants their Doctor, and their Doctor wants his
    feez.'

Up spoke Mr Hammill, sittin' at his desk,
'This year application does me much perplesk;
What I do adwise you, is to leave this babby
In the Parish where it was left by its mother shabby.'

The Doctor from his Worship sadly did depart –
He might have left the baby, but he hadn't got the heart
To go for to leave that Hinnocent, has the laws allows,
To the tender mussies of the Union House.

Mother, who left this little one on a stranger's knee,
Think how cruel you have been, and how good was he!
Think, if you've been guilty, innocent was she;
And do not take unkindly this little word of me:
Heaven be merciful to us all, sinners as we be!

                                        W. M. THACKERAY

192

The Ballad of the Oysterman

It was a tall young oysterman lived by the river-side,
His shop was just upon the bank, his boat was on the tide;
The daughter of a fisherman, that was so straight and slim,
Lived over on the other bank, right opposite to him.

It was the pensive oysterman that saw a lovely maid,
Upon a moonlight evening, a-sitting in the shade!
He saw her wave her handkerchief, as much as if to say,
'I'm wide awake, young oysterman, and all the folks away.'

Then up arose the oysterman, and to himself said he,
'I guess I'll leave the skiff at home, for fear that folks should see;
I read it in the story-book, that, for to kiss his dear,
Leander swam the Hellespont – and I will swim this here.'

And he has leaped into the waves, and crossed the shining stream,
And he has clambered up the bank, all in the moonlight gleam;
Oh, there were kisses sweet as dew, and words as soft as rain, –
But they have heard her father's step, and in he leaps again!

Out spoke the ancient fisherman: 'Oh, what was that, my
    daughter?'
' 'Twas nothing but a pebble, sir, I threw into the water.'
'And what is that, pray tell me, love, that paddles off so fast?'
'It's nothing but a porpoise, sir, that's been a-swimming past.'

Out spoke the ancient fisherman: 'Now bring me my harpoon!
I'll get into my fishing-boat, and fix the fellow soon.'
Down fell that pretty innocent, as falls a snow-white lamb!
Her hair drooped round her pallid cheeks, like seaweed on a clam.

Alas for those two loving ones! she waked not from her swouned,
And he was taken with the cramp, and in the waves was drowned!
But Fate has metamorphosed them, in pity of their woe,
And now they keep an oyster-shop for mermaids down below.

OLIVER WENDELL HOLMES

Hertfordshire Harmony

There was an old fellow of Tring
Who, when somebody asked him to sing,
   Replied, 'Ain't it odd?
   I can never tell *God*
Save the Weasel from *Pop goes the King.*'

                        ANON.

The Courtship of the Yonghy-Bonghy-Bò

On the Coast of Coromandel
   Where the early pumpkins blow,
      In the middle of the woods
Lived the Yonghy-Bonghy-Bò.
Two old chairs, and half a candle, –
One old jug without a handle, –
   These were all his worldly goods:
      In the middle of the woods,
   These were all the worldly goods,
Of the Yonghy-Bonghy-Bò,
Of the Yonghy-Bonghy-Bò.

2
Once, among the Bong-trees walking
   Where the early pumpkins blow,
      To a little heap of stones
Came the Yonghy-Bonghy-Bò.
There he heard a Lady talking,
To some milk-white Hens of Dorking, –
   ' 'Tis the Lady Jingly Jones!
      On that little heap of stones
   Sits the Lady Jingly Jones!'
Said the Yonghy-Bonghy-Bò.
Said the Yonghy-Bonghy-Bò.

3

'Lady Jingly! Lady Jingly!
  Sitting where the pumpkins blow,
    Will you come and be my wife?'
Said the Yonghy-Bonghy-Bò.
'I am tired of living singly, –
On this coast so wild and shingly, –
    I'm a-weary of my life;
    If you'll come and be my wife,
    Quite serene would be my life!' –
Said the Yonghy-Bonghy-Bò.
Said the Yonghy-Bonghy-Bò.

4

'On this Coast of Coromandel,
  Shrimps and watercresses grow,
    Prawns are plentiful and cheap,'
Said the Yonghy-Bonghy-Bò.
'You shall have my chairs and candle,
And my jug without a handle! –
    Gaze upon the rolling deep
    (Fish is plentiful and cheap);
    As the sea, my love is deep!'
Said the Yonghy-Bonghy-Bò.
Said the Yonghy-Bonghy-Bò.

5

Lady Jingly answered sadly,
  And her tears began to flow, –
    'Your proposal comes too late,
Mr Yonghy-Bonghy-Bò!
I would be your wife most gladly!'
(Here she twirled her fingers madly)
    'But in England I've a mate!
    Yes! you've asked me far too late,
    For in England I've a mate,
Mr Yonghy-Bonghy-Bò!
Mr Yonghy-Bonghy-Bò.

6

'Mr Jones — (his name is Handel, —
Handel Jones, Esquire, & Co.)
Dorking fowls delights to send,
Mr Yonghy-Bonghy-Bò!
Keep, oh! keep your chairs and candle,
And your jug without a handle, —
I can merely be your friend!
— Should my Jones more Dorkings send,
I will give you three, my friend!
Mr Yonghy-Bonghy-Bò!
Mr Yonghy-Bonghy-Bò!

7

'Though you've such a tiny body,
And your head so large doth grow, —
Though your hat may blow away,
Mr Yonghy-Bonghy-Bò!
Though you're such a Hoddy Doddy —
Yet I wish that I could modi-
fy the words I needs must say!
Will you please to go away?
That is all I have to say —
Mr Yonghy-Bonghy-Bò!
Mr Yonghy-Bonghy-Bò!'

8

Down the slippery slopes of Myrtle,
Where the early pumpkins blow,
To the calm and silent sea
Fled the Yonghy-Bonghy-Bò.
There, beyond the Bay of Gurtle,
Lay a large and lively Turtle: —
'You're the Cove,' he said, 'for me;
On your back beyond the sea,
Turtle, you shall carry me!'
Said the Yonghy-Bonghy-Bò,
Said the Yonghy-Bonghy-Bò.

9

Through the silent-roaring ocean
Did the Turtle swiftly go;
Holding fast upon his shell
Rode the Yonghy-Bonghy-Bò.
With a sad primaeval motion
Towards the sunset isles of Boshen
Still the Turtle bore him well.
Holding fast upon his shell,
'Lady Jingly Jones, farewell!'
Sang the Yonghy-Bonghy-Bò,
Sang the Yonghy-Bonghy-Bò.

10

From the Coast of Coromandel,
Did that Lady never go;
On that heap of stones she mourns
For the Yonghy-Bonghy-Bò.
On that Coast of Coromandel,
In his jug without a handle,
Still she weeps, and daily moans,
On that little heap of stones
To her Dorking Hens she moans,
For the Yonghy-Bonghy-Bò,
For the Yonghy-Bonghy-Bò.

EDWARD LEAR

Incidents in the Life of my Uncle Arly

O my agèd Uncle Arly!
Sitting on a heap of Barley
Through the silent hours of night, –
Close beside a leafy thicket: –
On his nose there was a Cricket, –
In his hat a Railway-Ticket; –
(But his shoes were far too tight).

Long ago, in youth, he squander'd
All his goods away and wander'd
   To the Tiniskoop-hills afar.
There on golden sunsets blazing,
Every evening found him gazing, –
Singing – 'Orb! you're quite amazing!
   How I wonder what you are!'

Like the ancient Medes and Persians,
Always by his own exertions
   He subsisted on those hills; –
Whiles, – by teaching children spelling, –
Or at times by merely yelling, –
Or at intervals by selling
   'Propter's Nicodemus Pills'

Later, in his morning rambles
He perceived the moving brambles
   Something square and white disclose; –
'Twas a First-class Railway-Ticket;
But, on stooping down to pick it
Off the ground, – a pea-green Cricket
   Settled on my uncle's Nose.

Never – never more, – oh! never,
Did that Cricket leave him ever, –
   Dawn or evening, day or night; –
Clinging as a constant treasure, –
Chirping with a cheerious measure, –
Wholly to my uncle's pleasure, –
   (Though his shoes were far too tight).

So for three-and-forty winters,
Till his shoes were worn to splinters,
   All those hills he wanders o'er, –
Sometimes silent; – sometimes yelling; –
Till he came to Borley-Melling,
Near his old ancestral dwelling: –
   (But his shoes were far too tight).

On a little heap of Barley
Died my agèd Uncle Arly,
    And they buried him one night: –
Close beside the leafy thicket; –
There, – his hat and Railway-Ticket; –
There, – his ever-faithful Cricket; –
    (But his shoes were far too tight).

EDWARD LEAR

The Ballad of Charity

It was in a pleasant deepô, sequestered from the rain,
That many weary passengers were waitin' for the train;
Piles of quite expensive baggage, many a gorgeous portmantó,
Ivory-handled umberellas made a most touristic show.

Whereunto there came a person, very humble was his mien,
Who took an observation of the interestin' scene;
Closely scanned the umberellas, watched with joy the mighty
    trunks,
And observed that all the people were securin' Pullman bunks:

Who was followed shortly after by a most unhappy tramp,
Upon whose features poverty had jounced her iron stamp;
And to make a clear impression, as bees sting you while they buzz,
She had hit him rather harder than she generally does.

For he was so awful ragged, and in parts so awful bare,
That the folks were quite repulsioned to behold him begging there;
And instead of drawing currency from out their pocket-books,
They drew themselves asunder with aversionary looks.

Sternly gazed the first newcomer on the unindulgent crowd,
Then in tones that pierced the deepô he solilicussed aloud: –
'I hev trevelled o'er this cont'nent from Quebec to Bogotáw,
But sech a lot of scallawags as these I never saw.

'Ye are wealthy, ye are gifted, ye have house and lands and rent,
Yet unto a suff'rin' mortal ye will not donate a cent;
Ye expend your missionaries to the heathen and the Jew,
But there isn't any heathen that is half as small as you.

'Ye are lucky – ye hev cheque-books and deeposits in the bank,
And ye squanderate your money on the titled folks of rank;
The onyx and the sardonyx upon your garments shine,
And ye drink at every dinner p'rhaps a dollar's wuth of wine.

'Ye are going for the summer to the islands by the sea,
Where it costs four dollars daily – setch is not for setch as me;
Iv'ry-handled umberellas do not come into my plan,
But I kin give a dollar to this suff'rin' fellow-man.

'Hand-bags made of Rooshy leather are not truly at my call,
Yet in the eyes of Mussy I am richer 'en you all,
For I kin give a dollar wher' you dare not stand a dime,
And never miss it nother, nor regret it any time.'

Sayin' this he drew a wallet from the inner of his vest,
And gave the tramp a daddy, which it was his level best;
Other people, havin' heard him, soon to charity inclined –
One giver soon makes twenty if you only get their wind.

The first who gave the dollar led the other one about,
And at every contribution he a-raised a joyful shout,
Exclaimin' how 'twas noble to relieviate distress,
And remarkin' that our duty is our present happiness.

Thirty dollars altogether were collected by the tramp,
When he bid 'em all good evenin' and went out into the damp,
And was followed briefly after by the one who made the speech,
And who showed by good example how to practise as to preach.

Which soon around the corner the couple quickly met,
And the tramp produced the specie for to liquidate his debt;
And the man who did the preachin' took his twenty of the sum,
Which you see that out of thirty left a tenner for the bum.

And the couple passed the summer at Bar Harbor with the rest,
Greatly changed in their appearance and most elegantly dressed.
Any fowl with change of feathers may a brilliant bird become:
And how hard is life for many! oh how sweet it is for some!

C. G. LELAND

Sir Guy the Crusader

SIR GUY was a doughty crusader,
 A muscular knight,
 Ever ready to fight,
A very determined invader,
 And DICKEY DE LION'S delight.

LENORE was a Saracen maiden,
 Brunette, statuesque,
 The reverse of grotesque,
Her pa was a bagman from Aden,
 Her mother she played in burlesque.

A coryphée, pretty and loyal,
 In amber and red
 The ballet she led;
Her mother performed at the Royal,
 LENORE at the Saracen's Head.

Of face and of figure majestic,
 She dazzled the cits –
 Ecstaticised pits; –
Her troubles were only domestic,
 But drove her half out of her wits.

Her father incessantly lashed her,
 On water and bread
 She was grudgingly fed;
Whenever her father he thrashed her
 Her mother sat down on her head.

GUY saw her, and loved her, with reason,
    For beauty so bright
    Sent him mad with delight;
He purchased a stall for the season,
    And sat in it every night.

His views were exceedingly proper,
    He wanted to wed,
    So he called at her shed
And saw her progenitor whop her –
    Her mother sit down on her head.

'So pretty,' said he, 'and so trusting!
    You brute of a dad,
    You unprincipled cad,
Your conduct is really disgusting,
    Come, come, now admit it's too bad!

'You're a turbaned old Turk, and malignant –
    Your daughter LENORE
    I intensely adore,
And I cannot help feeling indignant,
    A fact that I hinted before;

'To see a fond father employing
    A deuce of a knout
    For to bang her about,
To a sensitive lover's annoying.'
    Said the bagman, 'Crusader, get out.'

Says GUY, 'Shall a warrior laden
    With a big spiky knob,
    Sit in peace on his cob
While a beautiful Saracen maiden
    Is whipped by a Saracen snob?

'To London I'll go from my charmer.'
    Which he did, with his loot
    (Seven hats and a flute),
And was nabbed for his Sydenham armour
    At MR BEN-SAMUEL'S suit.

SIR GUY he was lodged in the Compter,
    Her pa, in a rage,
    Died (don't know his age),
His daughter, she married the prompter,
    Grew bulky and quitted the stage.

SIR W. S. GILBERT

Finnigin to Flannigan

Superintendent was Flannigan;
Boss av the siction wuz Finnigin;
Whiniver the kyars got offen the thrack,
An' muddled up things t' th' divil an' back,
Finnigin writ it to Flannigan,
After the wrick wuz all on ag'in;
    That is, this Finnigin
    Repoorted to Flannigan.

Whin Finnigin furst writ to Flannigan,
He writed tin pages – did Finnigin,
An' he tould jist how the smash occurred;
Full many a tajus blunderin' wurrd
Did Finnigin write to Flannigan
After the cars had gone on ag'in.
    That was how Finnigin
    Repoorted to Flannigan.

Now Flannigan knowed more than Finnigin –
He'd more idjucation, had Flannigan;
An' it wore'm clane an' complately out
To tell what Finnigin writ about
In his writin' to Muster Flannigan.
So he writed back to Finnigin:
    'Don't do sich a sin ag'in;
    Make 'em brief, Finnigin!'

When Finnigin got this from Flannigan,
He blushed rosy rid, did Finnigin;
An' he said: 'I'll gamble a whole month's pa-ay
That it will be minny and minny a da-ay
Befoore Sup'rintindint – that's Flannigan –
Gets a whack at this very same sin ag'in.
    From Finnigin to Flannigan
    Repoorts won't be long ag'in.'

*

Wan da'ay, on the siction av Finnigin,
On the road sup'rintinded by Flannigan,
A rail giv way on a bit av a curve,
An' some kyars went off as they made the swerve.
'There's nobody hurted', sez Finnigin,
'But repoorts must be made to Flannigan.'
    An' he winked at McGorrigan,
    As married a Finnigin.

He wuz shantyin' thin, wuz Finnigin,
As minny a railroader's been ag'in,
An' the shmoky ol' lamp wuz burnin' bright
In Finnigin's shanty all that night –
Bilin' down his repoort was Finnigin!
An' he writed this here: 'Muster·Flannigan:
    Off ag'in, on ag'in,
    Gone ag'in – Finnigin.'

S. W. GILLINAN

Lady Jane

SAPPHICS

Down the green hill-side fro’ the castle window
Lady Jane spied Bill Amaranth a workin’;
Day by day watched him go about his ample
        Nursery garden.

Cabbages thriv’d there, wi’ a mort o’ green-stuff –
Kidney beans, broad beans, onions, tomatoes,
Artichokes, seakale, vegetable marrows,
        Early potatoes.

Lady Jane cared not very much for all these:
What she cared much for was a glimpse o’ Willum
Strippin’ his brown arms wi’ a view to horti-
        Cultural effort.

Little guessed Willum, never extra-vain, that
Up the green hill-side, i’ the gloomy castle,
Feminine eyes could so delight to view his
        Noble proportions.

Only one day while, in an innocent mood,
Moppin’ his brow (’cos ’twas a trifle sweaty)
With a blue kerchief – lo, he spies a white ’un
        Coyly responding.

Oh, delightsome Love! Not a jot do *you* care
For the restrictions set on human inter-
course by cold-blooded social refiners;
        Nor do I, neither.

Day by day, peepin’ fro’ behind the bean-sticks,
Willum observed that scrap o’ white a-wavin’,
Till his hot sighs, out-growin’ all repression,
        Busted his weskit.

Lady Jane's guardian was a haughty Peer, who
Clung to old creeds and had a nasty temper;
Can we blame Willum that he hardly cared to
        Risk a refusal?

Year by year found him busy 'mid the bean-sticks,
Wholly uncertain how on earth to take steps.
Thus for eighteen years he beheld the maiden
        Wave fro' her window.

But the nineteenth spring, i' the Castle post-bag,
Came by book-post Bill's catalogue o' seedlings
Mark'd wi' blue ink at 'Paragraphs relatin'
        Mainly to Pumpkins.'

'W.A. can,' so the Lady Jane read,
'Strongly commend that very noble Gourd, the
Lady Jane, first-class medal, ornamental;
        Grows to a great height.'

Scarce a year arter, by the scented hedgerows –
Down the mown hillside, fro' the castle gateway –
Came a long train and, i' the midst, a black bier,
        Easily shouldered.

'Whose is yon corse that, thus adorned wi' gourd-leaves,
Forth ye bear with slow step?' A mourner answer'd,
' 'Tis the poor clay-cold body Lady Jane grew
        Tired to abide in.'

'Delve my grave quick, then, for I die tomorrow.
Delve it one furlong fro' the kidney bean-sticks,
Where I may dream she's goin' on precisely
        As she was used to.'

Hardly died Bill when, fro' the Lady Jane's grave,
Crept to his white death-bed a lovely pumpkin:
Clim' the house-wall and over-arched his head wi'
        Billowy verdure.

Simple this tale! – but delicately perfumed
As the sweet roadside honeysuckle. That's why,
Difficult though it's metre was to tackle,
                  I'm glad I wrote it.

SIR A. QUILLER-COUCH

Charles Augustus Fortescue,

WHO ALWAYS DID WHAT WAS RIGHT, AND SO ACCUMULATED AN IMMENSE FORTUNE

The nicest child I ever knew
Was Charles Augustus Fortescue.
He never lost his cap, or tore
His stockings or his pinafore:
    In eating Bread he made no Crumbs,
    He was extremely fond of sums,

To which, however, he preferred
The Parsing of a Latin Word –
He sought, when it was in his power,
For information twice an hour,
And as for finding Mutton-Fat
Unappetising, far from that!

He often, at his Father's Board,
Would beg them, of his own accord,
To give him, if they did not mind,
The Greasiest Morsels they could find –
His later years did not belie
The Promise of his Infancy.
In Public Life he always tried
To take a judgement Broad and Wide;
In Private, none was more than he
Renowned for quiet courtesy.
He rose at once in his Career,
And long before his Fortieth Year

Had wedded
Fifi,
     Only Child
Of Bunyan, First Lord Aberfylde,
He thus became immensely Rich,
And built the Spendid Mansion which
Is called
'𝕿𝖍𝖊 𝕮𝖊𝖉𝖆𝖗𝖘,
   𝕸𝖚𝖘𝖜𝖊𝖑𝖑 𝕳𝖎𝖑𝖑.'
Where he resides in Affluence still
To show what Everybody might
Become by
    SIMPLY DOING RIGHT.

           HILAIRE BELLOC

Dangerous Establishment

My favourite café – so I dreamed recently –
Stood amidst palm-trees in an island port.
Now, Margate is *my* holiday resort;
But dreams are rather apt to cross the sea.

I settled near the window, ill at ease;
Where once the number 2 bus used to stop
They'd set a kind of pristine jungle up
And apes – orang-outangs – hung on the trees.

I'm sure they'd not been there so very long:
You can't just change dimensions, yards and feet.
Before I came it was still Bishop Street;
You pick a place, and now it's Belitong

At first I felt like asking the head waiter.
But then I thought this wasn't any good.
What sort of comment should a man called Slater
Make on this business, even if he could?

Now the door opened. It was Dr Clare.
And, close behind him, a black panther who
Sat down as any Tom or Dick might do —
And at my table, on a vacant chair.

I asked him softly if he'd care to smoke.
He did not stir, but stared at me defiant.
Now the proprietor approached this client,
Solemnly tickled him, but never spoke.

The waiter brought us scrambled egg on toast.
He walked on tip-toe and seemed liverish.
The panther did not touch this wholesome dish
But ate poor Slater. Peace be with his ghost!

From up above came sounds of ball and cue.
The panther dined. He saw no need to hurry.
What could I do but sit there, watch and worry,
With jungle all around, no number 2?

Because they called me to the phone (old Deeping,
My senior clerk, to tell me he was sick).
I was obliged to make my exit quick.
When I came back I saw that I was sleeping.

ERICH KÄSTNER
(translated by MICHAEL HAMBURGER)

Repeat Performance

'False, false!' young Richard cried, and threw the stone
    Into the lake, and gave her in its stead
A single rose. Pacing the shore alone,
      'Deceived, deceived!' he cried: which done and said,
    He put the pistol up against his head
And, though he wasn't very good at gunnery,
    Could hardly miss. As soon as he was dead
Fair Isabel retired into a nunnery.

*

So ends my tale. In case you came in late,
    Where, when and why these various things were done,
      Whether the stone was his, or hers as well,
      And whether *it* was false or Isabel,
    And why he died and she became a nun,
I will recall and in due course relate.

P. M. HUBBARD

The Filbert

Nay, gather not that Filbert, Nicholas,
There is a maggot there . . . it is his house, . . .
His castle, . . . oh commit not burglary!
Strip him not naked, . . . 'tis his clothes, his shell,
His bones, the case and armour of his life,
And thou shalt do no murder, Nicholas!
It were an easy thing to crack that nut
Or with thy crackers or thy double teeth,
So easily may all things be destroy'd!
But 'tis not in the power of mortal man
To mend the fracture of a filbert shell.
There were two great men once amused themselves
Watching two maggots run their wriggling race,
And wagering on their speed; but Nick, to us
It were no sport to see the pamper'd worm
Roll out and then draw in his rolls of fat,
Like to some Barber's leathern powder-bag
Wherewith he feathers, frosts, or cauliflowers
Spruce Beau, or Lady fair, or Doctor grave.
Enough of dangers and of enemies
Hath Nature's wisdom for the worm ordain'd,
Increase not thou the number! Him the Mouse,
Gnawing with nibbling tooth the shell's defence,
May from his native tenement eject;
Him may the Nut-hatch, piercing with strong bill,
Unwittingly destroy; or to his hoard
The Squirrel bear, at leisure to be crack'd.
Man also hath his dangers and his foes
As this poor Maggot hath; and when I muse
Upon the aches, anxieties, and fears,
The Maggot knows not, Nicholas, methinks
It were a happy metamorphosis
To be enkernell'd thus: never to hear
Of wars, and of invasions, and of plots,
Kings, Jacobins, and Tax-commissioners;

To feel no motion but the wind that shook
The Filbert Tree, and rock'd us to our rest;
And in the middle of such exquisite food
To live luxurious! The perfection this
Of snugness! it were to unite at once
Hermit retirement, Aldermanic bliss,
And Stoic independence of mankind.

ROBERT SOUTHEY

To a Fish

You strange, astonished-looking, angle-faced,
    Dreary-mouthed, gaping wretches of the sea,
    Gulping salt-water everlastingly,
Cold-blooded, though with red your blood be graced,
And mute, though dwellers in the roaring waste;
    And you, all shapes beside, that fishy be, –
    Some round, some flat, some long, all devilry,
Legless, unloving, infamously chaste; –

O scaly, slippery, wet, swift, staring wights,
    What is't ye do? What life lead? eh, dull goggles?
How do ye vary your vile days and nights?
    How pass your Sundays? Are ye still but joggles
In ceaseless wash! Still nought but gapes, and bites,
    And drinks, and stares, diversified with boggles?

LEIGH HUNT

A Fish Answers

Amazing monster! that, for aught I know,
   With the first sight of thee didst make our race
   For ever stare! O flat and shocking face,
Grimly divided from the breast below!
Thou that on dry land horribly dost go
   With a split body and most ridiculous pace,
   Prong after prong, disgracer of all grace,
Long-useless-finned, haired, upright, unwet, slow!
O breather of unbreathable, sword-sharp air,
   How canst exist? How bear thyself, thou dry
And dreary sloth? What particle canst share
   Of the only blessed life, the watery?
I sometimes see of ye an actual *pair*
   Go by! linked fin by fin! most odiously.

LEIGH HUNT

The Walrus and the Carpenter

The sun was shining on the sea,
   Shining with all his might:
He did his very best to make
   The billows smooth and bright –
And this was odd, because it was
   The middle of the night.

The moon was shining sulkily,
   Because she thought the sun
Had got no business to be there
   After the day was done –
'It's very rude of him,' she said,
   'To come and spoil the fun!'

The sea was wet as wet could be,
   The sands were dry as dry.
You could not see a cloud, because
   No cloud was in the sky:
No birds were flying overhead –
   There were no birds to fly.

The Walrus and the Carpenter
   Were walking close at hand:
They wept like anything to see
   Such quantities of sand:
'If this were only cleared away,'
   They said, 'it would be grand!'

'If seven maids with seven mops
   Swept it for half a year,
Do you suppose,' the Walrus said,
   'That they could get it clear?'
'I doubt it,' said the Carpenter,
   And shed a bitter tear.

'O Oysters, come and walk with us!'
   The Walrus did beseech.
'A pleasant walk, a pleasant talk,
   Along the briny beach:
We cannot do with more than four,
   To give a hand to each.'

The eldest Oyster looked at him,
   But never a word he said:
The eldest Oyster winked his eye,
   And shook his heavy head –
Meaning to say he did not choose
   To leave the oyster-bed.

But four young Oysters hurried up,
   All eager for the treat:

Their coats were brushed, their faces washed,
   Their shoes were clean and neat –
And this was odd, because you know,
   They hadn't any feet.

Four other Oysters followed them,
   And yet another four;
And thick and fast they came at last,
   And more, and more, and more –
All hopping through the frothy waves,
   And scrambling to the shore.

The Walrus and the Carpenter
   Walked on a mile or so,
And then they rested on a rock
   Conveniently low:
And all the little Oysters stood
   And waited in a row.

'The time has come,' the Walrus said,
   'To talk of many things:
Of shoes – and ships – and sealing wax –
   Of cabbages – and kings –
And why the sea is boiling hot –
   And whether pigs have wings.'

'But wait a bit,' the Oysters cried,
   'Before we have our chat;
For some of us are out of breath,
   And all of us are fat!'
'No hurry!' said the Carpenter.
   They thanked him much for that.

'A loaf of bread,' the Walrus said,
   'Is what we chiefly need:
Pepper and vinegar besides
   Are very good indeed –
Now, if you're ready, Oysters dear
   We can begin to feed.'

'But not on us!' the Oysters cried,
   Turning a little blue.
'After such kindness, that would be
   A dismal thing to do!'
'The night is fine,' the Walrus said,
   'Do you admire the view?

'It was so kind of you to come!
   And you are very nice!'
The Carpenter said nothing but
   'Cut us another slice.
I wish you were not quite so deaf —
   I've had to ask you twice!'

'It seems a shame,' the Walrus said,
   'To play them such a trick.
After we've brought them out so far,
   And made them trot so quick!'
The Carpenter said nothing but
   'The butter's spread too thick!'

'I weep for you,' the Walrus said:
   'I deeply sympathize.'
With sobs and tears he sorted out
   Those of the largest size,
Holding his pocket-handkerchief
   Before his streaming eyes.

'O Oysters,' said the Carpenter,
   'You've had a pleasant run!
Shall we be trotting home again!'
   But answer came there none —
And this was scarcely odd, because
   They'd eaten every one.

LEWIS CARROLL

The Lobster-Quadrille

'Will you walk a little faster?' said a whiting to a snail,
'There's a porpoise close behind us, and he's treading on my tail.
See how eagerly the lobsters and the turtles all advance!
They are waiting on the shingle – will you come and join the dance?
Will you, won't you, will you, won't you, will you join the dance?
Will you, won't you, will you, won't you, won't you join the
        dance?

'You can really have no notion how delightful it will be
When they take us up and throw us, with the lobsters, out to sea!'
But the snail replied 'Too far, too far!' and gave a look askance –
Said he thanked the whiting kindly, but he would not join the
        dance.
        Would not, could not, would not, could not, could
          not join the dance.
        Would not, could not, would not, could not, could
          not join the dance.

'What matters it how far we go?' his scaly friend replied.
'There is another shore, you know, upon the other side.
The further off from England, the nearer is to France.
Then turn not pale, beloved snail, but come and join the dance.
        Will you, won't you, will you, won't you, will you
          join the dance?
        Will you, won't you, will you, won't you, will you
          join the dance?'

LEWIS CARROLL

A Sea Dirge

There are certain things – a spider, a ghost,
   The income-tàx, gout, an umbrella for three –
That I hate, but the thing that I hate the most
   Is a thing they call the SEA.

Pour some cold water over the floor –
   Ugly I'm sure you'll allow it to be:
Suppose it extended a mile or more,
   That's very like the SEA.

Beat a dog till it howls outright –
   Cruel, but all very well for a spree:
Suppose that one did so day and night,
   That would be like the SEA.

I had a vision of nursery-maids;
   Tens of thousands passed by me –
All leading children with wooden spades,
   And this was by the SEA.

Who invented those spades of wood?
   Who was it cut them out of the tree?
None, I think, but an idiot could –
   Or one that loved the SEA.

It is pleasant and dreamy, no doubt, to float
   With 'thoughts as boundless, and souls as free';
But suppose you are very unwell in a boat,
   How do you like the SEA?

There is an insect that people avoid
   (Whence is derived the verb 'to flee')
Where have you been by it most annoyed?
   In lodgings by the SEA.

If you like coffee with sand for dregs,
   A decided hint of salt in your tea,
And a fishy taste in the very eggs –
   By all means choose the SEA.

And if, with these dainties to drink and eat,
   You prefer not a vestige of grass or tree,
And a chronic state of wet in your feet,
   Then – I recommend the SEA.

For *I* have friends who dwell by the coast,
   Pleasant friends they are to me!
It is when I'm with them I wonder most
   That anyone likes the SEA.

They take me a walk: though tired and stiff,
   To climb the heights I madly agree:
And, after a tumble or so from the cliff,
   They kindly suggest the SEA.

I try the rocks, and I think it cool
   That they laugh with such an excess of glee,
As I heavily slip into every pool
   That skirts the cold, cold SEA.

LEWIS CARROLL

The Pelican Chorus

King and Queen of the Pelicans we;
No other birds so grand as we!
None but we have feet like fins!
With lovely leathery throats and chins!
      Ploffskin, Pluffskin, Pelican jee!
      We think no birds so happy as we!
      Plumpskin, Ploshkin, Pelican Jill!
      We think so then, and we thought so still!

We live on the Nile. The Nile we love.
By night we sleep on the cliffs above.
By day we fish, and at eve we stand
On long bare islands of yellow sand.
And when the sun sinks slowly down
And the great rock walls grow dark and brown,
Where the purple river rolls fast and dim
And the ivory Ibis starlike skim,
Wing to wing we dance around, –
Stamping our feet with a flumpy sound, –
Opening our mouths as Pelicans ought,
And this is the song we nightly snort
  Ploffskin, etc. (*as before*).

Last year came out our Daughter, Dell;
And all the birds received her well.
To do her honour, a feast we made
For every bird that can swim or wade.
Herons and Gulls, and Cormorants black,
Cranes, and Flamingoes with scarlet back,
Plovers and Storks, and Geese in crowds.
Thousands of Birds in wondrous flight!
They ate and drank and danced all night,
And echoing back from the rocks you heard
Multitude-echoes from Bird and Bird, –
  Ploffskin, etc. (*as before*).

Yes, they came; and among the rest,
The King of the Cranes all grandly dressed.
Such a lovely tail! Its feathers float
Between the ends of his blue dress-coat;
With pea-green trowsers all so neat,
And a delicate frill to hide his feet, –
(For though no one speaks of it, everyone knows,
He had got no webs between his toes!)
As soon as he saw our Daughter Dell,
In violent love that Crane King fell, –
On seeing her waddling form so fair,

With a wreath of shrimps in her short white hair,
And before the end of the next long day,
Our Dell had given her heart away;
For the King of the Cranes had won that heart,
With a Crocodile's egg and a large fish-tart.
She vowed to marry the King of the Cranes,
Leaving the Nile for stranger plains;
And away they flew in a lengthening cloud.
  Ploffskin, etc. (*as before*).

And far away in the twilight sky,
We heard them singing a lessening cry, –
Farther and farther till out of sight,
And we stood alone in the silent night!
Often since, in the nights of June,
We sit on the sand and watch the moon; –
She has gone to the great Gromboolian plain,
And we probably never shall meet again!
Oft, in the long still nights of June,
We sit on the rocks and watch the moon; –
– She dwells by the streams of the Chankly Bore,
And we probably never shall meet her more.
  Ploffskin, etc. (*as before*).

EDWARD LEAR

The Irish Pig

'Twas an evening in November,
As I very well remember,
I was strolling down the street in drunken pride,
But my knees were all aflutter,
So I landed in the gutter,
And a pig came up and lay down by my side.

Yes, I lay there in the gutter
Thinking thoughts I could not utter,
When a colleen passing by did softly say,
'Ye can tell a man that boozes
By the company he chooses.' –
At that the pig got up and walked away!

ANON.

Ah, Who?

Who comes so damp by grass and grave
   At ghastly twilight hour,
And bubbles forth his pois'nous breath
   On ev'ry shudd'ring flow'r?

Who dogs the houseless wanderer
   Upon the wintry wold;
And kisses – with his frothy lips –
   The clammy brow and cold?

Who, hideous, trails a slimy form
   Betwixt the moonlight pale,
And the pale, fearful, sleeping face?
   Our little friend – the Snail.

H. CHOLMONDELEY-PENNELL

The Python

A Python I should not advise, –
It needs a doctor for its eyes,
And has the measles yearly.
However, if you feel inclined
To get one (to improve your mind,

And not for fashion merely),
Allow no music near its cage;
And when it flies into a rage
Chastise it, most severely.

I had an aunt in Yucatan
Who bought a Python from a man
    And kept it for a pet.
She died, because she never knew
These simple little rules and few; —
    The snake is living yet.

HILAIRE BELLOC

The Pretender

In the greens of the wilds of Seringapatam
Is the haunt of an ancient redoubtable ram,
    With sharp-pointed horns on its head;
When it snuffs out a Brahmin it scoops with its hooves,
Till the jungle around it is jungle in grooves,
    And then it pretends to be dead.

O White Man, beware of such tactics as these,
For if in compassion thou sink to thy knees,
    All thought of mere safety forgot,
With a jerk of its horns the fell creature comes to,
And smiles, as if saying, 'Ah, friend, is it you?'
    When there's none to reply, 'It is not'.

WALTER DE LA MARE

The Legend of the First Cam-u-el

AN ARABIAN APOLOGUE

Across the sands of Syria,
Or, possibly, Algeria,
Or some benighted neighbourhood of barrenness and drouth,
There came the prophet Sam-u-el
Upon the only Cam-u-el –
A bumpy, grumpy Quadruped of discontented mouth.

The atmosphere was glutinous;
The Cam-u-el was mutinous;
He dumped the pack from off his back; with horrid grunts and
   squeals
He made the desert hideous;
With strategy perfidious
He tied his neck in curlicues, he kicked his paddy heels.

Then quoth the gentle Sam-u-el,
'You rogue, I ought to lam you well!
Though zealously I've shielded you from every grief and woe,
It seems, to voice a platitude,
You haven't any gratitude.
I'd like to know what cause you have for doing thus and so!'

To him replied the Cam-u-el,
'I beg your pardon, Sam-u-el.
I know that I'm a Reprobate, I know that I'm a Freak;
But oh! this utter loneliness!
My too distinguished Onliness!
Were there but other Cam-u-els I wouldn't be Unique.'

The Prophet beamed beguilingly.
'Aha', he answered smilingly,
'You feel the need of company? I clearly understand.

We'll speedily create for you
The corresponding mate for you –
Ho! presto, change-o, dinglebat!' – he waved a potent hand,

And, lo! from out Vacuity
A second Incongruity,
To wit, a Lady Cam-u-el was born through magic art.
Her structure anatomical,
Her form and face were comical;
She was, in short, a Cam-u-el, the other's counterpart.

As Spaniards gaze on Aragon,
Upon that Female Paragon
So gazed the Prophet's Cam-u-el, that primal Desert Ship.
A connoisseur meticulous,
He found her that ridiculous
He grinned from ear to auricle *until he split his lip!*

Because of his temerity
That Cam-u-el's posterity
Must wear divided upper lips through all their solemn lives!
A prodigy astonishing
Reproachfully admonishing
Those wicked, heartless married men who ridicule their wives.

ARTHUR GUITERMAN

Our Pond

I am fond
Of our pond,
Of the superfine gloss
On its moss,
Its pink lilies and things
And the wings
     Of its duck.

I am keen
On the green
Soupy surface of some
Of its scum,
Its water-waved weeds,
Its three reeds
    And its muck.

Yesterday,
As I lay
And admired its thick skin,
I fell in;
I went walloping down
Till I stuck.

I am fond
Of our pond,
But I like it much more
From the shore.
It was quite out of place
On my face,
    Where it stuck.

DANIEL PETTIWARD

Nottamun Town

In Nottamun Town not a soul would look up,
Not a soul would look up, not a soul would look down,
Not a soul would look up, not a soul would look down
To tell me the way to Nottamun Town.

I rode a big horse that was called a grey mare,
Grey mane and tail, grey stripes down his back,
Grey mane and tail, grey stripes down his back,
There weren't a hair on him but what was called black.

She stood so still, she threw me to the dirt,
She tore my hide and bruised my shirt;
From stirrup to stirrup, I mounted again
And on my ten toes I rode over the plain

Met the King and the Queen and a company of men
A-walking behind and a-riding before.
A stark naked drummer came walking along
With his hands in his bosom a-beating his drum.

Sat down on a hot and cold frozen stone,
Ten thousand stood round me and I was alone.
Took my heart in my hand to keep my head warm.
Ten thousand got drowned that never were born.

ANON.

Susan Simpson

Sudden swallows swiftly skimming,
Sunset's slowly spreading shade,
Silvery songsters sweetly singing
Summer's soothing serenade.

Susan Simpson strolled sedately,
   Stifling sobs, suppressing sighs.
Seeing Stephen Slocum, stately
   She stopped, showing some surprise.

'Say', said Stephen, 'sweetest sigher;
   Say, shall Stephen spouseless stay?'
Susan, seeming somewhat shyer,
   Showed submissiveness straightway.

Summer's season slowly stretches,
   Susan Simpson Slocum she –
So she signed some simple sketches –
   Soul sought soul successfully.

*

Six Septembers Susan swelters;
   Six sharp seasons snow supplies;
Susan's satin sofa shelters
   Six small Slocums side by side.

ANON.

Elegy

to the Memory of Miss Emily Kay, cousin to Miss Ellen Gee, of Kew
who died lately at Ewell, and was buried in Essex

'They fool me to the top of my bent.' – SHAKESPEARE

Sad nymphs of UL, U have much to cry for,
   Sweet MLEKU never more shall C!
OSX Maids! come hither and D, O,
   With tearful I, this MTLEG.

Without XS she did XL alway,
   Ah me! it truly vexes 12C,
How soon so DR a creature may DK,
   And only leave behind XUVE!

Whate'er 10 to do she did discharge,
  So that an NME it might NDR:
Then why an SA write? – then why N
  Or with my briny tears BDU her BR?

When her Piano-40 she did press,
  Such heavenly sounds did MN8, that she
Knowing her Q, soon IU2 confess
  Her XLNC in an XTC.

Her hair was soft as silk, not YRE,
  It gave no Q, nor yet 2P to view:
She was not handsome: shall I tell UY?
  UR2 know her I was all SQ.

L8 she was, and prattling like a J;
  How little, MLE! did you 4C,
The grave should soon MUU, cold as clay,
  And you should cease to be an NTT!

While taking T at Q with LNG,
  The MT grate she rose to put a:
Her clothes caught fire – no I again shall see
  Poor MLE; who now is dead as Solon.

OLNG! in vain you set at O
  GR and reproach her for suffering 2B
Thus sacrificed; to JLU should be brought,
  Or burnt UO2B in FEG.

Sweet MLEK into SX they bore,
  Taking good care the monument 2Y10,
And as her tomb was much 2 low B4,
  They lately brought fresh bricks the walls to 10
    (heighten).

HORACE SMITH
(or HORATIO)

Sonnet to Vauxhall

The cold transparent ham is on my fork –
   It hardly rains – and hark the bell! – ding-dingle –
Away. Three thousand feet at gravel work,
   Mocking a Vauxhall shower! – Married and Single
Crush – rush! – Soaked Silks with wet white Satin mingle.
   Hengler! Madame! round whom all bright sparks lurk,
Calls audibly on Mr and Mrs Pringle
   To study the Sublime, &c. – (vide Burke)
All noses are upturn'd! Whish – ish! – On high
   The rocket rushes – trails – just steals in sight –
Then droops and melts in bubbles of blue light –
   And Darkness reigns – Then balls flare up and die –
Wheels whiz – smack crackers – serpents twist – and then
   Back to the cold transparent ham again.

THOMAS HOOD

Evening

BY A TAILOR

Day hath put on his jacket, and around
His burning bosom buttoned it with stars.
Here will I lay me on the velvet grass,
That is like padding to earth's meagre ribs,
And hold communion with the things about me.
Ah me! how lovely is the golden braid
That binds the skirt of night's descending robe!
The thin leaves, quivering on their silken threads,
Do make a music like to rustling satin,
As the light breezes smooth their downy nap.

Ha! what is this that rises to my touch,
So like a cushion? Can it be a cabbage?
It is, it is that deeply injured flower
Which boys do flout us with; – but yet I love thee,
Thou giant rose, wrapped in a green surtout.
Doubtless in Eden thou didst blush as bright
As these, thy puny brethren; and thy breath
Sweetened the fragrance of her spicy air:
But now thou seemst like a bankrupt beau,
Stripped of his gaudy hues and essences,
And growing portly in his sober garments.

Is that a swan that rides upon the water?
O no, it is that other gentle bird,
Which is the patron of our noble calling.
I well remember, in my early years,
When these young hands first closed upon a goose;
I have a scar upon my thimble finger,
Which chronicles the hour of young ambition.
My father was a tailor, and his father,
And my sire's grandsires, all of them were tailors;
They had an ancient goose, – it was an heirloom
From some remoter tailor of our race.
It happened I did see it on a time
When none was near, and I did deal with it,
And it did burn me – oh, most fearfully!

It is a joy to straighten out one's limbs,
And leap elastic from the level counter,
Leaving the petty grievances of earth,
The breaking thread, the din of clashing shears,
And all the needles that do wound the spirit,
For such a pensive hour of soothing silence.
King Nature, shuffling in her loose undress,
Lays bare her shady bosom; – I can feel
With all around me; – I can hail the flowers
That sprig earth's mantle, – and yon quiet bird,
That rides the stream, is to me as a brother.

The vulgar know not all the hidden pockets
Where Nature stows away her loveliness.
But this unnatural posture of the legs
Cramps my extended calves, and I must go
Where I can coil them in their wonted·fashion.

OLIVER WENDELL HOLMES

Jabberwocky

'Twas brillig, and the slithy toves
    Did gyre and gimble in the wabe:
All mimsy were the borogoves,
    And the mome raths outgrabe.

'Beware the Jabberwock, my son!
    The jaws that bite, the claws that catch!
Beware the Jubjub bird, and shun
    The frumious Bandersnatch!'

He took his vorpal sword in hand:
    Long time the manxome foe he sought –
So rested he by the Tumtum tree,
    And stood awhile in thought.

And, as in uffish thought he stood,
    The Jabberwock, with eyes of flame,
Came whiffling through the tulgy wood,
    And burbled as it came!

One, two! One, two! And through and through
    The vorpal blade went snicker-snack!
He left it dead, and with its head
    He went galumphing back.

'And hast thou slain the Jabberwock?
  Come to my arms, my beamish boy!
O frabjous day! Callooh! Callay!'
  He chortled in his joy.

'Twas brillig, and the slithy toves
  Did gyre and gimble in the wabe:
All mimsy were the borogoves,
  And the mome raths outgrabe.

LEWIS CARROLL

Belagcholly Days

Chilly Dovebber with his boadigg blast
  Dow cubs add strips the bedow add the lawd,
Eved October's suddy days are past –
    Add Subber's gawd!

I kdow dot what it is to which I cligg
  That stirs to sogg add sorrow, yet I trust
That still I sigg, but as the liddets sigg –
    Because I bust.

Add now, farewell to roses add to birds,
  To larded fields and tigkligg streablets eke;
Farewell to all articulated words
    I fain would speak.

Farewell, by cherished strolliggs od the sward,
  Greed glades and forest shades, farewell to you;
With sorrowing heart I, wretched add forlord,
    Bid you – achew!!!

ANON.

The Parterre

I don't know any greatest treat
As sit him in a gay parterre,
And sniff one up the perfume sweet
Of every roses buttoning there.

It only want my charming miss
Who make to blush the self red rose;
Oh! I have envy of to kiss
The end's tip of her splendid nose.

Oh! I have envy of to be
What grass 'neath her pantoffle push,
And too much happy seemeth me
The margaret which her vestige crush.

But I will meet her nose at nose,
And take occasion for her hairs,
And indicate her all my woes,
That she in fine agree my prayers.

I don't know any greatest treat
As sit him in a gay parterre,
With Madame who is too more sweet
Than every roses buttoning there.

E. H. PALMER

The Rhyme of the Rusher

IN APPROPRIATE RHYMING SLANGUAGE

I was out one night on the strict teetote,
　　'Cause I couldn't afford a drain;
I was wearing a leaky I'm afloat,
　　And it started to France and Spain.
But a toff was mixed in a bull and cow,
　　And I helped him to do a bunk;
He had been on the I'm so tap, and now
　　He was slightly elephant's trunk.

He offered to stand me a booze, so I
　　Took him round to the 'Mug's Retreat';
And my round the houses I tried to dry
　　By the Anna Maria's heat.
He stuck to the I'm so to drown his cares,
　　While I went for the far and near,
Until the clock on the apples and pears
　　Gave the office for us to clear.

Then round at the club we'd another bout,
　　And I fixed him at nap until
I had turned his skyrockets inside out,
　　And had managed my own to fill.
Of course I had gone on the half-ounce trick
　　And we quarrelled and came to blows;
But I fired him out of the Rory quick,
　　And he fell on his I suppose.

And he laid there, weighing out prayers at me,
　　Without hearing the plates of meat
Of a slop, who pinched him for 'd. and d.'
　　And disturbing a peaceful beat.
And I smiled as I closed my two mince pies
　　In my insect promenade;
For out of his nibs I had taken a rise,
　　And his stay on the spot was barred.

Next morning I brushed up my Barnet Fair,
  And got myself up pretty smart;
Then I sallied forth with a careless air,
  And contented raspberry tart.
At the first big pub I resolved, if pos.,
  That I'd sample my lucky star;
So I passed a flimsy on to the boss
  Who served drinks at the there you are.

He looked at the note, and the air began
  With his language to pen and ink
For the mug I'd fleeced had been his head man
  And had done him for lots of chink.
I'm blessed if my luck doesn't hum and ha,
  For I argued the point with skill;
But the once a week made me go ta-ta
  For a month on the can't keep still.

DOSS CHIDERDOSS

The Bees' Song

Thousandz of thornz there be
On the Rozez where gozez
The Zebra of Zee:
Sleek, striped and hairy,
The steed of the Fairy
Princess of Zee.
Heavy with blossomz be
The Rozez that growzez
In the thickets of Zee.
Where grazez the Zebra,
Marked Abracadeebra
Of the Princess of Zee.

And he nozez the pozies
Of the Rozez that growzez
So luvez'm and free,
With an eye, dark and wary,
In search of a Fairy,
Whose Rozez he knowzez
Were not honeyed for he,
But to breathe a sweet incense
To solace the Princess
Of far-away Zee.

WALTER DE LA MARE

The Lass o' the Lab

A MODERN FOLKSONG

On being asked by an F.R.S. – no less – why modern poetry was so little
inspired by Science. To the tune of *The Bailiff's Daughter of Islington.*

Now there once was a lass and a very pretty lass,
    And she was an isotope's daughter
And they called her Ethyl-Methyl, for her mother was a gas
    Made of Ch_{17} and water.

She was built on such lines, perhaps parallel lines,
    (For Einstein says they'll never meet),
And her lips resembled the most delicate sines,
    And her cheeks were like cosines sweet.

Her hair it was like transformers in a way,
    And her eyes like two live coils,
While as for her spectrum, I always used to say,
    'I could watch it till it boils'.

Though at making of love I never was a dab,
    We were soon on the best of terms,
In fact the first time that I saw her in the lab.
    We generated n^2 therms.

Her metabolisms I shall never forget
    Nor her parallaxes till I die,
But the sad thing is that, whenever we met,
    The sparks they used to fly.

Alas and alack! it was ever, ever thus;
    We had perforce to part,
For she – she was a *minus*, and I – I was a *plus*;
    In fact we were poles apart.

ENVOI

Still, Scientists all, I am sorry I was wrong,
    And $\pm$ 0·3
With the Higher Hydrocarbons now shall decorate my song
    Instead of the willow-tree.

SIR J. C. SQUIRE

'*Il est Cocu – Le Chef de Gare*'

The Teuton sang the 'Wacht am Rhein'
    And 'Lieber Augustin', while we
Had 'Long Long Trail' and 'Clementine'
    And 'Old Kit-Bag' (to give but three):
    Good songs, and yet, you must agree,
The *Poilu*'s theme was richer, vaster,
    Double-distilled felicity!
'He has been duped – the station-master!'

A joyous thought, an anodyne
    For gelignite and T.N.T.;
A song to cure those saturnine
    Red singing-men of Battersea;
    And, whosoever wrote it, he
Deserves a tomb of alabaster,
    Graven on which these words should be:
'He has been duped – the station-master!'

When I am tired of Gertrude Stein
   ('She said she said that she said she ... !')
When the expressionistic line
   Has palled and Sitwells weary me,
   When bored with psycho-prosody,
Obscurist and grammaticaster,
   Give me that song of Picardy:
'He has been duped – the station-master!'

ENVOI

   Prince, did you hear the soldiery
   Singing of that obscure disaster –
   (Zenith of Gallic pleasantry!)
'He has been duped – the station-master!'

H. S. MACKINTOSH

Ballade of Unexampled Erudition

How many people know an Asymptote?
   How many know the rules of village whist?
Or grasp the import of a *table d'hôte*
   When *Potage Président Truman* heads the list?
   I know them all: I know how ants exist,
And how to hold a golf-club or a bat:
   And how to be a prosperous dramatist –
I've got a little book which tells me that.

In a debate at Hove on 'Serb *v.* Croat',
   There up and spake Lord Bilge, economist,
But question-time arrived before the vote
   And then things took a very tiresome twist:
   When asked: 'Are *you* an Ultramontanist?'
And: 'When and why and what's a thermostat?'
   The fool was stumped and all the audience hissed.
I've got a little book which tells me that!

243

But knowledge is Romance's antidote:
  I know the stuff of which the stars consist,
That H_2O's prismatic drops promote
    The moonbow and the ocean's amethyst,
      And that each lover who has 'toyed and kissed'
And each whose heart has beat Love's pit-a-pat
    Tends to become a Galactophagist –
I've got a little book which tells me that.

ENVOI

  Prince, when you feel my fervent foot and fist,
How nice to quote 'Bis dat qui cito dat!'
  That means . . . but there, that's something that you've missed:
I've got a little book which tells me that.

H. S. MACKINTOSH

What'll Be the Title?

O to scuttle from the battle and to settle on an atoll far from brutal
  mortal neath a wattle portal!
To keep little mottled cattle and to whittle down one's chattels and
  not hurtle after brittle yellow metal!
To listen, non-committal, to the anecdotal local tittle-tattle on a
  settle round the kettle,
Never startled by a rattle more than betel-nuts a-prattle or the
  myrtle-petals' subtle throttled chortle!
But I'll bet that what'll happen if you footle round an atoll is you'll
  get in rotten fettle living totally on turtle, nettles, cuttle-fish or
  beetles, victuals fatal to the natal *élan-vital,*
And hit the bottle.
I guess I'd settle
For somewhere ethical and practical like Bootle.

JUSTIN RICHARDSON

Soldier

When the Sex War ended with the slaughter of the Grandmothers
They found a bachelor's baby suffocating under them;
Somebody called him George and that was the end of it:
    They hitched him up to the Army.
    George, you old débutante,
    How did you get in the army?

In the Retreat from Reason he deserted on his rocking-horse
And lived on a fairy's kindness till he tired of kicking her;
He smashed her spectacles and stole her cheque-book and
    mackintosh
    Then cruised his way back to the Army.
    George, you old numero,
    How did you get in the Army?

Before the Diet of Sugar he was using razor-blades
And exited soon after with an allergy to maidenheads;
He discovered a cure of his own, but no one would patent it,
    So he showed up again in the Army.
    George, you old flybynight,
    How did you get in the Army?

When the Vice Crusades were over he was hired by some Mus-
    covites
Prospecting for deodorants among the Eskimos;
He was caught by a common cold and condemned to the whiskey
    mines,
    But schemozzled back to the Army.
    George, you old Emperor,
    How did you get in the Army?

Since Peace was signed with Honour he's been minding his
    business;
But, whoops, here comes His idleness, buttoning his uniform;

Just in tidy time to massacre the Innocents;
    He's come home to roost in the Army.
    George, you old matador
    Welcome back to the Army.

W. H AUDEN

The Roadside Littérateur

There's a little old fellow and he has a little paintpot,
And a paucity of brushes is something that he ain't got,
And when he sees a road sign, the road sign he betters,
And expresses of himself by eliminating letters.

    Thus THROUGH ROAD
    Becomes ROUGH ROAD
    And CURVES DANGEROUS
    Is transformed to CURVES ANGER US
    And 24-HOUR SERVICE
    Turns into 24-HOUR VICE
    And MEN AT WORK IN ENTRANCE
    Is reduced to MEN AT WORK IN TRANCE
    And SLOW DOWN BRIDGE ONE WAY
    Is triumphantly condensed to
    LOW DOWN BRIDE ON WAY

But the old fellow feels a slight dissatisfaction
With the uninspiring process of pure subtraction.
The evidence would indicate he's taken as his mission
The improvement of the road signs by the process of addition.

    Thus TRAFFIC LIGHT AHEAD
    Becomes TRAFFIC SLIGHT AHEAD
    And GAS AND OIL
    Is improved to GASP AND BOIL
    And simple REST ROOMS
    Appear as QUEEREST ROOMS

And UNDERPASS ONE WAY
Emerges as UNDERPASS GONE AWAY
And (perhaps his masterpiece)
                    RIGHT
              EAST BOUND
                  TUNNEL
Is elaborated to
                  FRIGHTENED
              BEASTS ABOUND
                  IN TUNNEL
Thus we see the critical mood
Becomes the creative attitude.

MORRIS BISHOP

A Reunion in Kensington

As I was sticking hand-bills on Prince Albert's prim anatomy
A green-faced naval colonel friend came waltzing round the back
  of me,
And since I'd often flown with him, I thought it quite absurd
To let him just dance on again without a single word.

I hailed him rather noisily by tweaking my suspenderses
And asked if he remembered that I used to be a friend of his,
He said he did with ecstasy, and warmly shook my feet,
At which I offered him a half-smoked harvest-mouse to eat.

We hailed a sliding staircase which went up into the Underground.
We missed one train quite easily, but caught it as it turned around.
We lay down on the ceiling and, with quite undue contempt,
Tore up the blue advertisements for smell-less onion scent.

He said he spent his years abroad in growing sal-volatile,
He'd always stuck the seeds in wrong, since he preferred philately.
He had a daughter now, it seemed, and three dear little wives,
Who helped him making pin-cushions, and jam from unripe chives.

247

But as we talked the major shaved in a far-off pomposity,
Then turning a flaming eye on me, that froze me with ferocity.
'You're not the man you was,' he says, and slid under the door,
Leaving a smell of camembert and a lucky monkey's paw.

S. J. COHEN

To T.M. S – E

CATECHISED IN HIS EPISTLE TO MR POPE

'What makes you write at this odd rate?'
'Why, Sir, it is to intimate.'
'What makes you steal and trifle so?'
'Why, 'tis to do as others do.'
'But there's no meaning to be seen,'
'Why, that's the very thing I mean.'

ALEXANDER POPE

Abroad and at Home

As Thomas was cudgel'd one day by his wife,
He took to the street, and fled for his life:
Tom's three dearest friends came by in the squabble,
And sav'd him at once from the shrew and the rabble;
Then ventur'd to give him some sober advice;
But Tom is a person of honour so nice,
Too wise to take counsel, too proud to take warning,
That he sent to all three a challenge next morning:
Three duels he fought, thrice ventur'd his life;
Went home, and was cudgel'd again by his wife.

JONATHAN SWIFT

Against Education

Accursed the man, whom Fate ordains, in spite,
And cruel parents teach, to read and write!
What need of letters? wherefore should we spell?
Why write our names? A mark will do as well.
Much are the precious hours of youth misspent,
In climbing Learning's rugged, steep ascent;
When to the top the bold adventurer's got,
He reigns, vain monarch, o'er a barren spot;
Whilst in the vale of Ignorance below,
Folly and Vice to rank luxuriance grow;
Honours and wealth pour in on every side,
And proud Preferment rolls her golden tide.
O'er crabbed authors life's gay prime to waste.
To cramp wild genius in the chains of taste,
To bear the slavish drudgery of schools,
And tamely stoop to every pedant's rules;
For seven long years debarr'd of liberal ease,
To plod in college trammels to degrees;
Beneath the weight of solemn toys to groan,
Sleep over books, and leave mankind unknown;
To praise each senior blockhead's threadbare tale,
And laugh till freedom blush and spirits fail;
Manhood with vile submission to disgrace,
And cap the fool, whose merit is his place,
Vice-Chancellors, whose knowledge is but small,
And Chancellors, who nothing know at all.

CHARLES CHURCHILL

King George III enters Heaven

Saint Peter sat by the celestial gate,
    And nodded o'er his keys; when, lo! there came
A wondrous noise he had not heard of late –
    A rushing sound of wind, and stream, and flame;
In short, a roar of things extremely great,
    Which would have made aught save a saint exclaim;
But he, with first a start and then a wink,
    Said, 'There's another star gone out, I think!'

But ere he could return to his repose,
    A cherub flapp'd his right wing o'er his eyes –
At which St Peter yawn'd, and rubb'd his nose:
    'Saint porter', said the angel, 'prithee rise!'
Waving a goodly wing, which glow'd, as glows
    An earthly peacock's tail, with heavenly dyes:
To which the saint replied, 'Well, what's the matter?
    Is Lucifer come back with all this clatter?'

'No,' quoth the cherub: 'George the Third is dead.'
    'And who *is* George the Third?' replied the apostle:
'What George? What Third?' 'The king of England,' said
    The angel. 'Well, he won't find kings to jostle
Him on his way; but does he wear his head?
    Because the last we saw here had a tustle.
And ne'er would have got into heaven's good graces
Had he not flung his head in all our faces

'He was, if I remember, king of France;
    That head of his, that could not keep a crown
On earth, yet ventured in my face to advance
    A claim to those of martyrs – like my own:
If I had had my sword, as I had once
    When I cut ears off, I had cut him down;
But having but my *keys*, and not my brand,
I only knock'd his head from out his hand.

'And then he set up such a headless howl,
   That all the saints came out and took him in;
And there he sits by St Paul, cheek by jowl;
   That fellow Paul – the parvenu! The skin
Of St Bartholomew, which makes his cowl
   In heaven, and upon earth redeem'd his sin,
So as to make a martyr, never sped
Better than did this weak and wooden head.

But had it come up here upon its shoulders,
   There would have been a different tale to tell:
The fellow-feeling in the saint's beholders
   Seems to have acted on them like a spell,
And so this very foolish head heaven solders
   Back on its trunk: it may be very well,
And seems the custom here to overthrow
Whatever has been wisely done below.'

The angel answer'd, 'Peter! do not pout:
   The king who comes has head and all entire,
And never knew much what it was about –
   He did as doth the puppet – by its wire,
And will be judged like all the rest, no doubt:
   My business and your own is not to inquire
Into such matters, but to mind our cue –
Which is to act as we are bid to do.'

GEORGE GORDON, LORD BYRON

Rhymes on the Road

And is there then no earthly place
   Where we can rest, in dream Elysian,
Without some curst, round English face
   Popping up near, to break the vision?
'Mid northern lakes and southern vines,
   Unholy cits we're doomed to meet;
Nor highest Alps nor Appenines
   Are sacred from Threadneedle Street!

If up the Simplon's path we wind,
Fancying we leave this world behind,
Such pleasant sounds salute one's ear
As – 'Baddish news from 'Change, my dear –
The Funds – (phew, curse this ugly hill) –
Are low'ring fast – (what, higher still?)
And – (zooks, we're mounting up to heaven!) –
Will soon be down to sixty-seven.'

Go where we may – rest where we will,
Eternal London haunts us still.
The trash of Almack's or Fleet Ditch –
And scarce a pin's head difference *which* –
Mixes, though ev'n to Greece, we run,
With every rill from Helicon!
And, if this rage for travelling lasts,
If Cockneys, of all sects and castes,
Old maidens, aldermen, and squires,
Will leave their puddings and coal fires,
To gape at things in foreign lands,
No soul among them understands;

If Blues desert their coteries,
To show off 'mong the Wahabees;
If neither sex nor age controls,
   Nor fear of Mamelukes forbids

Young ladies, with pink parasols,
   To glide among the Pyramids –
Why, then, farewell all hope to find
A spot that's free from London-kind!
Who knows, if to the West we roam,
But we may find some *Blue* 'at home'
   Among the *Blacks* of Carolina –
Or, flying to the Eastward, see
     Some Mrs HOPKINS taking tea
       And toast upon the Wall of China!

THOMAS MOORE

Cologne

In Köln, a town of monks and bones,
And pavements fang'd with murderous stones
And rags, and hags, and hideous wenches;
I counted two and seventy stenches,
All well defined, and several stinks!
Ye Nymphs that reign o'er sewers and sinks,
The river Rhine, it is well known,
   Doth wash your city of Cologne;
But tell me, Nymphs, what power divine
Shall henceforth wash the river Rhine?

S. T. COLERIDGE

Swans sing before they die – 'twere no bad thing
Should certain persons die before they sing.

S. T. COLERIDGE

On a Rhine Steamer

Republic of the West,
   Enlightened, free, sublime,
Unquestionably best
   Production of our time.

The telephone is thine,
   And thine the Pullman Car,
The caucus, the divine
   Intense electric star.

To thee we likewise owe
   The venerable names
Of Edgar Allen Poe,
   And Mr Henry James.

In short it's due to thee,
   Thou kind of Western star,
That we have come to be
   Precisely what we are.

But every now and then,
   It cannot be denied,
You breed a kind of men
   Who are not dignified,

Or courteous or refined,
   Benevolent or wise,
Or gifted with a mind
   Beyond the common size,

Or notable for tact,
   Agreeable to me,
Or anything, in fact,
   That people ought to be.

J. K. STEPHEN

To Julia, in Envy of her Toughness

When I, in such revolting weather
  As permeates the Arctic zone,
Just keep my soul and flesh together
  By wearing things that weigh a stone,
And find that you go undefeated
  In clothes that let the blast blow through,
I marvel why my sex is treated
  As much the tougher of the two.

When Earth is wrapt in frosty vapour
  And barren boughs with snow are fledged,
Your callous legs still love to caper
  In summer hose of silk (alleged);
While I, if thus I mocked the blizzard
  Or rashly dared the bitter rime –
I should be stricken in the gizzard,
  I should be dead in three days' time.

Having survived the day's exposure
  At eve you bare your hardy spine,
Marking that exhibition's closure
  At well below the old waist-line;
This seems to cause your lungs no trouble,
  Yet if I danced *sans* shirt and vest
I should incur pneumonia (double)
  And in a week or so go West.

How comes it you enjoy a measure
  Of nudity to me denied?
Is it because your frame, my treasure,
  Is coated with a coarser hide?
I fear you'll deem this view abhorrent,
  So let me add, to break, the blow
You are – and will remain, I warrant –
  The nicest pachyderm I know.

SIR OWEN SEAMAN

By Deputy

As Shakespeare couldn't write his plays
  (If Mrs Gallup's not mistaken)
I think how wise in many ways
  He was to have them done by Bacon;
They might have mouldered on the shelf,
  Mere minor dramas (and he knew it!)
If he had written them himself
  Instead of letting Bacon do it.

And if it's true, as Brown and Smith
  In many learned tomes have stated,
That Homer was an idle myth
  He ought to be congratulated,
Since thus, evading birth, he rose
  For men to worship at a distance:
He might have penned inferior prose
  Had he achieved a real existence.

To him and Shakespeare men agree
  In making very nice allusions;
But no one thinks of praising me,
  For I compose my own effusions:
As others wrote *their* works divine
  And they immortal thus today are,
Perhaps had some one written mine
  I might have been as great as they are.

A. ST JOHN ADCOCK

Satire on Paying Calls in August

When I was young, throughout the hot season
There were no carriages driving about the roads.
People shut their doors and lay down in the cool:
Or if they went out, it was not to pay calls.
Nowadays – ill-bred, ignorant fellows,
When they feel the heat, make for a friend's house.
The unfortunate host, when he hears someone coming
Scowls and frowns, but can think of no escape.
'There's nothing for it but to rise and go to the door,'
And in his comfortable seat he groans and sighs.

*

The conversation does not end quickly:
Prattling and babbling, what a lot he says!
Only when one is almost dead with fatigue
He asks at last if one isn't finding him tiring.
(One's arm is almost in half with continual fanning:
The sweat is pouring down one's neck in streams.)
Do not say that this is a small matter:
I consider the practice a blot on our social life.
I therefore caution all wise men
That August visitors should not be admitted.

CH'ĒNG HSIAO
(translated by ARTHUR WALEY)

On the Prevalence of Literary Revivals

It's hard
Keeping up with the *avant-garde*.
There was the time when Donne
Had a place in the sun.
His *lettres* were *belles* of pure gold
And they tolled and they tolled and they tolled,
Until critics in suitable haunts
Took up Kafka (Franz).
Then everyone wanted to herald
The genius of Scott Fitzgerald.
After that, among Prominent Names,
It was utterly Henry James.

In between, of course, there was room
For a Melville boom,
For a peek at Poe, for a dollop
Of Trollope,
And currently people report on
A scrambling aboard
The elegant wagons of Wharton
and Ford Madox Ford.

Oh, it's perfectly clear
That there's change when the critics forgather.
Last year was a Hawthorne year.
Coming up – Willa Cather?
And I'm happy the great ones are thriving,
But what puzzles my head
Is the thought that they needed reviving.
I had never been told they were dead.

PHYLLIS McGINLEY

On a Female Snob, Surprised

Now, when you cut me dead and say that I'm
Not kennel-bred, nor pure of pedigree,
I'll think how often that old Mongrel, Time,
Has cocked a leg against your Family Tree.

PATRIC DICKINSON

Dumb Friends' Corner

She was a Phantom of Delight
When first she gleamed upon my sight;
Now for her portrait I can't fancy a
Better all-round man than Landseer.

D. B. WYNDHAM LEWIS

STUDIED IRREVERENCE

A Catch

BY A MIMIC OF MODERN MELODY

If you were queen of bloaters
    And I were king of soles,
The sea we'd wag our fins in,
Nor heed the crooked pins in,
The water, dropped by boaters
    To catch our heedless joles;
If you were queen of bloaters
    And I were king of soles.

If you were Lady Mile-End
    And I were Duke of Bow,
We'd marry and we'd quarrel,
And then, to point the moral,
Should Lord Penzance his file lend,
    Our chains to overthrow;
If you were Lady Mile-End
    And I were Duke of Bow.

If you were chill November
    And I were sunny June;
I'd not with love pursue you;
For I should be to woo you
(You're foggy, pray remember)
    A most egregious spoon;
If you were chill November
    And I were sunny June.

If you were cook to Venus
    And I were J. 19;
When missus was out dining,
Our suppertites combining,
We'd oft contrive between us
    To keep the platter clean;
If you were cook to Venus
    And I were J. 19.

If you were but a jingle
   And I were but a rhyme;
We'd keep this up for ever,
Nor think it very clever
A grain of sense to mingle
   At times with simple chime;
If you were but a jingle
   And I were but a rhyme.

THOMAS HOOD, jun.

Culture in the Slums

Now ain't they utterly too-too
   (She ses, my missus mine, ses she),
Them flymy little bits of Blue?

Joe, just you kool 'em – nice and skew
   Upon our old meogginee,
Now ain't they utterly too-too?

They're better than a pot'n a screw,
   They're equal to a Sunday spree,
Them flymy little bits of Blue!

Suppose I put 'em up the flue,
   And booze the profits, Joe? Not me.
Now ain't they utterly too-too?

I do the 'Igh Art fake, I do.
   Joe, I'm consummate; and I see
Them flymy little bits of Blue.

Which, Joe, is why I ses to you –
   Aesthetic-like, and limp, and free –
Now ain't they utterly too-too,
Them flymy little bits o' Blue?

W. E. HENLEY

Ballad

BY HANS BREITMANN

Der noble Ritter Hugo
    Von Schwillensaufenstein,
Rode out mit shpeer and helmet,
    Und he coom to de panks of de Rhine.

Und oop der rose a meermaid,
    Vot hadn't got nodings on,
Und she say, 'Oh, Ritter Hugo,
    Vhere you goes mit yourself alone?'

And he says, 'I rides in de creenwood,
    Mit helmet und mit shpeer,
Till I cooms into em Gasthaus,
    Und dere I trinks some beer.'

Und den outshpoke de maiden
    Vot hadn't got nodings on:
'I don't dink mooch of beoplesh
    ⁓Dat goes mit demselfs alone.

'You'd petter coom down in de wasser,
    Vhere dere's heaps of dings to see,
Und hafe a shplendid tinner
    Und drafel along mit me.

'Dere you sees de fisch a schwimmin',
    Und you catches dem efery von': –
So sang dis wasser maiden
    Vot hadn't got nodings on.

'Dere ish drunks all full mit money
    In ships dat vent down of old;
Und you helpsh yourself, by dunder!
    To shimmerin' crowns of gold.

'Shoost look at dese shpoons und vatches!
    Shoost see dese diamant rings!
Coom down and fill your bockets,
    Und I'll giss you like efery dings.

'Vot you vantsh mit your schnapps und lager?
    Coom down into der Rhine!
Der ish pottles der Kaiser Charlemagne
    Vonce filled mit gold-red wine!'

Dat fetched him – he shtood all shpell pound;
    She pooled his coat-tails down,
She drawed him oonder der wasser,
    De maiden mit nodings on.

C. G. LELAND

The Poets in the Nursery

OMAR KHAYYAM

A Sixpence and a Pocketful of Rye.
So sing I, and must sing until I die,
    And not the Garnered Wisdom of the years
Nor all the Wheeling Stars can tell me why.

Ye know the time-worn tale – a score or so
Of Blackbirds, piping plaintively below
    The Brooding horror of a monstrous Crust,
Close-huddled in a Wilderness of dough.

Yet soon the darkness lightens. For the king
Cuts deeply, and the birds are on the wing,
    The mellow-throated warblers of the woods
Burst from their flaky Prison House to sing.

I sometimes count this marvel not the least
Of all the magic splendours of the East;
    I sometimes think there never was prepared
A daintier dish to grace a Monarch's feast.

List to the solemn burden of my cry,
Ah, what it means I know not, no, not I,
    Unknown, unknowable, it haunts me still,
A Sixpence and a Pocketful of Rye.

G. F. FORREST

RUDYARD KIPLING

O this I ha' heard, and this I ha' read in a book o' nursery lore,
And I make no doubt ye ha' found it out and read it all before.
But I care not, I; to the shivering sky I will bellow the tale anew,
How the shameless sheep o' the fair Bo-Peep had vanished and left
    no clue.
In a flood of tears, through the clanging spheres, to the Nethermost
    Gloom she hied,
Till she caught in despair at a comet's hair, and took up her tale and
    cried:
'O I ha' been east, and I ha' been west, I ha' waked wi' a fiendish
    yell
The Shapes that fit i' the seething Pit, I ha' sat on the rim o' Hell.
I ha' stopped to ask o' the souls that bask i' the sheen o' the Milky
    Way,
But for all my gain comes the grim refrain, "No Sheep have passed
    this way".'
From the fluttering silence stole a voice, the voice o' the Tortured
    Star,
(Ye may see his glare, if ye enter there, where the Naughty Devils
    are);
'Get hence, get hence, till ye win more sense than to climb to the
    Stars to weep.

And to vex my soul at the midmost pole for the sake o' your
    shiftless sheep.
Let be, let be. They shall yet win free and, if promise o' mine avails,
Ye shall find ('tis strange) no radical change i' the site o' their
    several tails.'

G. F. FORREST

If Gray had had to write his Elegy in the Cemetery of Spoon River instead of in that of Stoke Poges

The curfew tolls the knell of parting day,
    The whippoorwill salutes the rising moon,
And wanly glimmer in her gentle ray
    The sinuous windings of the turbid Spoon.

Here where the flattering and mendacious swarm
    Of lying epitaphs their secrets keep,
At last incapable of further harm,
    The lewd forefathers of the village sleep.

The earliest drug of half-awakened morn,
    Cocaine or hashish, strychnine, poppy-seeds
Or fiery produce of fermented corn
    No more shall start them on the day's misdeeds.

For them no more the whetstone's cheerful noise,
    No more the sun upon his daily course
Shall watch them savouring the genial joys
    Of murder, bigamy, arson and divorce.

Here they all lie; and, as the hour is late,
    O stranger, o'er their tombstones cease to stoop,
But bow thine ear to me and contemplate
    The unexpurgated annals of the group.

Here are two hundred only: yet of these
   Some thirty died of drowning in the river,
Sixteen went mad, ten others had D.T.'s,
   And twenty-eight cirrhosis of the liver.

Several by absent-minded friends were shot,
   Still more blew out their own exhausted brains,
One died of a mysterious inward rot,
   Three fell off roofs, and five were hit by trains.

One was harpooned, one gored by a bull-moose,
   Four on the Fourth fell victims to lock-jaw,
Ten in electric chair or hempen noose
   Suffered the last exaction of the law.

Stranger, you quail, and seem inclined to run;
But, timid stranger, do not be unnerved;
I can assure you that there was not one
   Who got a tithe of what he had deserved.

Full many a vice is born to thrive unseen,
   Full many a crime the world does not discuss,
Full many a pervert lives to reach a green
   Replete old age, and so it was with us.

Here lies a parson who would often make
   Clandestine rendezvous with Claflin's Moll,
And 'neath the druggist's counter creep to take
   A sip of surreptitious alcohol.

And here a doctor, who had seven wives,
   And, fearing this *ménage* might seem grotesque,
Persuaded six of them to spend their lives
   Locked in a drawer of his private desk.

And others here there sleep who, given scope,
   Had writ their names large on the Scrolls of Crime,
Men who, with half a chance, might haply cope
   With the first miscreants of recorded time.

Doubtless in this neglected spot was laid
  Some village Nero who had missed his due,
Some Bluebeard who dissected many a maid,
  And all for naught, since no one ever knew.

Some poor bucolic Borgia here may rest
  Whose poisons sent whole families to their doom.
Some hayseed Herod who, within his breast,
  Concealed the sites of many an infant's tomb.

Types that the Muse of Masefield might have stirred,
  Or waked to ecstasy Gaboriau,
Each in his narrow cell at last interred,
  All, all are sleeping peacefully below.

*

Enough, enough! But, stranger, ere we part,
  Glancing farewell to each nefarious bier,
This warning I would beg you to take to heart,
  'There is an end to even the worst career!'

SIR J. C. SQUIRE

The Everlasting Percy
or Mr Masefield on the Railway Centenary

I used to be a fearful lad,
The things I did were downright bad;
And worst of all were what I done
From seventeen to twenty-one
On all the railways far and wide
From sinfulness and shameful pride.

For several years I was so wicked
I used to go without a ticket,
And travelled underneath the seat
Down in the dust of people's feet,

Or else I sat as bold as brass
And told them 'Season' in first class.
In 1921, at Harwich,
I smoked in a non-smoking carriage;
I never knew what Life nor Art meant,
I wrote 'Reserved' on my compartment,
And once (I was a guilty man)
I swapped the labels in guard's van.
From 1922 to 4
I leant against the carriage door
Without a-looking at the latch;
And once, a-leaving Colney Hatch,
I put a huge and heavy parcel
Which I were taking to Newcastle,
Entirely filled with lumps of lead,
Up on the rack above my head;
And when it tumbled down, oh Lord!
I pulled communication cord.
The guard came round and said, 'You mule!
What have you done, you dirty fool?'
I simply sat and smiled, and said
'Is this train right for Holyhead?'
He said 'You blinking blasted swine,
You'll have to pay the five-pound fine.'
I gave a false name and address,
Puffed up with my vaingloriousness.
At Bickershaw and Strood and Staines
I've often got on moving trains,
And once alit at Norwood West
Before my coach had come to rest.
A window and a lamp I broke
At Chipping Sodbury and Stoke
And worse I did at Wissendine:
I threw out bottles on the line
And other articles as be
Likely to cause great injury
To persons working on the line –
That's what I did at Wissendine.

I grew so careless what I'd do
Throwing things out, and dangerous too,
That, last and worst of all I'd done,
I threw a great sultana bun
Out of the train at Pontypridd –

*

It hit a platelayer, it did.
I thought that I should have to swing
And never hear the sweet birds sing.
The jury recommended mercy,
And that's how grace was given to Percy.

And now I have a motor-bike
And up and down the road I hike,
Seeing the pretty birds and flowers,
And windmills with their sails and towers,
And all the wide sweep of the downs,
And villages and country towns,
And hear the mowers mowing hay,
And smell the great sea far away!
And always keeping – cars be blowed! –
Well on the wrong side of the road,
And never heeding hoots nor warners,
Especially around the corners,
For even down the steepest hill
Redemption saves me from a spill.

I have a flapper on my carrier
And some day I am going to marry her.

E. V. KNOX

Morning Song

(AFTER SHAKESPEARE–SCHUBERT)

Horch, horch, die Bell am Backdoor ringt!
Get up! Es iss das Ice.
Ich hoff der Crook von Iceman bringt
A Piece von decent size.
Denn dass gibt shure a Scorcher heut,
Ich fühl alreddy heiss.
Und schlam die Shcreen-thür gut und tight,
Das Haus wird voll mit Flies.
Arise! Arise!
Eh's melten tut, arise!

KURT M. STEIN

BALLADS TO HARP
ACCOMPANIMENT

The Maid's Longing

A maiden of late
Whose name was Sweet Kate,
She dwelt in London near Aldersgate;
   Now list to my ditty, declare it I can,
   She would have a child without help of a man.

To a doctor she came,
A man of great fame,
Whose deep skill in physick report did proclaim.
   Quoth she: 'Mr Doctor, shew me if you can
   How I may conceive without help of a man.'

'Then listen,' quoth he,
'Since it must be,
This wondrous strange med'cine I'll shew presently;
   Take nine pound of thunder, six legs of a swan,
   And you shall conceive without help of a man.

'The love of false harlots,
The faith of false varlets,
With the truth of decoys that walk in their scarlet,
   And the feathers of a lobster, well fry'd in a pan,
   And you shall conceive without help of a man.

'Nine drops of rain
Brought hither from Spain,
With the blast of a bellows quite over the main,
   With eight quarts of brimstone brew'd in a can,
   And you shall conceive without help of a man.

'Six pottles of lard,
Squeez'd from rock hard,
With nine turkey eggs, each as long as a yard,
   With pudding of hailstones well bak'd in a pan,
   And you shall conceive without help of a man.

'These med'cines are good,
And approved have stood,
Well temper'd together with a pottle of blood
Squeez'd from a grasshopper and the nail of a swan,
To make maids conceive without help of a man.'

ANON.

Here's the Man A-coming!

In Lunnon town each day, strange sayings will be springing,
But, if you list to me, a new one I'll be singing,
As you go through the town, the people will be funning,
One cries out, 'Put it down, here's the man a-coming!'

'Twas only t'other day, as sure as I'm a sinner,
A leg of pork I bought, to have a slap-up dinner;
When, half way down the street, a young scamp came by, running,
Says he, 'Guvner, drop that meat, here's the man a-coming!'

Young married folks, I fear, to extremes often dash on,
They're always in a fright, through studying the fashion;
Each day with fear and dread, the tradesmen they are shunning.
'Jem, get under the bed, here's the tally man a-coming!'

There's lots of ups and downs, and lots of rummy dodgings,
But I do it quite brown, in taking furnish'd lodgings;
I own I'm very poor, to pay there is no fun in,
So I always bolt the door when I hear the landlord coming!

It's pleasant, in this place, to see your smiling faces.
And, gents, too, I presume, you're in your proper places;
Now, there's one stands there so sly, I know he's very cunning,
I say, 'Mind what you're at, here's the man a-coming!'

ANON.

Blow Me Eyes!

When I was young and full o' pride,
    A-standin' on the grass
And gazin' o'er the water-side,
    I seen a fisher lass.
'O fisher-lass, be kind awhile,'
    I asks 'er quite unbid.
'Please look into me face and smile' –
    And blow me eyes, she did!

O blow me light, and blow me blow,
I didn't think she'd charm me so –
    But, blow me eyes, she did!

She seemed so young and beautiful
    I *had* to speak perlite,
(The afternoon was long and dull,
    But she was short and bright).
'This ain't no place', I says, 'to stand –
    Let's take a walk instid,
Each holdin' of the other's hand' –
    And, blow me eyes, she did!

O, blow me light and blow me blow,
I sort o' thunk she wouldn't go –
    But, blow me eyes, she did!

As we walked along a lane
    With no one else to see,
My heart was filled with sudden pain,
    And so I says to she:
'If you would have me actions speak
    The words what can't be hid,
You'd sort o' let me kiss yer cheek' –
    And, blow me eyes, she did!

O, blow me light and blow me blow,
How sweet she was I didn't know —
  But, blow me eyes, *she* did!

But pretty soon me shipmate Jim
  Came strollin' down the beach,
And she began a-oglin' him
  As pretty as a peach.
'O fickle maid o' false intent,'
  Impulsively I chid,
'Why don't you go and wed that gent?'
  And, blow me eyes, she did!

O, blow me light and blow me blow,
I didn't think she'd treat me so —
  But, blow me eyes, she did!

WALLACE IRWIN

Mule

My Mammy was a wall-eyed goat,
My Old Man was an ass,
And I feed myself off leather boots
And dynamite and grass;
For I'm a mule, a long-eared fool
And I ain't never been to school —
    Mammeee! Ma-ha-mam-hee!
    Heee-haw! Mamaah!
    Ma-ha-mee!

ANON.

Not Tonight, Josephine

Though I have an admiration for your charming resignation
(There appears no limitation to your constant animation)
And a deep appreciation of your warm cooperation,
And I find a consolation in the pleasing contemplation
Of a coy anticipation quite beyond articulation,
Yet forgive the implication if I plead disinclination
For the sweet exhilaration of a brief amalgamation.
I'll tell you in a phrase, my sweet, exactly what I mean:
          ... Not tonight, Josephine.

COLIN CURZON

SHORT MEASURE

I

AUGUSTAN MALICE

Woman

A *Woman* is a book, and often found
To prove far better in the Sheets than bound:
No marvel then why men take such delight
Above all things to *study in the night*.

ANON.

On a Musician and Dancing-Master who Decamped with Cash subscribed for a Musical Publication

His *time* was quick, his *touch* was fleet;
　Our gold he neatly *finger'd*:
Alike alert with *hand* and *feet*,
　His *movements* have not linger'd.
Where lies the wonder of the case?
　A moment's thought detects it:

His practice has been *thorough-bass*,
　A *chord* will be his exit.
Yet, while we blame his hasty flight,
　Our censure may be rash.
A traveller is surely right
　To change his *notes* for cash.

ANON.

The Wife's Epitaph

To follow you I'm not content.
How do I know which way you went?

ANON.

An Empty House

You beat your pate, and fancy wit will come:
Knock as you please, there's nobody at home.

ALEXANDER POPE

Verses on the 4th of November

Tonight's the night, I speak it with great sorrow,
That we were all to have been blown up tomorrow;
Therefore take care of fires and candle-light,
'Tis a cold frosty morning, and so good-night.

An Impromptu by the BEADLE OF ST PATRICK'S
(reported by Jonathan Swift)

From the German of Lessing

You hesitate if you shall take a wife.
Do as your father did – live single all your life.

ANON.

To a Lawyer

Trapped by my neighbour in his clover,
Three pigs I fee'd you to recover.
Before the court you gravely stand,
And stroke your wig and smooth your band;
Then, taking up the kingdom's story,
You ope your case with Alfred's glory;
Of Norman William's curfew bell
And Coeur de Lion's prowess tell;
How through the ravaged fields of France
Edwards and Henries shook the lance;
How great Eliza o'er the main
Pursu'd the shatter'd pride of Spain,
And Orange broke a tyrant's claim.
    All this, good sir, is mighty fine;
But now, an please you, to my swine!

ANON.

When I call'd you a blockhead, I candidly own
It was hastily done, for I could not have shown
    Such proof as would warrant conviction:
But, thanks to the anger my boldness has raised,
You're an author become, and now, Fortune be prais'd,
    I've proof that defies contradiction.

R. A. D.
(from the French of Fabian Pillet)

289

On John Dove, Innkeeper, Mauchline

Here lies Johnnie Pigeon;
What was his religion,
   Whe'er desires to ken,
To some other warl
Maun follow the carl,
   For here Johnnie Pigeon had nane.

Strong ale was ablution,
Small beer persecution,
   A dram was *memento mori*;
But a full flowing bowl
Was the saving his soul,
   And port was celestial glory.

ROBERT BURNS

We men have many faults.
   Poor women have but two: –
There's nothing good they say;
There's nothing good they do.

ANON.

Inscribed on a Pint-Pot

There are several reasons for drinking,
And one has just entered my head;
If a man cannot drink when he's living
How the Hell can he drink when he's dead?

ANON.

On a Vicious Person

He called thee vicious, did he? lying elf!
Thou art not vicious; thou art vice itself.

FLETCHER

I shudder if perchance I meet
Long-winded Dromio in the street,
For surely no man living says
So little in so tedious phrase.
Dromio, it seems, is doomed by fate
On nothing evermore to prate: –
But destiny, by the same decree,
Assigns a heavier lot to me;
Me, who, whenever I come near him
Am doomed eternally to hear him.

SAMUEL BISHOP

A Bon Mot

ON A LADY'S WEDDING BEING ON THE 21ST OF DECEMBER

Return'd from the opera, as lately I sat,
Indifferently chatting of this and of that,
My Chloe I asked how it entered her head
To fix on St Thomas, of all days to wed
To which she replied, with reason the strongest,
'Tho' shortest the day is – the night, sir, is longest.'

VAUGHAN

On Ale

Of this strange drink, so like the Stygian lake,
Which men call Ale, I know not what to make.
Folk drink it thick and void it very thin.
Therefore much dregs must needs remain within.

ANON.

John sobbed and whimpered when he saw
His wife lie squalling in the straw;
'I suffer much', quoth she, ' 'tis true;
But don't weep, John – I don't blame you.'

E. WALSH

In vino veritas, they say,
  Yet lying is so much the custom
Of certain folk, the safest way
  Is, drunk or sober, not to trust 'em.

ANON.

Tom found a trinket in his bed,
Which he'd to Stephen's mistress given:
'What's this, dear wife?' – 'Only (she said)
Your *gift* to *Ann* – returned by Stephen.'

ANON.

On Seeing a Lady's Garter

Why blush, dear girl, pray tell me why?
　　You need not, I can prove it;
For though your garter met my eye,
　　My thoughts were far above it.

ANON.

On Taking a Wife

'Come, come,' said Tom's father, 'at your time of life,
　There's no longer excuse for thus playing the rake.
It's time you should think, boy, of taking a wife.'
　'Why so it is, father. Whose wife shall I take?'

THOMAS MOORE

Epitaph

Posterity will ne'er survey
　　A nobler grave than this:
Here lie the bones of Castlereagh:
　　Stop, traveller, *** ****.

GEORGE GORDON, LORD BYRON

Epitaph on John Adams of Southwell

A CARRIER WHO DIED OF DRUNKENNESS

John Adams lies here, of the parish of Southwell,
A *Carrier* who *carried* his can to his mouth well;
He *carried* so much and he *carried* so fast,
He could *carry* no more – so was *carried* at last;
For the liquor he drank, being too much for one,
He could not *carry off*; so he's now *carry-on.*

GEORGE GORDON, LORD BYRON

Here lies Pat Steel,
    That's very true.
Who was he? what was he?
    What is that to you?

ANON.

Epigram

After such years of dissension and strife,
Some wonder that Peter should weep for his wife:
But his tears on her grave are nothing surprising, –
He's laying her dust, for fear of its rising.

THOMAS HOOD

'To this night's masquerade,' quoth Dick,
    'By pleasure I am beckon'd,
And think 'twould be a pleasant trick
    To go as Charles the Second.'

294

Tom felt for repartee a thirst,
    And thus to Richard said: –
'You'd better go as Charles the First,
    For that requires no head.'

HORACE SMITH

II

ROMANTIC NONSENSE

On the Death of the Giraffe

They say, God wot,
She died upon the spot:
But then in spots she was so rich, –
I wonder which?

THOMAS HOOD

Two Aboriginal Poems

Chackaboo, chickaboo, chuckaboo, chew,
Mark baby over with pretty tattoo;
Cut in the pattern like openwork tart:
Rub in the powder and make baby smart.

*

What, cry when I cook you, not like to be stewed?
Then go and be raw, and not fit to be food.
Until you leave off, and I see that you've smiled,
I shan't take the trouble to eat such a child.

SHIRLEY BROOKS

Here's a little proverb that you surely ought to know:
Horses sweat and men perspire, but ladies only glow.

ANON.

King David and King Solomon
  Led merry, merry lives,
With many, many lady friends
  And many, many wives;
But when old age crept over them,
  With many, many qualms,
King Solomon wrote the Proverbs,
  And King David wrote the Psalms.

J. B. NAYLOR

To the Moon

Oh Moon, when I look on thy beautiful face,
Careering along through the boundaries of space,
The thought has quite frequently come to my mind,
If ever I'll gaze on thy glorious behind.

ANON.

III

THREE LIMERICKS

A simple young fellow named Hyde
In a funeral procession was spied.
  When asked, 'Who is dead?'
  He tittered and said,
'I don't know. I just came for the ride.'

ANON.

There was an old man from Darjeeling,
Who boarded a bus bound for Ealing.
    He saw on the door:
    'Please don't spit on the floor',
So he stood up and spat on the ceiling.

ANON.

There was an old man of Khartoum
Who kept a tame sheep in his room.
'To remind me', he said,
'Of someone who's dead,
But I never can recollect whom'.

ANON.

IV

A BUNCH OF CLERIHEWS

The Empress Poppaea
Was really rather a dear,
Only no one could stop her
From being improper.

ANON.

Cecil B. de Mille,
Rather against his will,
Was persuaded to leave Moses
Out of 'The Wars of the Roses'.

NICOLAS BENTLEY

Diodorus Siculus
Made himself ridiculous.
He thought a thimble
Was the phallic symbol.

ANON.

Jonathan Swift
Never went up in a lift;
Nor did the author of 'Robinson Crusoe'
Do so.

ANON.

Abraham Lincoln
Never read the 'Pink 'un';
He preferred
God's Word.

E. K. BENNETT

On British Films

Isn't it funny
How they never make any money,
While everyone *in* the racket
Cleans up such a packet?

J. B. BOOTHROYD

298

V

MORE OR LESS TOPICAL

Weather Forecast

The Rain it raineth every day,
    Upon the just and unjust fellow,
But more upon the just, because
    The unjust has the just's umbrella.

ANON.

What is a Basket?

'Oh, Daddy dear, what is a basket?'
Said a youthful and mischievous elf:
'All baskets, me boy, are children of joy.
In fact you're a basket yourself.'

ANON.

As I was laying on the green
A little book it chanced I seen.
Carlyle's *Essay on Burns* was the edition –
I left it laying in the same position.

ANON.

Fatigue

I'm tired of Love: I'm still more tired of Rhyme.
But Money gives me pleasure all the time.

HILAIRE BELLOC

Sui Prodigus

We constantly hear O'Flannagan say
  'I gave him a piece of my mind,'
Which is why, when so much has been given away,
  So little remains behind.

A. B. RAMSAY

Epitaph on a Syndic

No teacher I of boys or smaller fry,
No teacher I of teachers, no, not I.
Mine was the distant aim, the longer reach,
To teach men how to teach men how to teach.

A. B. RAMSAY

Carelessness

A window-cleaner in our street
Who fell (five storeys) at my feet
Impaled himself on my umbrella
I said: 'Come, come, you careless fella!
If my umbrella had been shut
You might have landed on my nut.'

HARRY GRAHAM

Compensation

Weep not for little Léonie,
Abducted by a French *Marquis*!
Though loss of honour was a wrench,
Just think how it's improved her French.

HARRY GRAHAM

Mr Jones

'There's been an accident,' they said,
'Your servant's cut in half; he's dead!'
'Indeed!' said Mr Jones, 'and please
Send me the half that's got my keys.'

HARRY GRAHAM

To a Lady Who wanted a Penny for Two Ha'pennies

Look lidy, foller Olive Snell,
To 'oom yore accident befell.
It 'appened, as it does to many,
That *Olive* went to spend a penny.

She searched 'er bag, and 'ad jist one –
An' that wus bent – so wot she done?
She went and found a spinney shidy. . . .
An saved 'erself the penny, lidy!

ARNOLD SILCOCK

Poem

(BASED ON AN OLD FRENCH PROVERB)

People who live in Chateaux
Shouldn't throw tomateaux.

J. B. MORTON

Song of the Ballet

Lift her up tenderly,
  Raise her with care,
Catch hold of one leg,
  And a handful of hair;
Swing her round savagely,
And when this palls,
Heave-Ho! Away with her
  Into the stalls.

J. B. MORTON

Footnote to Tennyson

I feel it when the game is done,
I feel it when I suffer most.
'Tis better to have loved and lost
Than ever to have loved and won.

GERALD BULLETT

So you'll to the Psychiatrist,
  Your little psyche's queer?
You need, I think, to see a good
  Psmackbottomist, my dear!

ANON.

Envoi

I warmed both hands before the fire of Life,
I thought the heat and smoke were pretty swell;
Yet now I cannot cease from mental strife –
Should I have warmed my poor old feet as well?

D. B. WYNDHAM LEWIS

On Nevski Bridge a Russian stood
Chewing his beard for lack of food.
Said he, 'It's tough this stuff to eat
But a darn sight better than shredded wheat!'

ANON.

Take Heart, Illiterates

AN EPIGRAM

For years a secret shame destroyed my peace –
I'd not read Eliot, Auden or MacNeice.
But now I think a thought that brings me hope:
Neither had Chaucer, Shakespeare, Milton, Pope.

JUSTIN RICHARDSON

Eisteddfod Piece

'What is the matter with that Druid, Daddy?
Why is he whistling and limping so?'
'He's whistling to summon up his bardic spirit,
And he's probably got gout in his mistletoe.'

A. G. PRYS-JONES

303

Business as Usual

When Gabriel's starting trumpet rends the skies,
And all arise for that last race of man,
Dai Jones, the bookie, glasses to his eyes,
Will spot the winners, and the also ran.

A. G. PRYS-JONES

Useful Higher Education

A Harvard man named Wilbur Crats
Made a career of burgling flats:
But owed his prowess, so to speak,
Entirely to his Yale technique.

A. G. PRYS-JONES

Quite So

Within the whispering gallery of St Paul's
The merest whisper travels round the walls:
But in the parts where I was born and bred
Folk hear things long before they're even said.

A. G. PRYS-JONES

The Perfect Husband

He tells you when you've got on
    too much lipstick
And helps you with your girdle
    when your hips stick.

OGDEN NASH

Reflection on Babies

A bit of talcum
Is always walcum.

OGDEN NASH

The Parent

Children aren't happy with nothing to ignore,
And that's what parents were created for.

OGDEN NASH

The Persistence of Memory

FROM THE SPANISH OF A PICTURE BY SALVADOR DALI

Timepieces flow from table edge –
Trick glutinous toward the shore
From blasted tree and what the dredge
Dragged up from sea's subconscious floor.
Back of beyond runs out bright cliff
Where time and times are frozen stiff.

GEOFFREY TAYLOR

MORAL INSTRUCTION

The Nobleman

A noble lord once passed away –
A debt all noble lords must pay,
 Although they find this world delightful.
 And that is frightful,
 To die, when life is so delightful.

The noble lord my tale's about,
Poor wretch, when Death had sought him out,
 Came where you try in vain to freeze.
 And that's hard cheese,
 When people try in vain to freeze.

He met his coachman, and a yell
Escaped him: 'What! John too in Hell?
 I hardly can believe my eyes' –
 And that's unwise,
 To see, and disbelieve your eyes.

'The reason why I'm in this mess
I'm loth to tell you, though I guess
 You know too well the full particulars' –
 And that's ridiculous,
 To try to hide well-known particulars.

'My son spent such a pile on dice,
Women, and other kinds of vice,
 He drained the pockets of his dad' –
 And that is bad,
 To drain the pockets of your dad.

'To help that precious rascal, I
Confess I squeezed my tenants dry,
 And turned a deaf ear to their wailing' –
 And that's a failing,
 To disregard your tenants' wailing.

'But you, who were so very pi,
And wouldn't even hurt a fly,
　　To know why *you* are here, I'm curious' –
　　And that's injurious,
　　Always to be so very curious.

'I'm here', said John, 'because of one
Success I had where you had none,
　　Although you did your level best' –
　　And that's a pest,
　　To fail when you have done your best.

'That son, for whom you've earned damnation,
I grieve to say, was my creation.
　　The lady's wish was not deniable' –
　　And that's too pliable,
　　To find no lady's wish deniable.

The moral for a lively lad is:
Never to make your neighbours daddies,
　　Not if their wives are quite importunate.
　　And that's unfortunate,
　　When neighbours' wives are quite importunate.

JOHAN HERMAN WESSEL
(translated by O. G. W. STALLYBRASS)

My Familiar

'ECCE ITERUM CRISPINUS!'

Again I hear that creaking step! –
　　He's rapping at the door! –
Too well I know the boding sound
　　That ushers in a bore.
I do not tremble when I meet
　　The stoutest of my foes,
But Heaven defend me from the Friend
　　Who comes – but never goes!

He drops into my easy-chair,
    And asks about the news;
He peers into my manuscript,
    And gives his candid views;
He tells me where he likes the line,
    And where he's forced to grieve;
He takes the strangest liberties, –
    But never takes his leave!

He reads my daily paper through
    Before I've seen a word;
He scans the lyric (that I wrote)
    And thinks it quite absurd;
He calmly smokes my last cigar,
    And coolly asks for more;
He opens everything he sees –
    Except the entry door!

He talks about his fragile health,
    And tells me of the pains
He suffers from a score of ills
    Of which he ne'er complains;
And how he struggled once with death
    To keep the fiend at bay;
On themes like those away he goes, –
    But never goes away!

He tells me of the carping words
    Some shallow critic wrote;
And every precious paragraph
    Familiarly can quote;
He thinks the writer did me wrong;
    He'd like to run him through!
He says a thousand pleasant things, –
    But never says, 'Adieu!'

Whene'er he comes, – that dreadful man, –
   Disguise it as I may,
I know that, like an Autumn rain,
   He'll last throughout the day.
In vain I speak of urgent tasks;
   In vain I scowl and pout;
A frown is no extinguisher, –
   It does not put him out!

I mean to take the knocker off,
   Put crape upon the door,
Or hint to John that I am gone
   To stay a month or more.
I do not tremble when I meet
   The stoutest of my foes,
But Heaven defend me from the friend
   Who never, never goes!

J. G. SAXE

Don't Ask for Bread

A wretched man walked up and down
To buy his dinner in the town.

At last he found a wretched place
And entered in with modest grace,

Took off his coat, took off his hat,
And wiped his feet upon the mat,

Took out his purse to count his pence
And found he had but two half-cents.

The bill of fare, he scanned it through
To see what two half-cents would do.

The only item of them all
For two half-cents was one fishball.

So to the waiter he did call
And gently whispered: One fishball.

The waiter bellowed down the hall;
This gentleman here wants one fishball.

The diners looked both one and all
To see who wanted one fishball.

The wretched man, all ill at ease
Said: A little bread, sir, if you please.

The waiter bellowed down the hall:
We don't serve bread with one fishball.

The wretched man, he felt so small,
He quickly left the dining hall.

The wretched man, he went outside
And shot himself until he died.

This is the moral of it all,
Don't ask for bread with one fishball.

ANON.

The Reverend Simon Magus

A rich advowson, highly prized,
For private sale was advertised;
And many a parson made a bid;
The Reverend Simon Magus did.

He sought the agent's: 'Agent, I
Have come prepared at once to buy
(If your demand is not too big)
The Cure of Otium-cum-Digge.'

'Ah!' said the agent, '*there*'s a berth –
The snuggest vicarage on earth;
No sort of duty (so I hear),
And fifteen hundred pounds a year!

'If on the price we should agree,
The living soon will vacant be;
The good incumbent's ninety-five,
And cannot very long survive.

'See – here's his photograph – you see,
He's in his dotage.' 'Ah, dear me!
Poor soul!' said Simon. 'His decease
Would be a merciful release!'

The agent laughed – the agent blinked –
The agent blew his nose and winked
And poked the parson's ribs in play –
It was that agent's vulgar way.

The Reverend Simon frowned: 'I grieve
This light demeanour to perceive;
It's scarcely *comme il faut*, I think:
Now – pray oblige me – do not wink.

'Don't dig my waistcoat into holes –
Your mission is to sell the souls
Of human sheep and human kids
To that divine who highest bids.

'Do well in this, and on your head
Unnumbered honours will be shed.'
The agent said, 'Well, truth to tell,
I *have* been doing pretty well.'

'You should,' said Simon, 'at your age;
But now about the parsonage.
How many rooms does it contain?
Show me the photograph again.

'A poor apostle's humble house
Must not be too luxurious;
No stately halls with oaken floor –
It should be decent and no more.

'No billiard-rooms – no stately trees –
No croquet-grounds or pineries.'
'Ah!' sighed the agent, 'very true;
This property won't do for you.

'All these about the house you'll find' –
'Well,' said the parson, 'never mind;
I'll manage to submit to these
Luxurious superfluities.

'A clergyman who does not shirk
The various calls of Christian work,
Will have no leisure to employ
These "common forms" of worldly joy.

'To preach three times on Sabbath days –
To wean the lost from wicked ways –
The sick to soothe – the sane to wed –
The poor to feed with meat and bread;

'These are the various wholesome ways
In which I'll spend my nights and days
My zeal will have no time to cool
At croquet, archery, or pool.'

The agent said, 'From what I hear,
This living will not suit, I fear –
There are no poor, no sick at all;
For services there is no call.'

The reverend gent looked grave. 'Dear me!
Then there is *no* "society"? –
I mean, of course, no sinners there
Whose souls will be my special care?'

The cunning agent shook his head,
'No, none – except' – (the agent said) –
'The Duke of A., the Earl of B.,
The Marquis C., and Viscount D.

'But you will not be quite alone,
For, though they've chaplains of their own,
Of course this noble well-bred clan
Receive the parish clergyman.'

'Oh, silence, sir!' said Simon M.,
'Dukes – earls! What should I care for them?
These worldly ranks I scorn and flout!'
'Of course,' the agent said, 'no doubt.'

'Yet I might show these men of birth
The hollowness of rank on earth.'
The agent answered, 'Very true –
But I should not, if I were you.'

'Who sells this rich advowson, pray?'
The agent winked – it was his way –
'His name is Hart; 'twixt me and you,
He is, I'm griev'd to say, a Jew!'

'A Jew?' said Simon, 'happy find!
I purchase this advowson, mind.
My life shall be devoted to
Converting that unhappy Jew!'

W. S. GILBERT

Visionary

ON THE ADVANTAGES OF AN 'ASTRAL BODY'

It is told, in Buddhi-theosophic Schools
    There – are rules
By observing which when mundane matter irks
   Or the world has gone amiss, you
   Can incontinently issue
   From the circumscribing tissue
    Of your Works.

That the body and the gentleman inside
    Can divide,
And the latter, if acquainted with the plan,
   Can alleviate the tension
   By remaining 'in suspension'
   As a kind of fourth dimension
    Bogie man.

And to such as mourn an Indian Solar Crime
    At its prime,
'Twere a stratagem so luminously fit,
   That, tho' doctrinaires deny it,
   And Academicians guy it,
   I, for one, would like to try it
    For a bit.

Just to leave one's earthly tenement asleep
    In a heap,
And detachedly to watch it as it lies,
   With an epidermis pickled
   Where the prickly heat has prickled,
   And a sense of being tickled
    By the flies.

And to sit and loaf and idle till the day
    Dies away,
In a duplicate ethereally cool,
   Or around the place to potter,
   (Tho' the flesh could hardly totter,)
   As contented as an otter
    In a pool!

Let the pestilent mosquito do his worst
    Till he burst,
Let him bore and burrow, morning, noon and night,
   If he finds the diet sweet, oh,
   Who am *I* to place a veto
   On the pestilent mosquito?
    Let him bite!

O my cumbersome misfit of bone and skin,
    Could I win
To the wisdom that would render me exempt
   From the grosser bonds that tether
   You and Astral Me together,
   I should simply treat the weather
    With contempt;

I should contemplate its horrors with entire
    Lack of ire,
And pursuant to my comfortable aim,
   With a snap at every shackle
   I should quit my tabernacle,
   And serenely sit and cackle
    At the game!

But, alas! the 'mystic glory swims away',
    And the clay
Is as vulgarly persistent as of yore,
   And the cuticle is pickled
   Where the prickly heat has prickled,
   And the nose and ears are tickled
    As before;

And until the Buddhi-theosophic Schools
    Print the rules
That will bring our tale of sorrows to a close,
  Body mine, though others chide thee,
  And consistently deride thee,
  I shall have to stay inside thee,
    I suppose!

J. S. KENDALL (DUM-DUM)

Marron Rechauffé

Proud the Solicitor –
Family Solicitor –
All aboard for Calais and
  The glass set fair,
With Mrs Solicitor
And Miss Solicitor
Snug abaft the paddle-box
  In gay salt air.

Firm the Solicitor
With the Calais Customs:
Letter-to-*The-Times*-and-
  He-Would-Not-Pay;
Mrs Solicitor
Bridled at their poking;
Miss Solicitor
  Looked the other way.

Lordly the Solicitor
At the gilded Crillon:
No-Feather-Beds-and-
    The-Bells-Must-Ring;
Mrs Solicitor
Couldn't bear the Bidet;
Miss Solicitor
    Marvelled at the thing.

Brusque the Solicitor
With the Crillon waiters.
Damning alien messes
    In phrase condign;
Mrs Solicitor
Detected Garlic;
Miss Solicitor
    Partook of Wine.

Grave the Solicitor
Conferring with the Porter
As to entertainment
    That would not cause
Vestal embarrassment
To Miss Solicitor,
Nor would be subversive of
    His Country's laws.

Blithe the Solicitor
Learning from the Porter
All about the Odéon
    And what they played:
Sublimated sentiment,
Flawless Alexandrines,
Totally innocuous
    To man or maid.

Troubled the Solicitor
Rattling to the Odéon –
We-Have-Got-Your-Number-You-
    Must-Drive-With-Care-
By inward stirrings
Not to be mistaken,
Wrathfully ascribable
    To Gallic fare.

Deft the Solicitor,
Desperate-retentive,
Planting loved ones in
    The foremost row;
Quitting them abruptly
To seek mysterious regions
To which Solicitors
    Must sometimes go.

Purged the Solicitor
Affable-informative
Of Aristotle's Unities
    And much beside;
Dwelling on Purgation
By Horror and Compassion,
And on the ancient tracing
    Of Sin from Pride.

Calm the Solicitor,
Relying on the Porter,
When to ghostly thumpings
    The act-drop rose
On rites most unsuggestive
To Miss Solicitor,
On lantern jaws, on ageing limbs
    In spun-silk hose.

Vexed the Solicitor
To hear above the booming
Of flawless Alexandrines an
   Insistent beat,
A hoarse obbligato,
Pervasive and continuing;
To see a Hag, with claw outheld,
   Beside his seat . . .

Chastened the Solicitor,
Gallic mirth about him,
And Miss Solicitor
   Rosy in dismay:
Monsieur n'a pas payé,
The Beldam chanted,
Monsieur n'a pas payé,
   Son Cabinet.

W. BRIDGES-ADAMS

Polterguest, My Polterguest

I've put Miss Hopper upon the train,
And I hope to do so never again,
For must I do so, I shouldn't wonder
If, instead of upon it, I put her under.

Never has host encountered a visitor
Less desirabler, less exquisiter,
Or experienced such a tangy zest
In beholding the back of a parting guest.

Hoitiful-toitiful Hecate Hopper,
Haunted our house and haunted it proper,
Hecate Hopper left the property
Irredeemably Hecate Hopperty.

322

MORAL INSTRUCTION

The morning paper was her monopoly
She reads it first, and Hecate hopperly,
Handing on to the old subscriber
A wad of Dorothy Dix and fiber.

Shall we coin a phrase for 'to uncooperate'?
How about trying 'to Hecate Hopperate'?
On the maid's days off she found it fun
To breakfast in bed at quarter to one.

Not only was Hecate on a diet,
She insisted that all the family try it,
And all one week-end we gobbled like pigs
On rutabagas and salted figs.

She clogged the pipes and she blew the fuses,
She broke the rocker that Grandma uses,
She left stuff to be posted or expressed,
Hecate Hopper, the Polterguest.

If I pushed Miss Hopper under the train
I'd probably have to do it again,
For the time that I pushed her off the boat
I regretfully found Miss Hopper could float.

OGDEN NASH

323

Grandmer's Busy Day

BEING A SMALL EXCERPT FROM THE GREAT
AMERICAN LOVE STORY

Grandmer loves granddaughter Beta
But teenage Beta plays with Alpha —
A teenage youth 'clapt Alfred Pie,
We call him Alpha and for why?
For why he were the very first
Would do with Beta that he durst —
And had, but Grandmer hobbling by
Saw them coupling, raised sad cry
'Alack, alas! Alfred! Beta! Stop this inster!
'Two childer about to make a childer!
'Wretched Beta! Art, gal, bust?
'Or didst they Granny hap here fust?'

A frogman with great hands of mutton
Who smacks the sea's broad marble bottom
Could not have walloped Beta so!
But Grandmer could, and she knew how!
What time creek frogs intoned the skies
'Better Grandmer's hand than Pie's'.

Over Grandmer's knees bow bent
First red, then white, our Beta went —
A sight to charm young Alfred Pie
That deeming not his personal safety
But inveigled to a closer view
(Panties by Haver Dash & Co.)

He sidled close to Grandmer's arm!
When, gosh! Granny with a ruggled frown
Seized, debagged, and flung him down,
And proceeded in a merry din
Alternately biffing Beta, and biffing him.

324

The goggling frogs who heard their groans
While holding humans sorry loons
As Grandmer's flailing arm beat time
Sang in creek refrain this rhyme:

'Promise you'll never do it again
'Do it again
'Do it again
'Promise you'll never do it again
'You limbs of Satan, you!'

Since Granny marked their homework copies
Have A and B found greater glories,
And checked their lustful appetites
By douching the afflicted parts?
So keeping Alpha's inches flaccid
And Beta's Mound of Venus placid?

Alas! For our most earnest hopes
It is not thus they learnt the ropes –
I'd like to show them heavenward bent
With priest's robe, nun's robe, Book, and scent,
Or in a chariot lifted up
(Elevators by Neverstop Incorp.)

But not to sell you any pup
I ween it is between those twain
That once is seen: that twice is not seen!
For now when Grandmer nods *they* wink . . .
They're up to something, I should think.

EWART MILNE

The Bleed'n' Sparrer

We 'ad a bleed'n' sparrer wot
Lived up a bleed'n' spaht,
One day the bleed'n' rain came dahn
An' washed the bleeder aht.

An' as 'e layed 'arf drahnded
Dahn in the bleed'n' street
'E begged that bleed'n' rainstorm
To bave 'is bleed'n' feet.

But then the bleed'n' sun came aht –
Dried up the bleed'n' rain –
So that bleed'n' little sparrer
'E climbed up 'is spaht again.

But, Oh! – the crewel sparrer'awk,
'E spies 'im in 'is snuggery,
'E sharpens up 'is bleed'n' claws
An' rips 'im aht by thuggery!

Jist then a bleed'n' sportin' type
Wot 'ad a bleed'n' gun
'E spots that bleed'n' sparrer'awk
An' blasts 'is bleed'n' fun.

The moral of this story
Is plain to everyone –
That them wot's up the bleed'n' spaht
Don't get no bleed'n' fun.

ANON.

Galoshes

I am having a *rapprochement* with galoshes
And some would say this heralds middle age;
Yes, sneering they would say
'Does he also wear pince-nez?'
Old jossers wore galoshes when ladies' hats were cloches,
Ha! Woollen combinations are this dodderer's next stage!'
Well, let these people snigger
Just because my feet look bigger,
For, colossal in galoshes, they are dry among the sploshes;
A story that won't wash is this notion that galoshes,
So snug at slushy crossings, make a man a sloppy figure.

Oh, crossly, and still crosslier,
I have bought shoes ever costlier
Which, still quite new, let water through before I've crossed the
      street:
There's nothing manly, I repeat,
In always having cold wet feet;
Galoshlessness is foolishness when sharply slants the sleet –
And I utterly refuse
The expression 'overshoes',
To make galoshes posher I would scorn this feeble ruse.
The word 'galosh' is strong, not weak,

It comes from *kalopous*, the Greek
For 'cobbler's last', and thus it's classed with hero times antique.
Come, Muse, through slush and sleet dry-footed with me trip so
That I may praise galoshes in a *kalopous* calypso.
   Oh, when swishing buses splash
   And the rush-hour masses clash
   When it's marshy as molasses, how galoshes cut a dash!
   It makes me quite impassioned
   When they're dubbed unsmart, old-fashioned –
   (For such, by gosh, the bosh is that's talked about galoshes)

327

Since the very finest leather
Is outsmarted altogether
By the classy, glossy polish of galoshes in such weather.

Come, galoshers, be assertive,
Drop that air discreet and furtive!
Let galosh shops' stocks be lavish
With designs and hues that ravish –
Men's galoshes black and British, but for ladies colours skittish
(And galoshes could make rings
Round those silly plastic things
Which tie up with clumsy strings) –
Let us *all* have this *rapprochement* with galoshes
And see what health and happiness it brings!

PAUL JENNINGS

Advice to a Young Lady on the Subject of Alcohol

Beware the man who keeps you late
When Mum said to be in by ate,
And shun the chap who, at the Palais,
Invites you to inspect his chalais.
Behave, then, as you really ought,
Refuse that second glass of pought.
Supping unaccustomed liquor
Will only make you fall the quicor;
Drinking brandies at 'The Mitre'
Is sure to go and make you titre;
And oh! that headache in the dawn
Will make you wish you'd not been bawn.
Remember, then, a maiden oughter
Shun all drink, and stick to woughter.

ERIC PARROTT

UNNATURAL HISTORY

The Coelacanth

A DIALOGUE ON EVOLUTION

'*Melania Anjouani*, the Coelacanth, has never evolved.'
— Professor Smith

There lived a happy coelacanth
In dim, primordial seas,
He ate and mated, hunted, slept,
Completely at his ease.
Dame Nature urged: 'Evolve!'
He said: 'Excuse me, Ma'am,
You get on making Darwin,
I'm staying as I am.'

The fishes changed their fishy shapes,
The reptiles stormed the land,
The algae turned to trees, the apes
To men, we understand.
The Coelacanth remained
A monster and a myth;
He said: 'There's nothing to be gained
By my becoming Smith.'

Dame Nature urged: 'You must desire,
And what you wish you'll be it.
Surely, "we needs must love the higher",'
She quoted, ' "when we see it.".'
The Coelacanth said: 'Hark!
It all depends on what
You mean by "higher": Me, Lamarck,
Or Alfred, does it not?

'To be a whirlpool of Pure Mind
That surely is the goal,'
She begged, 'Until you are, you find,
No body, but all soul.'

The Coelacanth just set
His square, determined jaw.
'Then leave me out,' he snapped, 'and get
On with Bernard Shaw.'

So for a hundred million years
While Nature worked out man the
Obdurate Coelacanth appears
The same, and simply perseveres
In being Coelacanthi.

HORACE SHIPP

Noah

After all the flood-storm's dark
A southern sun shone on the ark.

From the foreland of Hawaii
Floated voices soft and sighy,

From the beaches called: 'Aloha,'
Sweetly called: 'Aloha, Noah,

'Come and be forever harbored.'
Other voices came from starboard,

Called: 'This isle is Noa-Noa;
Welcome, Noah, and aloha;

'Live with us and furl your sail.'
Noah went up to the rail,

(Shouting to an upraised boa:
'Down! you naughty so-and-soa!')

Said: 'How keep my charges waiting?
Spite of orders, they've been mating.

'I've been doing some detecting;
All the ladies are expecting;

'And we've not an inch of space.
This crowded cruise is now a race.

'I must get my charges home,
Have no time for even Rome;

'And you're all so loving here.'
Noah turned to hide a tear;

Said: 'The answer must be noa.
I am Noah; I must goa.'

So he left the siren seas,
Left the luring melodies,

Left the loving maidens flat;
Ran aground on Ararat.

O those islands! O those seas!
O those siren melodies!

Hark! I hear that sweet Aloha,
Am I yes or am I Noah?

CLARK STILLMAN

Hall and Knight

OR

$$z + b + x = y + b + z$$

When he was young his cousins used to say of Mr Knight:
'This boy will write an Algebra – or looks as if he might.'
And sure enough when Mr Knight had grown to be a man,
He purchased pen and paper and an inkpot, and began.

But he very soon discovered that he couldn't write at all,
And his heart was filled with yearnings for a certain Mr Hall;
Till, after thirty years of doubt, he sent his friend a card:
'Have tried to write an Algebra, but find it very hard.'

Now Mr Hall himself had tried to write a book for schools,
But suffered from a handicap: he didn't know the rules.
So when he heard from Mr Knight and understood his gist,
He answered him by telegram: 'Delighted to assist.'

So Mr Hall and Mr Knight they took a house together,
And they worked away at algebra in any kind of weather,
Determined not to give it up until they had evolved
A problem so constructed that it never could be solved.

'How hard it is,' said Mr Knight, 'to hide the fact from youth
That x and y are equal: it is such an obvious truth!'
'It is,' said Mr Hall, 'but if we gave a b to each,
We'd put the problem well beyond our little victims' reach.

'Or are you anxious, Mr Knight, lest any boy should see
The utter superfluity of this repeated b?'
'I scarcely fear it,' he replied, and scratched his grizzled head,
'But perhaps it *would* be safer if to b we added z.'

'A brilliant stroke!' said Hall, and added z to either side;
Then looked at his accomplice with a flush of happy pride.
And Knight, he winked at Hall (a very pardonable lapse).
And they printed off the Algebra and sold it to the chaps.

E. V. RIEU

Life of a Scientist

Isaac Newton, it is reckoned,
Lived in the time of Charles the Second.
Charles's forte was depravity
But Isaac came out strong for gravity.

I. KENVYN EVANS

Hengist and Horsa

Hengist was coarser than Horsa,
And Horsa was awfully coarse.
Horsa drank whiskey,
Told tales that were risqué,
But Hengist was in a divorce.
Horsa grew coarser and coarser,
But Hengist was coarse all his life.
That reprobate Horsa
Drank tea from a saucer,
But Hengist ate peas with his knife.

DESMOND CARTER

The Snail

Where is the poet fired to sing
     The snail's discreet degrees,
A rhapsody of sauntering,
     A gloria of ease,
Proclaiming theirs the baser part
     Who consciously forswear
The delicate and gentle art
     Of never getting there.

E. V. LUCAS

A centipede was happy quite,
  Until a frog in fun
Said, 'Pray, which leg comes after which?'
This raised her mind to such a pitch,
She lay distracted in a ditch
  Considering how to run.

MRS EDMUND CRASTER

Anxious Lines on a New Kitten

Is this small ball of fur a noedipus,
Or just a budding feline Oedipus?
Will he, with lavish milk by me supplied,
Quickly forget his new-left mother's side?
Or, complex-fixed, become a – groedipus?

PENDENNIS CASTLE

The Octopus

Tell me, O Octopus, I begs,
Is those things arms, or is they legs?
I marvel at thee, Octopus;
If I were thou, I'd call me Us.

OGDEN NASH

The Ant

The ant has made himself illustrious
Through constant industry industrious.
So what?
Would you be calm and placid
If you were full of formic acid?

OGDEN NASH

The Jellyfish

Who wants my jellyfish?
I'm not sellyfish!

OGDEN NASH

The Fly

The Lord in His wisdom made the fly,
And then forgot to tell us why.

OGDEN NASH

The Dog

The truth I do not stretch or shove
When I state the dog is full of love.
I've also found, by actual test,
A wet dog is the lovingest.

OGDEN NASH

337

The Frog

What a wonderful bird the frog are!
When he stand he sit almost;
When he hop he fly almost.
He ain't got no sense hardly;
He ain't got no tail hardly either.
When he sit, he sit on what he ain't got almost.

ANON.

The Elephant

OR

The Force of Habit

A tail behind, a trunk in front,
Complete the usual elephant.
The tail in front, the trunk behind,
Is what you very seldom find.
If you for specimens should hunt
With trunks behind and tails in front,
That hunt would occupy you long;
The force of habit is so strong.

A. E HOUSMAN

The Squid

The squid has an id;
Id is not nice, but the squid loves id.

CLARK STILLMAN

The Oocuck

'The cuckoo!' cried my child, the while I slept;
  'Sweet pop, the cuckoo! o, its cries impinge!
The harbinger is here!' And up I leapt
  To hear the thing harbinge.

I flung the casement, thrust the visage through,
  Composed the features in rhapsodic look,
Cupped the left ear and ... lo! I heard an 'oo',
  Soon followed by a 'cuck'.

Another 'oo'! A 'cuck'! An 'oo' again.
  A 'cuck'. 'Oocuck'. 'Oocuck' Ditto. Repeat.
I tried to pick the step up but in vain –
  I'd ... 'oo' ... missed ... 'Cuck' ... the beat.

I'd missed the beat. And this would last till June
  And nothing could be done now to catch up –
This fowl would go on hiccuping its tune,
  Hic after beastly cup.

'Oocuck!' ... 'Oocuck!' ... that was four weeks ago,
  Four non-stop weeks of contrapuntal blight.
My nerves are ... what was that? ... Ah, no! Ah, no!
  Spare me the ingalenight!

JUSTIN RICHARDSON

The Daddy Long-Legs and the Fly

Once Mr Daddy Long-Legs,
   Dressed in brown and gray,
Walked about upon the sands
   Upon a summer's day;
And there among the pebbles,
   When the wind was rather cold,
He met with Mr Floppy Fly,
   All dressed in blue and gold.
And as it was too soon to dine,
They drank some Periwinkle-wine,
And played an hour or two, or more,
At battlecock and shuttledore.

Said Mr Daddy Long-Legs
   To Mr Floppy Fly,
'Why do you never come to court?
   'I wish you'd tell me why.
'All gold and shine, in dress so fine,
   'You'd quite delight the court.
'Why do you never go at all?
   'I really think you *ought!*
'And if you went, you'd see such sights!
'Such rugs! and jugs! and candle-lights!
'And more than all, the King and Queen,
'One in red, and one in green!'

'O Mr Daddy Long-Legs,'
   Said Mr Floppy Fly,
'It's true I never go to court,
   'And I will tell you why.
'If I had six long legs like yours,
   'At once I'd go to court!
'But Oh! I can't, because *my* legs
   'Are so extremely short.

'And I'm afraid the King and Queen
'(One in red and one in green)
'Would say aloud, "You are not fit,
'"You Fly, to come to court a bit!"

'O Mr Daddy Long-Legs,'
  Said Mr Floppy Fly,
'I wish you'd sing one little song!
  'One mumbian melody!
'You used to sing so awful well
  'In former days gone by,
'But now you never sing at all;
  'I wish you'd tell me why:
'For if you would, the silvery sound
'Would please the shrimps and cockles round,
'And all the crabs would gladly come
'To hear you sing, "Ah, Hum di Hum!"'

Said Mr Daddy Long-Legs,
  'I can never sing again!
'And if you wish, I'll tell you why,
  'Although it gives me pain.
'For years I could not hum a bit,
  'Or sing the smallest song;
'And this the dreadful reason is,
  'My legs are grown too long!
'My six long legs, all here and there,
'Oppress my bosom with despair;
'And if I stand, or lie, or sit,
'I cannot sing one single bit!'

So Mr Daddy Long-Legs
  And Mr Floppy Fly
Sat down in silence by the sea,
  And gazed upon the sky.
They said, 'This is a dreadful thing!
  'The world has all gone wrong,
'Since one has legs too short by half,
  'The other much too long!

341

'One never more can go to court,
'Because his legs have grown too short;
'The other cannot sing a song,
'Because his legs have grown too long!'

Then Mr Daddy Long-Legs
   And Mr Floppy Fly
Rushed downward to the foaming sea
   With one sponge-taneous cry;
And there they found a little boat
   Whose sails were pink and gray;
And off they sailed among the waves
   Far, and far away.
They sailed across the silent main
And reached the great Gromboolian plain;
And there they play for evermore
At battlecock and shuttledore.

EDWARD LEAR

THE SADNESS OF THINGS

In Isas Bed

I love in Isas bed to lie
O such a joy and luxury
The bottom of the bed I sleep
And with great care I myself keep
Oft I embrace her feet of lillys
But she has goton all the pillies
Her neck I never can embrace
But I do hug her feet in place
But I am sure I am contented
And of my follies am repented

I am sure I'd rather be
In a small bed at liberty

MARJORY FLEMING

The Ballad of the Green Old Man

It was a balmeous day in May, when spring was springing high
And all among the buttercups the bees did butterfly;
While the butterflies were being enraptured in the flowers,
And winsome frogs were singing soft morals to the showers.

Green were the emerald grasses which grew upon the plain,
And green too were the verdant boughs which rippled in the rain,
Far green likewise the apple hue which clad the distant hill,
And at the station sat a man who looked far greener still.

An ancient man, a boy-like man, a person mild and meek,
A being who had little tongue, and nary bit of cheek.
And while upon him pleasant-like I saw the ladies look,
He sat a-counting money in a brownsome pocket-book.

Then to him a policeman spoke: 'Unless you feel too proud,
You'd better stow away that cash while you're in this here crowd;
There's many a chap about this spot who'd clean you out like ten.'
'And can it be', exclaimed the man, 'there are such wicked men?'

'Then I will put my greenbacks up all in my pocket-book,
And keep it buttoned very tight, and at the button look.'
He said it with a simple tone, and gave a simple smile –
You never saw a half-grown shad one-half so void of guile.

And the bumble-bees kept bumbling away among the flowers,
While distant frogs were frogging amid the summer showers,
And the tree-toads were tree-toadying in accents sharp or flat –
All nature seemed a-naturing as there the old man sat.

Then up and down the platform promiscuous he strayed,
Amid the waiting passengers he took his lemonade,
A-making little kind remarks unto them all at sight,
Until he met two travellers who looked cosmopolite.

Now even as the old was green, this pair were darkly-brown;
They seemed to be of that degree that sports about the town
Amid terrestrial mice, I ween, their destiny was Cat;
If ever men were gonoffs,* I should say these two were that.

And they had watched that old man well with interested look,
And gazed him counting greenbacks in that brownsome pocket-
    book;
And the elder softly warbled with benevolential phiz,
'Green peas has come to market, and the veg'tables is riz.'

Yet still across the heavenly sky the clouds went clouding on,
The rush upon the gliding brook kept rushing all alone,
While the ducks upon the water were a-ducking just the same,
And every mortal human man kept on his little game.

* Yiddish for crooks.

And the old man to the strangers very affable let slip
How that zealousy policeman had given him the tip,
And how his cash was buttoned in his pocket dark and dim,
And how he guessed no man alive on earth could gammon him.

In ardent conversation ere long the three were steeped,
And in that good man's confidence the younger party deeped.
The p'liceman, as he shadowed them, exclaimed in blooming rage,
'They're stuffin' of that duck, I guess, and leavin' out the sage'.

He saw the game distinctly, and inspected how it took,
And watched the reappearance of that brownsome pocket-book,
And how that futile ancient, ere he buttoned up his coat,
Had interchanged, obliging-like, a greensome coloured note,

And how they parted tenderly, and how the happy twain
Went out into the Infinite by taking of the train:
Then up the blue policeman came, and said, 'My ancient son,
Now you have gone and did it; say what you have been and done?'

And unto him the good old man replied in childish glee,
'They were as nice a two young men as I did ever see;
But they were in such misery their story made me cry;
So I lent 'em twenty dollars – which they'll pay me bye-and-bye.

'But as I had no twenty, we also did arrange,
They got from me a fifty bill, and gimme thirty change;
But they will send that fifty back, and by to-morrow's train –'
'That note,' out cried the constable, 'you'll never see again.'

'And that', exclaimed the sweet old man, 'I hope I never may,
Because I do not care a cuss how far it keeps away;
For if I'm a judge of money, and I *reether* think I am,
The one I shoved was never worth a continental dam.

'They hev wandered with their sorrers into the sunny South,
They hev got uncommon swallows and an extry lot of mouth.
In the next train to the North'ard I expect to widely roam,
And if any come inquirin', jist say I ain't at home.'

347

The p'liceman lifted up his glance unto the sunny skies,
I s'pose the light was fervent, for a tear were in his eyes,
And said, 'If in your travels a hat store you should see,
Just buy yourself a beaver tile and charge that tile to me.'

While the robins were a robbing acrost the meadow gay,
And the pigeons still a-pigeoning among the gleam of May,
All out of doors kept out of doors as suchlike only can,
A-singing of an endless hymn about that good old man.

C. G. LELAND

The Duel

A SERIOUS BALLAD

'Like the two Kings of Brentford smelling at one nosegay.'

In Brentford town, of old renown,
    There lived a Mister Bray,
Who fell in love with Lucy Bell,
    And so did Mr Clay.

To see her ride from Hammersmith,
    By all it was allow'd,
Such fair outsides are seldom seen,
    Such Angels on a Cloud.

Said Mr Bray to Mr Clay,
    You choose to rival me,
And court Miss Bell, but there your court
    No thoroughfare shall be.

Unless you now give up your suit,
    You may repent your love;
I who have shot a pigeon match,
    Can shoot a turtle dove.

348

So pray before you woo her more,
   Consider what you do;
If you pop aught to Lucy Bell, –
   I'll pop it into you.

Said Mr Clay to Mr Bray,
   Your threats I quite explode;
One who has been a volunteer
   Knows how to prime and load.

And so I say to you unless
   Your passion quiet keeps,
I who have shot and hit bulls' eyes,
   May chance to hit a sheep's.

Now gold is oft for silver changed,
   And that for copper red;
But these two went away to give
   Each other change for lead.

But first they sought a friend a-piece,
   This pleasant thought to give –
When they were dead, they thus should have
   Two seconds still to live.

To measure out the ground not long
   The seconds then forebore,
And having taken one rash *step*,
   They took a dozen more.

They next prepared each pistol-pan
   Against the deadly strife,
By putting in the prime of death
   Against the prime of life.

Now all was ready for the foes,
   But when they took their stands,
Fear made them tremble so they found
   They both were shaking hands.

Said Mr C. to Mr B.,
  Here one of us may fall,
And like St Paul's Cathedral now,
  Be doom'd to have a ball.

I do confess I did attach
  Misconduct to your name;
If I withdraw the charge, will then
  Your ramrod do the same?

Said Mr B., I do agree –
  But think of Honour's Courts!
If we go off without a shot,
  There will be strange reports.

But look, the morning now is bright,
  Though cloudy it begun;
Why can't we aim above, as if
  We had call'd out the sun?

So up into the harmless air
  Their bullets they did send;
And may all other duels have
  That upshot in the end!

THOMAS HOOD

350

Dahn the Plug-'ole

A muvver was barfin' 'er biby one night,
The youngest of ten and a tiny young mite,
The muvver was pore and the biby was thin,
Only a skelington covered in skin;
The muvver turned rahnd for the soap orf the rack,
She was but a moment, but when she turned back,
The biby was gorn; and in anguish she cried,
'Oh, where is my biby?' – The angels replied:
'Your biby 'as fell dahn the plug-'ole,
Your biby 'as gorn dahn the plug;
The poor little thing was so skinny and thin
'E oughter been barfed in a jug;
Your biby is perfeckly 'appy,
'E won't need a barf any more,
Your biby 'as fell dahn the plug-'ole,
Not lorst, but gorn before.'

ANON.

Matrimony

'Matrimony – Advertiser would like to hear from well-educated Protestant lady, under thirty, fair, with view to above, who would have no objection to work Remington typewriter, at home. Enclose photo. T.99 this office.' – Cork newspaper

T.99 would gladly hear
    From one whose years are few,
A maid whose doctrines are severe,
    Of Presbyterian blue,
Also – with view to the above –
    Her photo he would see,
And trusts that she may live and love
    His Protestant to be!
But ere the sacred rites are done
    (And by no priest of Rome)
He'd ask if she a Remington
    Typewriter works – at home?
If she have no objections to
    This task, and if her hair –
In keeping with her eyes of blue –
    Be delicately fair,
Ah, *then*, let her a photo send
    Of all her charms divine,
To him who rests her faithful friend,
    Her own T.99.

ANDREW LANG

Saving a Train

'Twas in the year of 1869, and on the 19th of November,
Which the people in Southern Germany will long remember,
The great rain-storm which for twenty hours did pour down,
That the rivers were overflowed and petty streams all around.

The rain fell in such torrents as had never been seen before,
That it seemed like a second deluge, the mighty torrents' roar,
At nine o'clock at night the storm did rage and moan,
When Carl Springel set out on his crutches all alone –

From the handsome little hut in which he dwelt,
With some food to his father, for whom he greatly felt,
Who was watching at the railway bridge,
Which was built upon a perpendicular rocky ridge.

The bridge was composed of iron and wooden blocks,
And crossed o'er the Devil's Gulch, an immense cleft of rocks,
Two hundred feet wide and one hundred and fifty feet deep,
And enough to make one's flesh to creep.

Far beneath the bridge a mountain-stream did boil and rumble,
And on that night did madly toss and tumble;
Oh! it must have been an awful sight
To see the great cataract falling from such a height.

It was the duty of Carl's father to watch the bridge on stormy
    nights,
And warn the on-coming trains of danger with the red lights;
So, on this stormy night, the boy Carl hobbled along
Slowly and fearlessly upon his crutches, because he wasn't strong.

He struggled on manfully with all his might
Through the fearful darkness of the night,
And half-blinded by the heavy rain,
But still resolved the bridge to gain.

But, when within one hundred yards of the bridge, it gave way
    with an awful crash,
And fell into the roaring flood below, and made a fearful splash,
Which rose high above the din of the storm,
The like brave Carl never heard since he was born.

353

Then father! father! cried Carl in his loudest tone,
Father! father! he shouted again in very pitiful moans;
But no answering voice did reply,
Which caused him to heave a deep-fetched sigh.

And now to brave Carl the truth was clear
That he had lost his father dear,
And he cried, My poor father's lost, and cannot be found;
He's gone down with the bridge, and has been drowned.

But he resolves to save the on-coming train.
So every nerve and muscle he does strain,
And he trudges along dauntlessly on his crutches,
And tenaciously to them he clutches.

And just in time he reaches his father's car
To save the on-coming train from afar,
So he seizes the red light, and swings it round,
And cries with all his might, The bridge is down! The bridge is
    down!

So forward his father's car he drives,
Determined to save the passengers' lives,
Struggling hard with might and main,
Hoping his struggle won't prove in vain.

And so on comes the iron-horse, snorting and rumbling,
And the mountain-torrent at the bridge kept roaring and tumbling;
While brave Carl keeps shouting, The bridge is down! The bridge
    is down!
He cried with a pitiful wail and sound.

But, thank heaven, the engine-driver sees the red light
That Carl keeps swinging round his head with all his might;
But bang! bang! goes the engine with a terrible crash,
And the car is dashed all to smash.

But the breaking of the car stops the train,
And poor Carl's struggle is not in vain;
But, poor soul, he was found stark dead,
Crushed and mangled from foot to head!

And the passengers were all loud in Carl's praise,
And from the cold wet ground they did him raise,
And tears for brave Carl fell silently around,
Because he had saved two hundred passengers from being drowned.

In a quiet village cemetery he now sleeps among the silent dead
In the south of Germany, with a tombstone at his head,
Erected by the passengers he saved in the train,
And which to his memory will long remain.

WILLIAM MCGONAGALL

The Mouse-Trap

I

Palmström is very ill at ease:
He has a mouse, but has no cheese.

Korf, answering his heart's desire,
Builds him a cabinet of wire,

And with a fine-toned violin
He sets his boon companion in.

The night descends, the dog-stars bark.
Palmström makes music in the dark.

And while the sweet strains come and go
The mouse comes walking on tip-toe.

No sooner in than from aloft
The gateway drops down, secret-soft.

Half-hidden in the shadows deep
Sinks Palmström's figure wrapped in sleep.

2

Next morning Korf, with gloves and gaiters,
Loads this elaborate apparatus

(Complete, that is, with mouse and man)
On to a strong removals van

Which powerful horses bear apace
Towards a distant woodland place.

Here, in the leafy silence, he
Sets this unusual couple free.

The mouse trots out to take the air
With Palmström bringing up the rear.

She looks once at her chaperone,
Then wags her whiskers and is gone.

Their task achieved the happy twain
Immediately go home again.

CHRISTIAN MORGENSTERN
(translated R. F. C. HULL)

The Bishop's Mistake

The bishop glanced through his window pane
On a world of sleet, and wind, and rain,
When a dreary figure met his eyes
That made the bishop soliloquize.

And as the bishop gloomily thought
He ordered pen and ink to be brought,
Then 'Providence Watches' he plainly wrote
And pinned the remark to a ten bob note.

Seizing his hat from his lordly rack
And wrapping his cloak around his back,
Across the road the bishop ran
And gave the note to the shabby man.

That afternoon was the bishop's 'at home'
When everyone gathered beneath his dome,
Curate and canon from far and near
Came to partake of the bishop's cheer.

There in the good old bishop's hall
Stood a stranger lean and tall,
'Your winnings, my lord' he cried. 'Well done
"Providence Watches", at ten to one.'

It is to be noted on Sunday next
The bishop skilfully chose his text,
And from the pulpit earnestly told
Of the fertile seed that returned tenfold.

ANON.

Second Philosopher's Song

If, O my Lesbia, I should commit,
Not fornication, dear, but suicide,
My Thames-blown body (Pliny vouches it)
Would drift face upwards on the oily tide
With the other garbage, till it putrefied.

But you, if all your lovers' frozen hearts
Conspired to send you, desperate, to drown –
Your maiden modesty would float face down,
And men would weep upon your hinder parts.

'Tis the Lord's doing. Marvellous is the plan
By which this best of world's is wisely planned.
One law He made for woman, one for man:
We bow the head and do not understand.

ALDOUS HUXLEY

His Hirsute Suit

A bristling beard wàs his peculiarity:
   He kissed. She thought it smacked of insincerity
   And bridling up remarked with great severity,
'Such misdemeanors are, I trust, a rarity;
Also your face, despite its angularity,
   Is hidden in a razorless asperity:
   Were it not so, I call it great temerity –
Our walks in life are not upon a parity.'
Wherefore he shaved, to give his chin the purity
   It knew ere he emerged from his minority.
The razor, naked, with no guard's security,
   Slipped. Gizzard cut, he joined the great majority.
Where he will pass the aeons of futurity –
Above – below – I can't say with authority.

F. SIDGWICK

The Grange

Oh there hasn't been much change
At The Grange.

Of course the blackberries growing closer
Make getting in a bit of a poser
But there hasn't been much change
At The Grange.

Old Sir Prior died
They say on the point of leaving for the seaside
They never found the body which seemed odd to some
(Not me, seeing as what I seen the butler done)

Oh there hasn't been much change
At The Grange.

The governess as got it now
Miss Ursy having moved down to The Green Cow
Seems proper done out of er rights a b. shame
And what's that the governess pushes round at nights in the old pram?

No there hasn't been much change
At The Grange.

The shops leave their stuff at the gates now – meat, groceries
Mostly old canned goods you know from McInnes's
They wouldn't go up to the door,
Not after what happened to Fred's pa.

Oh there hasn't been much change
At The Grange.

Passing there early this morning, cor lummy,
I hears a whistling sound coming from the old chimney
Whistling it was fit to bust and not a note wrong
The old pot, whistling *The Death of Nelson.*

Oh there hasn't been much change
At The Grange.

But few goes that way somehow
Not now.

STEVIE SMITH

Obituary

Life's little day is fading fast; upon the mountain's brow, the sink-
ing sun is gleaming red: the shadows lengthen now. The twilight
hush comes on apace, and soon the evening star will light us to
those chambers dim where dreamless sleepers are; and when the
curfew bell has rung that calls us all to rest, and we have left all
earthly things at Azrael's request, O may some truthful mourner
rise and say of you or me: 'Gee-whiz! I'm sorry that he's dead: he
was a honey-bee! Whate'er his job, he did his best: he put on all
his steam. In everything he had to do, he was a four-horse team.
He thought that man was placed on earth to help his fellow-guys:
he never wore a frosty face, and balked at weepy eyes. The hard-
luck pilgrim always got a handout at his door; and any friend
could help himself to all he had in store. He tried to make his
humble home the gayest sort of camp, till Death, the king of
bogies, came and slugged him in the lamp. There never was a
squarer guy existed in the land; and Death was surely off his base
when that galoot was canned.

WALT MASON

Notting Hill Polka

We've – had –
A Body in the house
   Since Father passed away:
He took bad on
Saturday night an' he
   Went the followin' day:

Mum's – pulled –
The blinds all down
   An' bought some Sherry Wine,
An' we've put the tin
What the Arsenic's in
   At the bottom of the Ser-pen-tine!

W. BRIDGES-ADAMS

I'm a Treble in the Choir

In the Choir I'm a treble
And my singing is the debbel!
I'm a treble in the Choir!
They sing high but I sing higher.
Treble singing's VERY high,
But the highest high am I!
Soon I'll burst like any bubble:
I'm a treble – that's the trouble!

EDMOND KAPP

Defenestration

I once had the honour of meeting a philosopher called McIndoe
Who had once had the honour of being flung out of an upstairs
    window.
During his flight, he said, he commenced an interesting train of
    speculation
On why there happened to be such a word as defenestration.

There is not, he said, a special word for being rolled down a roof
    into a gutter;
There is no verb to describe the action of beating a man to death
    with a putter;
No adjective exists to qualify a man bound to the buffer of the
    12.10 to Ealing,
No abstract noun to mollify a man hung upside down by his
    ankles from the ceiling.

Why, then, of all the possible offences so distressing to humani-
    tarians,
Should this one alone have caught the attention of the verbarians?
I concluded (said McIndoe) that the incidence of logodaedaly was
    purely adventitious.
About a thirtieth of a second later, I landed in a bush that my
    great-aunt brought back from Mauritius.

I am aware (he said) that defenestration is not limited to the
    flinging of men through the window.
On this occasion, however, it was so limited, the object defen-
    estrated being, I, the philosopher, McIndoe.

R. P. LISTER

The Drummer

He sold his soul
To the Devil he did –
The Devil he did!
For a couple of quid;
And really I think
He was very well rid
Of a soul like his
For a couple of quid.
I honestly think
He properly did
The Devil he did!

MICHAEL FLANDERS

Autobiography of an Honest Man

During the night
I was out of sight;
During the day
I was in the way.

CLARK STILLMAN

Garbled Gifts

From Florida to the Corinthian Isthmus
People give people gifts for Christmus;
Some give hampers from Mason (and Fortnum)
With the rarest viands that can be bortnum,
Some give a weighty tome of Nietzsche's,
Some give powder, for female fietzches,
Some give a fascist ham from Eire,
Some knit socks for a well-loved weire –

But some, who were never told what taste meant,
Buy terrible things from the bargain basement,
Things so tasteless that taste is minus,
For well was it said by St Thomas Aquinus
Sicut ens sicut unum, which, construed,
Means a thing is ONE, not a spawn or brood;
Yet people save up for monce and monce
For things that are several things at once –
The electric fire that is shaped like a yacht,
With copper sails round a mast red-hacht,
The fountain-pen-cum-cigarette-lighter
For the busy (and tasteless) smoker-wrighter,
The teapot shaped like a country cottage,
The razor that uses not soap but wattage,
The pourer of whisky, or even wyne,
Which when inverted plays Auld Lang Syne –
Not far removed, to the sensitive soul,
From (horror!) the musical toilet roul. . . .
Dear Reader, if you give things like these
Don't let this verse cause a goodwill-freeze;
The author's not arty, or over-zealous –
It's just that this year has made him jealous
By scoring the tally another notch
When nobody bought him

                               A Chiming watch.

                             PAUL JENNINGS

The Shrew

Once you were gentle and adoring,
As beautiful as a dove about my morning.
I never asked. But all the same you came
And trembling every moment spoke my name.

364

What's come over you? That now you sulk and pout
And every meeting seems to you so boring?
I have not changed. So need you shout
Or look at me with eyes quite so devouring?

Late as censorious as a judge you've grown.
Be off. You can no longer call my life your own.

LESLIE PAUL

La Beldam Sans Directoire

ON THE RECENSION OF THE TELEPHONE DIRECTORY, 1953

Picture me, my dear, alone and
Palely doing whatever one does alone,
Receiving, perhaps, an imaginary message,
Silent – like Cortez – on a telephone.

Emperorwise or clownlike listening
– In my dark glasses – to the nightingale
Threading, no doubt, its song through the sad heart
Of Truth reduced to tears amid the ale....

Preferring sorrow to a harvest home:
For now, to save a little L. s. d.,
Truth they compress and distance they compel
Who have retrenched the old Directory.

RICHARD TOLSON

The Wider Life

I once was a dull, narrow housewife
   With nothing to talk of at all
But the loves, the frustrations,
The rows, the relations
   Of the woman from over the wall.

But now I've a job, I'm quite different;
   I can talk with a sparkle like wine
Of the loves, the frustrations,
The rows, the relations,
   Of the girl at the desk next to mine.

CELIA FREMLIN

UNSOCIAL COMMENT

The Fate of Sergeant Thin

Weep for the fate of Sergeant Thin,
  A man of desperate courage was he,
More he rejoiced in the battle's din
  Than in all the mess-room's revelry;
But he died at last of no ugly gash, –
He choked on a hair of his own moustache!

Sergeant Thin was stern and tall,
  And he carried his head with a wonderful air;
He looked like a man who could never fall,
  For devil or don he did not care;
But death soon settled the Sergeant's hash,
He choked on a hair of his own moustache!

Sorely surprised was he to find
  That his life thus hung on a single hair;
Had he been drinking until he grew blind,
  It would have been something more easy to bear;
Or had he been eating a cartload of trash, –
But he choked on a hair of his own moustache!

The news flew quickly along the ranks,
  And the whiskered and bearded grew pale with fright;
It seemed the oddest of all death's pranks,
  To murder a Sergeant by means so slight, –
And vain were a General's state and cash,
If he choked on a hair of his own moustache!

They buried poor Thin when the sun went down,
  His cap and his sword on the coffin lay;
But many a one from the neighbouring town
  Came smilingly up to the sad array, –
For they said with a laughter they could not quash,
That he choked on a hair of his own moustache!

Now every gallant and gay hussar,
  Take warning by this mournful tale, –
It is not only bullet or scar
  That may your elegant form assail;
Be not too bold – be not too rash –
You may choke on a hair of your own moustache!

H. G. BELL

Early Rising

'God bless the man who first invented sleep!'
  So Sancho Panza said, and so say I:
And bless him, also, that he didn't keep
  His great discovery to himself; nor try
To make it – as the lucky fellow might –
  A close monopoly by patent-right!

Yes – bless the man who first invented sleep
  (I really can't avoid the iteration);
But blast the man, with curses loud and deep,
  Whate'er the rascal's name, or age, or station,
Who first invented, and went round advising,
That artificial cut-off, – Early Rising!

'Rise with the lark, and with the lark to bed,'
  Observes some solemn, sentimental owl;
Maxims like these are very cheaply said;
  But, ere you make yourself a fool or fowl,
Pray just inquire about his rise and fall,
And whether larks have any beds at all!

The time for honest folks to be abed
  Is in the morning, if I reason right;
And he who cannot keep his precious head
  Upon his pillow till it's fairly light,
And so enjoy his forty morning winks,
Is up to knavery; or else – he drinks!

370

Thomson, who sang about the 'Seasons', said
  It was a glorious thing to *rise* in season;
But then he said it – lying – in his bed,
  At ten o' clock A.M., – the very reason
He wrote so charmingly. The simple fact is
His preaching wasn't sanctioned by his practice.

'Tis, doubtless, well to be sometimes awake, –
  Awake to duty, and awake to truth, –
But when, alas, a nice review we take
  Of our best deeds and days, we find, in sooth,
The hours that leave the slightest cause to weep
Are those we passed in childhood or asleep!

'Tis beautiful to leave the world awhile
  For the soft visions of the gentle night;
And free, at last, from mortal care or guile,
  To live as only in the angels' sight,
In sleep's sweet realm so cosily shut in,
Where, at the worst, we only *dream* of sin!

So let us sleep, and give the Maker praise.
  I like the lad who, when his father thought
To clip his morning nap by hackneyed phrase
  Of vagrant worm by early songster caught,
Cried, 'Serve him right! – it's not at all surprising;
The worm was punished, sir, for early rising!'

J. G. SAXE

Sonnet by a Civil Servant to his Love

In th' enforcèd leisure of the hour when tea
   And biscuit sweet (supplied in duplicate)
   The schedules of the mind coördinate,
Some higher rule directs my thoughts to thee.
Then do I register sheer ecstasy
   For thou all lovelinesses integrate
   With charms but too redundant for thy fate
That meets small charm reciprocal in me.

O, might our ways bilateral twine in one,
   And, requisitioning one domicile,
     Share one inclusive, coinciding view!

The teacups' tinkle dies. Once more begun
   The high and changeless round; and here, on file,
     These lines for note and comment passed to you.

ALLAN M. LAING

A Slice of Wedding Cake

Why have such scores of lovely, gifted girls
   Married impossible men?
Simple self-sacrifice may be ruled out,
   And missionary endeavour, nine times out of ten.

Repeat 'impossible men' – not merely rustic,
   Foul-tempered, or depraved
(Dramatic foils chosen to show the world
   How well women behave, and always have behaved).

Impossible men: idle, illiterate,
   Self-pitying, dirty, sly,
For whose appearance even in City parks
   Excuses must be made to casual passers-by.

Has God's supply of tolerable husbands
   Fallen, in fact, so low?
Or do I always over-value woman
   At the expense of man?
       Do I?
           It might be so.

ROBERT GRAVES

Hymn

The Church's Restoration
   In eighteen-eighty-three
Has left for contemplation
   Not what there used to be.
How well the ancient woodwork
   Looks round the Rectr'y hall,
Memorial of the good work
   Of him who plann'd it all,

He who took down the pew-ends
   And sold them anywhere
But kindly spared a few ends
   Work'd up into a chair.
O worthy persecution
   Of dust! O hue divine!
O cheerful substitution,
   Thou varnishéd pitch-pine!

Church furnishing! Church furnishing!
   Sing art and crafty praise!
He gave the brass for burnishing,
   He gave the thick red baize,
He gave the new addition,
   Pull'd down the dull old aisle,
– To pave the sweet transition
   He gave th' encaustic tile.

373

Of marble brown and veinéd
  He did the pulpit make;
He order'd windows stainéd
  Light red and crimson lake.
Sing on, with hymns uproarious,
  Ye humble and aloof,
Look up! and oh how glorious
  He has restored the roof!

JOHN BETJEMAN

How to get on in Society

Phone for the fish-knives, Norman,
As cook is a little unnerved;
You kiddies have crumpled the serviettes
And I must have things daintily served.

Are the requisites all in the toilet?
The frills round the cutlets can wait
Till the girl has replenished the cruets
And switched on the logs in the grate.

It's ever so close in the lounge dear,
But the vestibule's comfy for tea
And Howard is out riding on horseback,
So do come and take some with me.

Now here is a fork for your pastries,
And do use the couch for your feet;
I know what I wanted to ask you –
Is trifle sufficient for sweet?

Milk and then just as it comes dear?
I'm afraid the preserve's full of stones;
Beg pardon, I'm soiling the doileys
With afternoon tea-cakes and scones.

JOHN BETJEMAN

A Question of Age

LINES WRITTEN AT AN EDUCATIONAL CONFERENCE

'How old are you?' the adult said
Patting the bratling on the head.
The earnest youngster dodged the imminent squeeze,
Patted the adult back, and snapped out 'Please,
Do tell me just precisely what it is you mean;
My age? By birth certificate or by Binet seen?
We cannot with sophisticate intelligence engage
On conversation round this theme of age
When you refuse to make it crystal clear
If you mean Mental, Chronological, or Reading here.
Let us be certain, sir, if we must use a pedagogic term
We use it right, in manner scientific, *juste*, and firm!'
Abashed the untaught adult turned and fled
And wished that ageless child, Methuselah – or even dead.

J. E. MORPURGO

Lines Composed in Fifth Row centre

Of all the kinds of lecturer
    The lecturer I most detest
Is he who finishes a page
    And places it behind the rest.

I much prefer the lecturer
    Who takes the pages as he finishes
And puts them on a mounting pile
    As the original pile diminishes.

But best of all the lecturer
    Who gets his papers in confusion
And prematurely lets escape
    The trumpet-phrase: 'And in conclusion . . .'

MORRIS BISHOP

375

A Grotesque

Dr Newman with the crooked pince-nez
Has studied in Vienna and Chicago,
Chess was his only relaxation.
And Dr Newman remained unperturbed
By every nastier manifestation
Of plutodemocratic civilization:
All that was cranky, corny, ill-behaved,
Unnecessary, askew, or orgiastic
Would creep unbidden to his side-door (hidden
Behind a poster in the Tube Station,
Nearly half-way up the moving-stairs),
Push its way in, to squat there undisturbed
Among box-files and tubular steel-chairs.
He was once seen at the Philharmonic Hall
Noting the reactions of two patients,
With pronounced paranoiac tendencies,
To old Dutch music. He appeared to recall
A tin of lozenges in his breast-pocket,
Put his hand confidently in –
And drew out a black imp, or sooterkin,
Six inches long, with one ear upside-down,
Licking at a vanilla ice-cream cornet –
Then put it back again with a slight frown.

ROBERT GRAVES

Mistaken Identity

The smiling film-star stood, to meet
The mob that surged along the street.
Before the man could say a word
They charged him like a maddened herd,
And knocked him down and trampled him,
And almost tore him limb from limb.

Then, laughing wildly through their tears,
They ripped his clothes for souvenirs,
Snatched bits of trouser, strips of shirt,
And left him lying in the dirt.
But one, whose wits were wide awake,
Knew they had made a slight mistake,
And thus addressed the hideous throng:
'Hi! Wait a bit! We've got it wrong!
Oh, damn it all! Take it from me,
He's not the one we came to see.'

J. B. MORTON

The Member for –

Though washed in public, and with great display,
His dirty linen's dirtier every day.

J. B. MORTON

Gilbertian Recipe for a Politician

Take a recipe now for that clot of inanity
    Known as the party political man:
From semi-humanity drain off the sanity,
    Dress it in vanity, stuff it with bran;
Add voice like a radio (nobody listening),
    Gobbledegookery, dull as a ditch
(No more to the point than a bull at a christening),
    Droning on – What is he, Labour or which?
The mind of a Marx (it is Groucho I'm thinking of),
Greedy for power that he longs to be stinking of,
Burning to build up an Orwell's Big Brotherland,
Yearning to sit for his portrait (not Sutherland!),
    Form of a Goering – face of a sphinx –
Fond of conferring (to learn what he thinks) –

377

Leach from these elements all that is soluble,
Toss in a lump of the valueless voluble,
    Pour off the liquid and store it in kegs,
    And a party political man is the *dregs!*

J. A. LINDON

To Miss X

AGE 9 OR THEREABOUTS

Some man one day, a better man than I am
    Will look into your eyes and lose his heart,
And quoting, maybe, bits of Omar Khayyam
    Will take you (sans the loaf of bread) apart
'Neath some convenient bough to sing your praises,
    And lover-like, still gazing in your eyes,
Inform you with a fierceness that amazes
    That you are ve *y* beautiful and wise.
But could he see you now aged nine or under,
    Your pleasant placid face untouched by care,
Would he not call, with me, on earth to sunder
    And swallow you complete with desk and chair?
Would he not share with me some fellow-feeling
    As I devise, with inward rage, a fate
That may convince you, though it lead to squealing,
    That $5 + 4$ does *not* result in 8!

F. A. V. MADDEN

The Food Fad

    Her relatives were all agreed
    That very, very large indeed
    There loomed in little Ermyntrude
    A faddiness about her food.

378

A puppy dog in half a trice
Will woffle anything that's nice,
And even cats, though more sedate,
Still leave a clean and polished plate,
But Ermyntrude, when she was small,
Could scarce be got to feed at all,
And never, at the table, cared
To eat those edibles prepared.
At breakfast, if her egg were fried,
'Oh, bring me boiled or poached,' she cried,
But boiled or poached, as you may guess,
Would satisfy her even less,
And likewise any other stuff
Received a similar rebuff.
Then, even if her parents hit
On anything she liked a bit,
She shunted it about her plate
And nodged it into such a state
The grisly and revolting sight
Quite robbed them of their appetite.
Each breakfast, therefore, tempers got
On every hand extremely hot,
A really most upsetting way
In which to start upon the day.
When lunch and, later, teatime came
Young Ermyntrude was just the same,
So scenes of violence and of hate
Raged regularly round her plate.

Now food should always, doctors find,
Be eaten with a tranquil mind,
For tums and organs that digest
In these conditions function best,
But otherwise incline to get
Most comprehensively upset.
No wonder then that pa and ma
Grew symptoms of dyspepsia,
And that's a very noted ill

For making tempers badder still.
Hence when one teatime mother said,
'You should, my darling, start with bread
And only after that partake
Of richer things like jam and cake,'
And Ermie thrust her plate aside
And contumaciously replied,
'I'll start my tea with what I like,
Or else I'll – yes, I'll hunger strike!'
Instead of wisely bringing forth
The soft reply that turneth wrath
Both parents gave their anger play
And shouted, 'Right then, strike away!'
And that, so wilful was the kid,
Was just precisely what she did!

The days dragged by and Ermyntrude
Shrank visibly through want of food,
But though her parents sighed a lot
To note how very thin she got,
And urged her, 'Ermie, start with bread,
Do hurry dear, before you're dead,'
They stayed resolved on no pretence
To suffer disobedience,
While Ermie, in her stupid way,
Would rather suffer than obey!

Her weight, when finally she starved,
Was actually more than halved,
Which meant, in coffin and in hearse,
A saving to her parents' purse.
This very clearly shows, or should,
The wind is ill that blows no good.

H. A. FIELD

Problem

The wind is in the north, the wind
Unfurls its fury at the door;
To turn the cat out seems unkind.

To use him ill I do abhor,
Yet this reflection comes to mind:
Suppose he desecrates the floor?

Though hateful what he'll leave behind,
(To cleanse which were a loathsome chore)
To turn the cat out seems unkind.

He eats a lot, and cries for more:
Roughage, alas, which does not bind:
Suppose he desecrates the floor?

But what if with the dawn I find
Him frozen stiff, and frosted o'er?
To turn the cat out seems unkind.

I'll leave my lino with a score
Of daily journals amply lined:
Suppose he desecrates the floor?
To turn the cat out seems unkind.

KENNETH LILLINGTON

In the Swim

No one enjoys more than I do
The pleasures of the swimming-pool, or Lido
When I lie on the concrete bordering this municipal moisture
The world is my oisture.
I do not talk, or read novels of detection,

No, what deep water produces in me is deep reflection;
I am one of the many chaps who
Have only to be at a swimming pool, and they start thinking of the
      primordial ocean, which the Egyptians called Nu and the
      Babylonians Apsu;
Water, says Jung, the sage of Switzerland,
Is an archetype of the Unconscious, from which our Conscious,
      the part that fills in income tax forms, rises in scattered
      peaks or bits o' land.
At swimming pools, when the weather is finer
I dream of broken aqueducts by ruined cities in Asia Minor.
Surrounded by laughing bathers, I am as old as Tiresias or Geron-
      tius
I swim through a green and chlorinated Unconscious,
I love all men –
    but what is this?
    Two golden men and a golden miss
    Seem to think they're admired by all
    For their solemn game with a medicine ball;
    They stand in poses we all have seen
    On the covers of many a health magazine,
    It's clear they think, from their graces and airs,
    We wish we could all have bodies like theirs.
    Sooner or later they drop their catches,
    The wet ball lands on my pipe and matches;
    My dreams no longer hatch out from their eggs
    When gymnasts trip on my outstretched legs.
    The view I take of their sport is dim,
    I crossly rise and dive in for a swim –
    But here again I am far from solo,
    I come up for air in a game of polo ...
Too late! too late! I was just a fool
To think I could dream at a swimming pool.

PAUL JENNINGS

Double Entente Cordiale

Consider for a moment the French
I mean, of course, the people themselves, not the stench
Of garlic in their underground trains nor their typically Gallic
    morals
Or the way in which their governments govern in a series of awful
    quarrels.
For instance the Frenchman is famous for drinking wine with his
    meals instead of water,
But I think he does this not so much because he likes it as because
    he thinks he oughter.
And also for having small black dogs called 'caniches'
Which if I had my way I would irrevocably banish
Because the caniche doesn't bark it contemptuously mutters
And also is excessively careless on the boulevards and in the gutters.
The Frenchman also has a reputation for designing women's
    clothing
A proceeding which any right-minded Englishman regards with
    loathing,
Because it seems fairly obvious that anyone who spends his time
    concocting things in satin
Can hardly be expected to distinguish himself at bowling or batin.
Which reminds me of another thing which strikes me as curious
And that is why, when Frenchmen play any sort of game, they
    always get absolutely furious,
In fact it is very much more
Like war.
But on the other hand when they really have a war and things get bad
They immediately think they're playing a game and start to cheer
    like mad;
But we should try to get used to the French
Because it would be such an awful wrench
If we had no one to say at the end of a long and successful war, 'Of
    course,
We would have won the whole thing much more quickly without
    the aid of the British Expeditionary Force.'

ALUN GWYNNE JONES

383

The Proper Study

Seated before her window Mrs Jones
Described the passers-by in ringing tones.
'Look,' she would say, 'the girl at Number Three
Has brought her latest boy-friend home to tea;
And, see, the woman at the upstairs flat
Has bought herself another summer hat.'
Her daughter Daphne, filled with deep disgust,
Expostulated 'Mother, really must
You pry upon the neighbours? Don't you know
Gossip is idle, empty-minded, low?'
And Mrs Jones would murmur 'Fancy, dear!
There's Mr Thompson going for his beer.'

Daphne, an earnest girl of twenty-three,
Read Sociology for her degree
And every Saturday she would repair,
Armed with her tutor's latest questionnaire,
To knock on doors, demanding 'Are you wed?
Have you a child? A car? A double bed?'
Poor Mrs Jones would remonstrate each week,
'Daphne, I wonder how you have the cheek.
And then to call me nosey!' Daphne sighed.
'Oh, will you never understand?' she cried.
'Mere curiosity is one thing, Mother:
Social Analysis is quite another.'

W. S. SLATER

I Dunno

I sometimes think I'd rather crow
And be a rooster than to roost
And be a crow. But I dunno.

A rooster he can roost also,
Which don't seem fair when crows can't crow
Which may help some. Still I dunno.

Crows should be glad of one thing though;
Nobody thinks of eating crow,
While roosters they are good enough
For anyone unless they're tough.

There's lots of tough old roosters though,
And anyway a crow can't crow,
So mebby roosters stand more show.
It looks that way. But I dunno.

ANON.

Sonnet on Steam

BY AN UNDER-OSTLER

I wish I livd a Thowsen year Ago
Wurking for Sober six and Seven milers
And dubble Stages runnen safe and slo
The Orsis cum in Them days to the Bilers
But Now by meens of Powers of Steem forces
A-turning Coches into Smoakey Kettels
The Bilers seam a Cumming to the Orses
And Helps and naggs Will sune be out of Vittels
Poor Bruits I wunder How we bee to Liv
When sutch a change of Orses is our Faits
No nothink need Be sifted in a Siv
May them Blowd ingins all Blow up their Grates
And Theaves of Oslers crib the Coles and Giv
Their blackgard Hannimuls a Feed of Slaits!

THOMAS HOOD

Amo, Amas

Amo, amas,
I love a lass,
As cedar tall and slender;
Sweet cowslip's face
Is her nominative case,
And she's of the feminine gender.
Horum quorum,
Sunt divorum,
Hafum, scarum, Divo;
Tag, rag, merry derry, periwig and hatband,
Hic, hoc, harum, genitivo.

JOHN O'KEEFE

The Werewolf

One night an errant Werewolf fled
His wife and child and visited
A village teacher's sepulchre
And begged him: 'Conjugate me, Sir!'

The village teacher then awoke
And standing on his scutcheon spoke
Thus to the beast, who made his seat
With crossed paws at the dead man's feet:

'The Werewolf', said that honest wight,
'The Willwolf – future, am I right?
The Wouldwolf – wolf conditional,
The Beowulf – father of them all!'

These tenses had a pleasing sound,
The Werewolf rolled his eyeballs round,
And begged him, as he'd gone so far,
Add plural to the singular.

The village teacher scratched his head;
He'd never heard of that, he said.
Though there were 'wolves' in packs and swarms,
Of 'were' could be no plural forms!

There Werewolf rose up blind with tears
– He'd had a wife and child for years!
But being ignorant of letters
He went home thankful to his betters.

CHRISTIAN MORGENSTERN
(translated R. F. C. HULL)

A Macaronic Poem

'The Kaiser spoke at length with the Baron de Haulleville, Director of the
Congo Museum in French, German, and English.' –

Newspaper report 1910 (?

Guten Morgen, mon ami,
  Heute ist es schönes Wetter!
Charmé de vous voir içi!
  Never saw you looking better!

Hoffentlich que la Baronne,
  So entzückend et so pleasant,
Ist in Brussels cet automne:
  Combien wünsch' ich she were present!

Und die Kinder, how are they?
  Ont-ils eu la rougeole lately?
Sind sie avec vous today?
  J'aimerais les treffen greatly.

Ich muss chercher mon hôtel.
  What a charming Schwätzerei, Sir!
Lebe wohl! adieu! Farewell!
  Vive le Congo! Hoch dem Kaiser!

H. G.

To a Friend Studying German

Si liceret te amare
Ad Suevorum magnum mare,
Sponsam te perducerem.
'Tristicia Amorosa', *Frau Aventiure*, J. V. von Scheffel

Will'st dou learn die deutsche Sprache?
  Denn set it on your card
Dat all the nouns have shenders
  Und de shenders all are hard,

390

Dere ish also dings called pronoms,
    Vitch id's shoost ash vell to know;
Boot ach! de verbs or time-words —
    Dey'll work you bitter woe.

Will'st dou learn de deutsche Sprache?
    Dann you allatag moost go
To sinfonies, sonatas,
    Or an oratorio.
Vhen you dinks you knows 'pout musik,
    More ash any other man,
Be sure de soul of Deutschland
    Into your soul is ran.

Will'st dou learn de deutsche Sprache?
    Dou moost eat apout a peck
A week, of stinging sauerkraut,
    Und sefen pfoundts of speck,
Mit Gott knows vot in vinegar,
    Und deuce knows vot in rum:
Dis ish de only cerdain vay
    To make de accents coom.

Will'st dou learn de deutsche Sprache?
    Brepare dein soul to shtand
Soosh sendences as ne'er vas heardt
    In any oder land.
Till dou canst make parentheses
    Intwisted — ohne zahl —
Dann wirst du erst deutschfertig seyn,
    For a languashe ideál.

Willst dou learn de deutsche Sprache?
    Du must mitout an fear
Trink afery tay an gallon dry,
    Of foamin Sherman bier.

Und de more you trinks, pe certain,
  More Deutsch you'll surely pe;
For Gambrinus ish de Emperor
  Of de whole of Germany.

Will'st dou learn de deutsche Sprache?
  Be sholly, brav, und treu,
For dat veller ish kein Deutscher
  Who ish not a sholly poy.
Find out vot means Gemüthlichkeit,
      Und do it mitout fail,
In Sang und Klang dein Lebenlang
  A brick – ganz kreuzfidél.

Will'st dou learn de deutsche Sprache?
  If a shendleman dou art,
Denn shtrike right indo Deutschland,
  Und get a schveetes heart.
From Schwabenland or Sachsen
  Vhere now dis writer pees;
Und de bretty girls all wachsen
  Shoost like aepples on de drees.

Boot if dou bee'st a laty
  Denn on de oder hand,
Take a blonde moustachioed lofer
  In de vine green Sherman land.
Und if you shoost kit married
  (Vood mit vood soon makes a vire),
You'll learn to sprechen Deutsch mein kind
  Ash fast ash you tesire.

C. G. LELAND

Gaudeamus and Igitur

Gaudeamus and Igitur
Were Romans inseparably.
Where Gaudeamus was wont to be,
He was wont with Igitur.

Never a night were the two at home,
Gaudeamus and Igitur;
It was Gaudeamus and Igitur
In the brightest spots of Rome.

Gaudeamus got gravel soon,
And gout got Igitur.
But 'Gaudeamus Igitur' –
The boys are still the tune.

CLARK STILLMAN

A Charm Against Indigestion

Absit ventus circum cor,
Likewise epigastric sore;
Absit dolor in jejuno,
Which, post prandium, not a few know;
Absit atrox vomitus
With its horrid sonitus;
Absit tum insomnia:
Bismuth vincit omnia.

H. A. C. EVANS

393

J'ai peur
Du Flu!
Toute à l'heure
J'ai bu
Un peu trop
D'whisky chaud,
Et j'ai vu
Trois faces
Dans la glace:
Trois 'moi'
À la fois;
Et – ma foi,
Tous les trois
Étaient moi!
J'ai peur
Du Flu!

ANON.

French Limerick

Il était un gendarme à Nanteuil,
Qui n'avait qu'une dent et qu'un œil;
   Mais cet œil solitaire
   Était plein de mystère,
Cette dent d'importance et d'orgueil.

GEORGE DU MAURIER

The Metric System Defied

Some talk of millimetres and some of kilogrammes,
And some of decilitres to measure beer and drams;
But I'm a British Workman, too old to go to school,
So by *pounds* I'll eat, and by *quarts* I'll drink,
And I'll work by my *three-foot* rule.

JOHN RANKINE

Pot-and-Pan and Trouble-and-Strife go Turnip-Topping

One day when I'd washed my old Jem Mace
    and combed my Barnet Fair,
My trouble-and-strife said what about
    a spot of the old grey mare?

Says I: It isn't a ball-of-chalk
    on which your mind is bent:
You're out for a day in the turnip-tops;
    so we'll borrow the Duke of Kent.

She bought herself some daisy roots
    and me a Peckham Rye,
Then a tit-for-tat, wiv fevvers, made
    a hole in me houses-sky.

Just past the Joan of Arc we scoffed
    a cup of you-and-me,
With a once-or-twice of Sexton Blake,
    in a nice little A.B.C.

Then out again on our plates-of-meat,
    spending the bees-and-honey,
She made me wait at the Rory O'Mores
    and seemed to think it funny!

But in a lark-and-linnet I
    shewed who was her heap-of-coke;
For when she fancies some almond-rocks,
    says I: I'm heart-of-oak.

ALLAN M. LAING

Jargon-Jingle

Tawdery! – faddery! – Feathers and fuss!
Mummery! – flummery! – wusser and wuss!
All o' Humanity – Vanity Fair! –
Heaven for nothin', and – nobody there!

J. W. RILEY

An Original Love-Story

He struggled to kiss her. She struggled the same
    To prevent him so bold and undaunted;
But, as smitten by lightning, he heard her exclaim,
    'Avaunt, Sir!' and off he avaunted.

But when he returned, with the fiendishest laugh,
    Showing clearly that he was affronted,
And threatened by main force to carry her off,
    She cried 'Don't!' and the poor fellow donted.

When he meekly approached, and sat down at her feet,
    Praying aloud, as before he had ranted,
That she would forgive him and try to be sweet,
    And said 'Can't you!' the dear girl recanted.

Then softly he whispered, 'How could you do so?
    I certainly thought I was jilted;
But come thou with me, to the parson we'll go;
    Say, wilt thou, my dear?' and she wilted.

ANON.

The Bus

You cannot cuss
The motor bus
And brilliant wit
Is lost on it.

W. J. TURNER (HENRY AIRBUBBLE)

[An Inge-nious Rhyme on the Gloomy Dean]

If you his temper would unhinge
And his most sacred rights infringe,
Or, excommunicated, singe
Where fiends forever writhe and cringe
Imploring that a drop of ginge-
R ale may on their tongues impinge
   Address him then as Doctor Inje;
But if you prize the proper thing
Be sure you him call Doctor Ing,
(Unless, your ignorance to screen
You temporise with Mister Dean)
But be advised by me, and cling
To the example of the King
   And fearlessly pronounce him Ing.
Then rush to hear him have his fling
In Pauls and places where they sing.

BERNARD SHAW

Chacun A Son Berlitz

French is easy.
At speaking French I am the champ of the Champs-Élysée,
And since I can speak Parisian without a flaw,
I will tell you why the crows, or les corbeaux, always win their
    battle against the scarecrows: it's on account of their esprit de
    caw.

OGDEN NASH

Nomenclaturik

There was a young fellow named Cholmondeley,
Whose bride was so mellow and colmondeley
That the best man, Colquhoun,
An inane young bolqufoun,
Could only stand still and stare dolmondeley.

The bridegroom's first cousin, young Belvoir,
Whose dad was a Lancashire welvoir,
Arrived with George Bohun
At just about nohun
When excitement was mounting to felvoir.

The vicar – his surname was Beauchamp –
Of marriage endeavoured to teauchamp,
While the bridesmaid, Miss Marjoribanks,
Played one or two harjoripranks;
But the shoe that she threw failed to reauchamp.

HARRY HEARSON

Huntingdonshire

If anyone asked me what there is about Hunts.,
I should have to proclaim myself a dunts.
The name itself is practically useless for rhyming; I don't dispute
That there are punts, stunts, shunts, and even Lunts, but how to
    drag them in is a point which is moot.
It isn't a garden of England like Kent, nor does it foucester
Young ladies of the type found in Gloucester;
Nobody writes songs about Hunts-by-the-sea, I fear,
Nor about Hunts., Glorious Hunts., or that they come up from
    Huntingdonshire.
Yorkshire, now, has a pudding, and bred the sisters Brontë;
And is the largest English conté;
That's what I call hot stuff,
Unlike that Oliver Cromwell and quads-at-St Neots stuff.
What Hunts. needs, beyond all doubt, is some chap
To put it on the map.

D. R. PEDDY

Rhyme for Remembering the Date of Easter

No need for confusion if we but recall
That Easter on the first Sunday after the full moon
    following the vernal equinox doth fall.

JUSTIN RICHARDSON

Spring in New York

Der spring is sprung,
Der grass is riz,
I wonder where dem boidies is?

Der little boids is on der wing,
Ain't dat absoid?
Der little wings is on der boid!

ANON.

Grace for a Cannibal Feast

Totem, votem very good showtem;
C. of E. religion not
Much cop!
Fine fine dish on – boss from mission!
Plenty lousy preacher but
Good chop!

D. R. PEDDY

I asked the maid in dulcet tone
To order me a buttered scone.
The silly girl has been and gone
And ordered me a buttered scone.

ANON

A 'Twiner'

What a curious sculptor is Moore!
What a very odd painter, Picasso!
What is granite with holes in it *for*?
What's the purpose of painting a lass so
    She's green and two-faced?
    Can it keep her more chaste?
    Is a twenty-foot lollabout
    Moll to your taste?
Or a butchered deformity? No, Mr Moore!
Good day to you, Pablo Picasso!

J. A. LINDON

400

Murie Sing

Plumber is icumen in;
Bludie big tu-du.
Bloweth lampe, and showeth dampe,
And dripth the wud thru.
Bludie hel, boo-hoo!

Thawth drain, and runneth bath;
Saw sawth, and scruth scru;
Bull-kuk squirteth, leakë spurteth;
Wurry springeth up anew,
Boo-hoo, boo-hoo.

Tom Pugh, Tom Pugh, well plumbës thu, Tom Pugh;
Better job I naver nu.
Therefore will I cease boo-hoo,
Woorie not, but cry pooh-pooh,
Murie sing pooh-pooh, pooh-pooh,
Pooh-pooh!

A. Y. CAMPBELL

Mr Smith Tries in vain to Telephone

Soe hee
His eager Steps pursu'd, with Purpose clere
And unfulfill'd Intent, nor turn'd, nor stay'd
His onward Course, impatient to inspire
With urgent Speech the Engin sensible
To Breath articulate. Yet al in vaine:
Him of his swift Converse unequall Fate
Bereft, and in the silent solitary Street
Left impotent. His angry Eyes aflame
Like living Coales the glassy Tower transfix'd,
Where unrepentant, careless, unashamed,

A son of *Belial* to the ekkoing Wire
—Outpour'd his foolish love, with sweet Delay
Entranc'd, al els forgot. He long in Hope
Kept faithfull watch, though vaine; as once of old
The hapless Mother from her Casement gaz'd
Al unavailing, for his glad Return
Whom in her Tent the avenging *Kenite* pierc'd
With sharp and bitter Nail; or *Ceres* fair
Awaited long her deare *Persephone*
By *Pluto's* guile ensnar'd. In deep Despaire,
And by Frustration rack'd, at last he turn'd
Unsatisfied away; what time the Other, stirr'd
By garrulous Emotion, straight renew'd
Interminable Speech and soft Discourse
Unending. . . .

G. H. VALLINS

The Curate to his Slippers

Take, oh take those boots away,
    That so nearly are outworn;
And those shoes remove, I pray –
    Pumps that but induce the corn!
But my slippers bring again,
      Bring again;
Works of love, but worked in vain,
      Worked in vain!

HORATIO SMITH

The Owl's Reply to Gray

Who, who has dared to treat us owls so ill?
(With us, of course it's U to use two whos)
To whomsoe'er it was, I take my quill
To twit him for his quite erroneous views.

Doubtless some elegiac poet grey,
Too witless and too wooden in the head
To understand a whit of what I say,
Has misconstrued my twilight serenade.

No, I did not complain, I'm not a grouse
(I do not give two hoots when I am blue)
You heard me call my love to share a mouse
For that's our owlish way, to wit, to woo.

F. SINCLAIR

From our Austerity Anthology

ELERGY W.I. A COUNTRY CHURCHYARD BY T. G.

The curfew t's the k. of parting day.
The village elders in the churchyard plot
Might have been famous men like (e.g.) Gray;
But famous people also die. So what?

JUSTIN RICHARDSON

Sonnet IV of the Amatory Poems of Abel Shufflebottom

I would I were that portly gentleman
With gold-laced hat and golden-headed cane,
Who hangs in Delia's parlour! But whene'er
From books or needlework her looks arise,
On him CONVERGE THE SUNBEAMS OF HER EYES
And he UNBLAMED may gaze upon MY FAIR,
And oft MY FAIR his FAVOUR'D form surveys.
O HAPPY PICTURE! still on HER to gaze;
I envy him! and jealous fear alarms,
Lest the STRONG *glance* of those *divinest* charms
WARM HIM TO LIFE, as in the ancient days,
When MARBLE MELTED in Pygmalion's arms.
I would I were that portly gentleman
With gold-laced hat and golden-headed cane.

ROBERT SOUTHEY

Brahma

If the wild bowler thinks he bowls,
   Or if the batsman thinks he's bowled,
They know not, poor misguided souls,
   They, too, shall perish unconsoled.
I am the batsman and the bat,
   I am the bowler and the ball,
The umpire, the pavilion cat,
   The roller, pitch, and stumps, and all.

ANDREW LANG

If thou wouldst visit fair Melrose aright,
Go visit it at pale moonlight.
If thou wouldst visit it awrong
Go visit it by charrybong.

ANON.

The Willow-Tree

Long by the willow-tree
  Vainly they sought her,
Wild rang the mother's screams
  O'er the gray water.
'Where is my lovely one?
  Where is my daughter?

'Rouse thee, sir constable —
  Rouse thee and look.
Fisherman, bring your net,
  Boatman, your hook;
Beat in the lily beds,
  Dive in the brook.'

Vainly the constable
  Shouted and called her;
Vainly the fisherman
  Beat the green alder;
Vainly he threw the net,
  Never it hauled her!

Mother beside the fire
  Sat, her night-cap in;
Father, in easy chair,
  Gloomily napping;
When at the window-sill
  Came a light tapping.

407

And a pale countenance
   Looked through the casement:
Loud beat the mother's heart,
   Sick with amazement,
And at the vision which
   Came to surprise her!
Shrieking in an agony –
   'Lor! it's Elizar!'

Yes, 'twas Elizabeth;
   Yes, 'twas their girl;
Pale was her cheek, and her
   Hair out of curl.
'Mother!' the loved one,
   Blushing, exclaimed,
'Let not your innocent
   Lizzy be blamed.

'Yesterday, going to Aunt
   Jones's to tea,
Mother, dear mother, I
   Forgot the door-key!
And as the night was cold,
   And the way steep,
Mrs Jones kept me to
   Breakfast and sleep.'

Whether her pa and ma
   Fully believed her,
That we shall never know;
   Stern they received her;
And for the work of that
   Cruel, though short night, –
Sent her to bed without
   Tea for a fortnight.

MORAL

Hey diddle diddlety,
    Cat and the fiddlety,
Maidens of England take
    Caution by she!
    Let love and suicide
    Never tempt you aside,
And always remember to take the door-key.

W. M. THACKERAY

The Heathen Pass-Ee

IN IMITATION OF BRET HARTE

Which I wish to remark,
    And my language is plain,
That for plots that are dark
    And not always in vain,
The heathen Pass-ee is peculiar,
    And the same I would rise to explain.

I would also premise
    That the term of Pass-ee
Most fitly applies,
    As you probably see,
To one whose vocation is passing
    The 'Ordinary B.A. degree'.

Tom Crib was his name.
    And I shall not deny
In regard to the same
    What the name might imply,
But his face it was trustful and childlike,
    And he had the most innocent eye.

Upon April the First
  The Little-Go fell,
And that was the worst
  Of the gentleman's sell,
For he fooled the Examining Body
  In a way I'm reluctant to tell.

The candidates came
  And Tom Crib soon appeared;
It was Euclid. The same
  Was 'the subject he feared',
But he smiled as he sat by the table
  With a smile that was wary and weird.

Yet he did what he could,
  And the papers he showed
Were remarkably good,
  And his countenance glowed
With pride when I met him soon after
  As he walked down the Trumpington Road.

We did not find him out,
  Which I bitterly grieve,
For I've not the least doubt
  That he'd placed up his sleeve
Mr Todhunter's excellent Euclid,
  The same with intent to deceive.

But I shall not forget
  How the next day at two
A stiff paper was set
  By Examiner U . . .
On Euripides' tragedy, Bacchae.
  A subject Tom 'partially knew'.

But the knowledge displayed
   By that heathen Pass-ee,
And the answers he made
   Were quite frightful to see,
For he rapidly floored the whole paper
   By about twenty minutes to three.

Then I looked up at U...
   And he gazed upon me.
I observed, 'This won't do.'
   He replied, 'Goodness me!
We are fooled by this artful young person,'
   And he sent for that heathen Pass-ee.

The scene that ensued
   Was disgraceful to view,
For the floor it was strewed
   With a tolerable few
Of the 'tips' that Tom Crib had been hiding
   For the 'subject he partially knew'.

On the cuff of his shirt
   He had managed to get
What we hoped had been dirt,
   But which proved, I regret,
To be notes on the rise of the Drama,
   A question invariably set.

In his various coats
   We proceeded to seek,
Where we found sundry notes
   And – with sorrow I speak –
One of Bohn's publications, so useful
   To the student of Latin or Greek.

In the crown of his cap
    Were the Furies and Fates,
And a delicate map
    Of the Dorian States,
And we found in his palms which were hollow,
    What are frequent in palms, – that is dates.

Which is why I remark,
    And my language is plain,
That for plots that are dark
    And not always in vain,
The heathen Pass-ee is peculiar,
    Which the same I am free to maintain.

A. C. HILTON

The Raven Replies to Poe

Charnel-minded Edgar Allan, surely you are nodding, shall an
Architect in planning put a lamp so far above the floor
As to shine down on a raven who has found a shaky haven
On the summit of a graven image higher than the door –
As to be above a bird above a bust above a door?
    They'd employ him nevermore!

It must make you even madder, Edgar, standing on your ladder,
When a visitor comes roaring in and flings you to the floor.
With your oil-can or your taper, you must cut a comic caper –
He'll suspect you are a japer lodging something on the door!
Oh, it's silly, Edgar, surely putting *props* above a door!
    Do not do it evermore!

J. A. LINDON

Alfred Lord Tennyson Forgets to Press Button B

'Button B. coins belong to P.M.G.' – Daily Paper

xxviii

I seized the dark machine, and spun
   With trembling hand the circle round,
   And listen'd; neither word nor sound
Was heard from Temple one two one.

Save, in the dark, a ghostly bell
   That echoed through the void of space,
   And measur'd, in that far-off place,
The beat of some vain sentinel.

You spoke not; in the mystic wire
   Nor wave, nor answering motion stirred;
   Within your silent room I heard
No voice to still my strong desire.

Shall we, I mused in sad despair,
   Who had sweet converse each with each
   And join'd in dear, familiar speech
Be sunder'd by the vacant air?

A keener sorrow fell; to me
   A sharper pain, beyond redress;
   Unthinking, I forgot to press
The secret spring of Button B.

Yet, if my wasted pledge should fall
   To him who rules both wire and post,
   'Tis better to have rung and lost
Than never to have rung at all.

G. H. VALLINS

In the Schools at Oxford

Butcher boys shouted without,
  – Within was writing for thee,
Shadows of three live men
  Talked as they walked into me,
Shadows of three live men and you were one of the three.

Butcher boys sang in the streets,
  The Bobby was far away,
Butcher boys shouted and sang
  In their usual maddening way.
Still in the Schools quite courteous you were torturing men all the
    day.

Two dead men I have known
  Examiners settled by me,
Two dead men I have scored,
  Now I will settle with thee.
Three dead men must I score, and thou art the last of the three.

ANON.

Disenchantment

He thought he saw Utopia
  As neatly planned as chess:
He looked again and saw it was
  Ubiquitous duress:
This does not gratify, he said,
  My bourgeois consciousness.

He thought he saw the truth of life
    As sex all unalloyed:
He looked again and saw it was
    A yarn of Sigmund Freud:
If this sprang from the *id*, he said,
    Its arguments are void.

He thought he saw full many a gem
    Of purest ray serene:
He looked again and saw it was
    A dose of Mescalin:
The price of visions is, he said,
    The headaches in between.

He thought he saw the Holy Ghost
    Lamenting in a mist:
He looked again and saw it was
    An existentialist:
It may be that he's right, he said,
    But what a pessimist.

He thought he saw some golden boys
    Our phoney world condemn:
He looked again and saw it was
    Some pimply A.Y.M.:
A dose of Epsom Salts, he said,
    Would ease the strain for them.

He thought he saw a projectile
    Descending from a height;
To blow the human race to bits
    And blast it out of sight:
He looked again and saw that he
    Was absolutely right.

KENNETH LILLINGTON

Octopus

IN IMITATION OF SWINBURNE

Strange beauty, eight-limbed and eight-handed,
    Whence camest to dazzle our eyes?
With thy bosom bespangled and banded
    With the hues of the seas and the skies;
Is thy home European or Asian,
    O mystica! monster marine?
Part molluscous and partly crustacean,
    Betwixt and between.

Wast thou born to the sound of sea-trumpets?
    Hast thou eaten and drunk to excess
Of the sponges – thy muffins and crumpets,
    Of the seaweed – thy mustard and cress?
Wast thou nurtured in caverns of coral,
    Remote from reproof or restraint?
Art thou innocent, art thou immoral,
    Sinburnian or Saint?

Lithe limbs, curling free, as a creeper
    That creeps in a desolate place,
To enrol and envelop the sleeper
    In a silent and stealthy embrace,
Cruel beak craning forward to bite us,
    Our juices to drain and to drink,
Or to whelm us in waves of Cocytus,
    Indelible ink!

O breast, that 'twere rapture to writhe on!
    O arms 'twere delicious to feel
Clinging close with the crush of the Python,
    When she maketh her murderous meal!
In thy eight-fold embraces enfolden,
    Let our empty existence escape;
Give us death that is glorious and golden,
    Crushed all out of shape!

Ah! thy red lips, lascivious and luscious,
    With death in their amorous kiss!
Cling round us, and clasp us, and crush us,
    With bitings of agonized bliss;
We are sick with the poison of pleasure,
    Dispense us the potion of pain;
Ope thy mouth to its uttermost measure
    And bite us again!

A. C. HILTON

A London Sparrow's

IF —

If you c'n keep alive when li'l bleeders
    Come arter y' wi' catapults an' stones;
If you c'n grow up unpertickler feeders,
    An' live on rubbidge, crumbs, an' 'addock bones;
If you c'n nest up in the bloomin' gutters,
    An' dodge the blinkin' tabby on the tiles;
Nip under wheels an' never git the flutters,
    Wear brahn an' no bright-coloured fevver-styles;
If you ain't blown b' nippers (Cor, I'd skin 'em!);
    Stop in y'r shells nah, warm-like, under me;
Yours is the eggs an' everyfink 'at's in 'em —
    An' when they 'atch, yor be cock-sparrers, see?

J. A. LINDON

In Memoriam

Here lies a woman, no man can deny it,
Who rests in peace although she lived unquiet,
Her husband prays you, if by her grave you walk
You gently tread, for if she wake she'll talk.

*

Here lies, cut down like unripe fruit,
The wife of Deacon Amos Shute.
She died of drinking too much coffee,
Anny Dominy, eighteen forty.

(FROM CONNECTICUT)

*

Reader, pass on! – don't waste your time
On bad biography and bitter rhyme;
For what I am, this cumbrous clay insures,
And what I was is no affair of yours.

*

Within this grave do lie,
Back to back, my wife and I;
When the last trump the air shall fill,
If she gets up, I'll just lie still.

*

Beneath this plain pine board is lying
   The body of Joshua Hight,
'Cheer up,' the parson told him, dying;
   'Your future's very bright.'

(AMERICAN)

*

Here lies the body of Mary Charlotte,
Born a virgin, died a harlot.
Until fifteen she kept her virginity,
Which is a record for this vicinity.

*

Poor Martha Snell, she's gone away,
She would if she could, but she couldn't stay;
She'd two bad legs and a baddish cough,
But her legs it was that carried her off.

*

Here lies one who for medicine would not give
A little gold, and so his life he lost:
I fancy now he'd wish again to live
Could he but guess how much his funeral cost.

*

'Parding, Mrs Harding,
Is my kitting in your kitching garding,
Gnawing of a mutting-bone?'
'No, he's gone to Londing.'
'How many miles to Londing?
Eleving? I thought it was only seving.
Heavings! what a long way from home!'

ANON.

Eighteenth-Century Epigrams

ADDRESSED TO A GENTLEMAN AT TABLE

WHO KEPT BOASTING OF THE COMPANY HE KEPT

What of lords with whom you've supped,
    And of dukes that you dined with yestreen!
A louse, sir, is still but a louse,
    Though it crawl on the locks of a queen.

ROBERT BURNS

ON THOMAS MOORE'S POEMS

Lallah Rookh
Is a naughty book
By Tommy Moore,
Who has written four,
Each warmer
Than the former.
So the most recent
Is the least decent.

SAMUEL ROGERS

My Bishop's eyes I've never seen
Though the light in them may shine;
For when he prays he closes his,
And when he preaches, mine.

ANON.

423

A Toast

Here's to a temperance supper,
   With water in glasses tall,
And coffee and tea to end with –
   And me not there at all!

ANON.

Predestination

We are the precious chosen few:
   Let all the rest be damned.
There's only room for one or two:
   We can't have Heaven crammed.

ANON.

Parson among the Pigeons

St Francis fed pigeons whenever he see 'em,
   But I saw a parson today
Who sat on the steps of the British Museum
   And frightened the pigeons away.

GEORGE MORROW

Quiet Fun

My son Augustus, in the street, one day,
  Was feeling quite exceptionally merry.
A stranger asked him: 'Can you tell me, pray,
  The quickest way to Brompton Cemetery?'
'The quickest way? You bet I can!' said Gus,
  And pushed the fellow underneath a bus.

*

Whatever people say about my son,
He does enjoy his little bit of fun.

HARRY GRAHAM

Indifference

When Grandmamma fell off the boat,
And couldn't swim (and wouldn't float),
Matilda just stood by and smiled.
I almost could have slapped the child.

HARRY GRAHAM

Late last night I slew my wife,
Stretched her on the parquet flooring.
I was loath to take her life,
But I had to stop her snoring.

HARRY GRAHAM

Horse Sense: a Triolet

Sir Alfred Munnings, P.R.A.,
Roundly condemns Matisse,
Who does not paint like (shall we say?)
Sir Alfred Munnings, P.R.A.,
In strong approval horses neigh:
Loud cackle human geese.
Sir Alfred Munnings, P.R.A.,
Roundly condemns Matisse.

ALLAN M. LAING

Toiling, rejoicing, sorrowing,
so I my life conduct.
Each morning see some job begun,
each evening see it chucked.

ANON.

Stag Night, Palaeolithic

Drink deep to Uncle Uglug,
That early heroic human,
The first to eat an oyster,
The first to marry a woman.

God's curse on him who murmurs
As the banquet waxes moister,
'Had he only eaten the woman,
Had he only married the oyster!'

OGDEN NASH

Sigmund Freud

Who's afreud of the big bad dream?
Things are never what they seem;
Daddy's bowler, Auntie's thimbles,
Actually are shocking symbols.
Still, I think, a pig's a pig –
Ah, there, symbol-minded Sig!

OGDEN NASH

Death

If Death were truly conquered, there would be
Too many great-great-great-great aunts to see.

L. E. JONES

The University Match

A thousand vicars prayed for a dry wicket;
When God sent rain they felt it wasn't cricket.

L. E. JONES

Gay birds

Cuckoos lead Bohemian lives,
They fail as husbands and as wives,
And so they cynically disparage
Everybody else's marriage.

ANON.

Translation from the Chinese

ANTHROPOMORPHIC

Even Jehovah
After Moses had got the Commandments
Committed to stone
Probably thought:
I always forget the things
I really intended to say.

CHRISTOPHER MORLEY

Sapphics

Exquisite torment, dainty Mrs Hargreaves
Trips down the High Street, slaying hearts a-plenty;
Stricken and doomed are all who meet her eye-shots!
   Bar Mr Hargreaves.

Grocers a-tremble bash their brassy scales down,
Careless of weight and hacking cheese regardless;
Postmen shoot letters in the nearest ashcan,
   Dogs dance in circles.

Leaving their meters, gas-inspectors gallop,
Water Board men cease cutting off the water;
Florists are strewing inexpensive posies
   In Beauty's pathway.

'O cruel fair!' groan butchers at their chopping,
'Vive la belle Hargreaves!' howls a pallid milkman;
Even the Vicar shades his eyes and mutters:
   '*O dea certe.*'

Back to 'Balmoral' trips the goddess lightly;
Night comes at length, and Mr Hargreaves with it,
Casting his bowler glumly on the sideboard:
   'Gimme my dinner.'

D. B. WYNDHAM LEWIS

Note on the Prevalence of Choristers

Nothing can glower
   Like a tourist throng
Trapped for an hour
   By Evensong.

PHYLLIS MCGINLEY

Epitaph

('Is your bed attractive? Buy Quillettes.' – *Advertisement*)

Now Poppy Pentonville is dead,
It can, indeed it should, be said:
She had a most attractive bed.

RICHARD USBORNE

Epitaph

ON A PARTY GIRL

Lovely Pamela, who found
One sure way to get around,
Goes to bed beneath this stone
Early, sober, and alone.

RICHARD USBORNE

On Growing Old

I hope I'll not be hairless
There's nothing I could bear less.
Disease of the follicle
Is diabollicle!

I. KENVYN EVANS

The Louse

The louse
Has very little 'nous',
It's only pursuit
Is the hirsute.

I. KENVYN EVANS

Vive le Roi

Grief at the Loved One's parting from this Life
Is doubled for the ill-provided Wife.
With more Philosophy the Widow bears
That Husband's Loss who leaves behind some Shares.
Life's Continuity demands this so:
The Breadwinner is dead – long live the Dough!

JUSTIN RICHARDSON

Lineage

His Family was very Old,
Hers Older still, they used to boast;
Yet when their child was born, I'm told,
It seemed about as young as most.

JUSTIN RICHARDSON

Limericks

There were once two young people of taste
Who were beautiful down to the waist;
   So they limited love
   To the regions above
And so remained perfectly chaste.

MONICA CURTIS

There was a young lady of Ryde,
Who ate some green apples and died.
   The apples fermented
   Inside the lamented,
And made cider inside her inside.

ANON.

There was a young girl of Madras
Who had the most beautiful ass,
   But not as you'd think
   Firm, round, and pink,
But grey, with long ears, and eats grass.

ANON.

Said a maid, 'I will marry for lucre,'
And her scandalized ma almost shucre.
   But when the chance came
   And she told the good dame,
I notice she didn't rebucre.

ANON.

There was a young lady of Tottenham,
Who'd no manners, or else she'd forgotten 'em;
    At tea at the vicar's
    She tore off her knickers
Because, she explained, she felt 'ot in 'em.

ANON.

There was an old man of Dunoon
Who always ate soup with a fork.
    For he said: 'As I eat
    Neither fish, fowl, nor flesh,
I should otherwise finish too quick.'

ANON.

There once was a person from Lyme
Who married three wives at a time.
    When asked, 'Why a third?'
    He replied, 'One's absurd,
And bigamy, sir, is a crime.'

ANON.

Five Clerihews

I am really rather annoyed
With Freud
For getting us all openly bumptious
About what had been secretly scrumptious.

One day Titian
Got into a somewhat equivocal position
When drawing from the nude.
She thought him just rude.

432

When Augustus John
Really did slap it on
His price was within 4d
Of Orpen's.

Henry Eight
Got up late.
Perhaps there was something to be said
For *his* staying in bed.

'Twas at Verona that Keats,
Finding strange company between the sheets,
To obviate future meetings
Invented Keatings.

EDMOND KAPP

And Two More

Watteau
Was painting a nymph in a grotto.
He put up a notice 'Défense de Toucher'
To warn off Boucher.

I. GRIFFITH FAIRFAX

Gilbert Scott
Might have been a lovesome thing, God wot,
If he had resisted the wiles
Of the manufacturers of encaustic tiles.

JOHN and ERNESTINE CARTER

The Higher Motive

'The lower classes are such fools
They waste their money on the pools.
I bet, of course, but that's misleading.
One must encourage bloodstock breeding.

BERNARD FERGUSSON

The old Feminist

Snugly upon the equal heights
    Enthroned at last where she belongs,
She takes no pleasure in her rights
    Who so enjoyed her wrongs.

PHYLLIS MCGINLEY

Eat slowly: only men in rags
And gluttons old in sin
Mistake themselves for carpet-bags
And tumble victuals in.

SIR WALTER RALEIGH

Health and Fitness

Bruised by the masseur's final whack,
The patient lay without a sound;
Then, coming to, he hit him back.
Now masseur's in the cold, cold ground.

J. B. MORTON

434

'Lord Stanley of Alderley wishes in future to be known by the title of his senior barony, Lord Sheffield.' – *The Times*

> Trusty as steel, more valuable than plate,
> Aspiring Sheffield knocked at Heaven's gate.
> Top Man, who reads *The Times*, pronounced his doom,
> Coldly remarking: 'Stanley, I presume?'

EVELYN WAUGH

Plain Murder

> I saw a wasp upon a wall
> And did not like his face at all:
> And so the creature had no time
> To wonder whether he liked mine.

A. G. PRYS-JONES

O (Modern) Helen!

> The face that could have launched a thousand ships
> And burnt the topless towers of Ilium
> Is happy, now, to feast on fish and chips
> With Harris, prior to the Odeon.

A. G. PRYS-JONES

Young Man of Porthcawl

> There was a young man of Porthcawl
> Who thought he was Samson or Saul:
> These thoughts so obscure
> Were due to the brewer,
> And not to his ego at all.

A. G. PRYS-JONES

INDEX OF POETS AND POEMS

INDEX

INDEX

INDEX

INDEX

INDEX

INDEX OF FIRST LINES

FOR THE BEST IN PAPERBACKS, LOOK FOR THE 🐧

In every corner of the world, on every subject under the sun, Penguin represents quality and variety – the very best in publishing today.

For complete information about books available from Penguin – including Pelicans, Puffins, Peregrines and Penguin Classics – and how to order them, write to us at the appropriate address below. Please note that for copyright reasons the selection of books varies from country to country.

In the United Kingdom: Please write to *Dept E.P., Penguin Books Ltd, Harmondsworth, Middlesex, UB7 0DA*

If you have any difficulty in obtaining a title, please send your order with the correct money, plus ten per cent for postage and packaging, to *PO Box No 11, West Drayton, Middlesex*

In the United States: Please write to *Dept BA, Penguin, 299 Murray Hill Parkway, East Rutherford, New Jersey 07073*

In Canada: Please write to *Penguin Books Canada Ltd, 2801 John Street, Markham, Ontario L3R 1B4*

In Australia: Please write to the *Marketing Department, Penguin Books Australia Ltd, P.O. Box 257, Ringwood, Victoria 3134*

In New Zealand: Please write to the *Marketing Department, Penguin Books (NZ) Ltd, Private Bag, Takapuna, Auckland 9*

In India: Please write to *Penguin Overseas Ltd, 706 Eros Apartments, 56 Nehru Place, New Delhi, 110019*

In Holland: Please write to *Penguin Books Nederland B.V., Postbus 195, NL–1380AD Weesp, Netherlands*

In Germany: Please write to *Penguin Books Ltd, Friedrichstrasse 10–12, D–6000 Frankfurt Main 1, Federal Republic of Germany*

In Spain: Please write to *Longman Penguin España, Calle San Nicolas 15, E–28013 Madrid, Spain*

In France: Please write to *Penguin Books Ltd, 39 Rue de Montmorency, F-75003, Paris, France*

In Japan: Please write to *Longman Penguin Japan Co Ltd, Yamaguchi Building, 2–12–9 Kanda Jimbocho, Chiyoda-Ku, Tokyo 101, Japan*

The Annotated Snark

Lewis Carroll

Edited by Martin Gardner

The inscrutable 'Snark'
leaves us all in the dark ...
It is psocial or filosofycle?
The dregs from the barrel
of *Alice's* Carroll?
Or a skit on the whole
business cycle?

Martin Gardner's advice
in his notes is concise.
(Once you've
purchased this volume, it's free.)
He reveals the whole core ...
but we mustn't say more,
for the Snark *was* a Boojum,
you see.

The Annotated Alice, Martin Gardner's
edition of the full text of
Lewis Carroll's two famous 'Alice' books,
is also published in Penguins.

Small Dreams of a Scorpion

Spike Milligan

They chop down 100ft trees
To make chairs
I bought one
I am six-foot one inch
When I sit in the chair
I'm four foot two
Did they really chop down a 100ft tree
To make me look shorter?

Here's a volume of Millipoems
on pollution, population and conversation
– serious subjects, overlaid
by the inimitable Milligan humour.

The Penguin Book of
Spanish Civil War Verse

Edited by Valentine Cunningham

This collection is the first comprehensive assembly of British poems (some never before published) which have to do with the Spanish Civil War. It includes also supporting prose reports and reviews by the poets, and a selection of poems – notably Spanish romanceros – in translation.

Some of this century's best-known literary figures – Auden, Spender, MacNeice and Orwell among them – are naturally represented, but the anthology also puts firmly on the map the work of several undeservedly neglected poets, such as Charles Donnelly, Clive Branson and Miles Tomalin.

In addition, the detailed and fascinating introduction is the first account of this war's relation to English literature that has been able to draw on the Archive of the International Brigade Association.

The Penguin Book of Hebrew Verse

Edited by T. Carmi

Hebrew poetry has been written virtually without interruption from biblical times to the present day, its centres spread through several continents. The result of many years of dedicated research by a poet and translator of international reputation, *The Penguin Book of Hebrew Verse* collects together for the first time the poetic riches from over three thousand years and presents the English translations alongside the Hebrew originals.

'A Book of Verses underneath the bough. . .'

The Penguin Book of Greek Verse

Edited by Constantine A. Trypanis

This selection of Greek verse in the original is the
first of its kind to be published in the English-
speaking world: it covers approximately three thousand
years – from Homer to the twentieth century.

The Penguin Book of English Verse

Edited by John Hayward

A choice of verse reflecting the richness and variety of
intellectual and emotional appeal made by the principal
poets – some 150 in all – who have written in English
throughout the four centuries dividing the first
Elizabethan age from the second.

The Penguin Book of Irish Verse

Introduced and edited by Brendan Kennelly

Brendan Kennelly explores the origins and development
of the Irish poetic tradition, tracing its growth to
show its tough capacity for survival despite long
silences and methodical oppression and indicating the directions
in which he believes it is likely to develop.

The Penguin Book of Turkish Verse

*Edited by Nermin Menemencioğlu in collaboration
with Fahir İz*

This anthology is the first published in the English-
speaking world to represent the whole span of Turkish
verse from the founding of the Ottoman Empire to the
present day.

*'Poetry . . . the opening and closing of a door,
leaving those who look through to guess about
what is seen during a moment . . .'*

The Penguin Book of Love Poetry

Introduced and edited by Jon Stallworthy

Set by theme rather than chronology, Jon Stallworthy's
delightful anthology explores men's and women's
changeless responses to the changeless changing seasons
of their hearts.

The Penguin Book of Ballads

Edited by Geoffrey Grigson

From both Britain and overseas, this rich and colourful
selection of traditional and modern ballads includes
stories of court, castle and manor, and themes of
social injustice, love and war.

The Penguin Book of
First World War Poetry

Edited by Jon Silkin

In this haunting collection of war poetry, poets who
were soldiers are joined by others like Kipling and
Hardy who were not combatants yet wrote poetry
concerned with the War.

'the priests of the invisible . . .'

Blaise Cendrars
Selected Poems

Translated by Peter Holden

Cendrars's poetry with its startling immediacy and intense visual quality made him a legendary underground figure in his lifetime.

Renga

A Chain of Poems by Octavio Paz, Jacques Roubaud, Edoardo Sanguineti, Charles Tomlinson

Based on the principle of the Japanese *renga* – a sequence of linked poems – this remarkable composition is the work of four poets of international stature.

Octavio Paz
Selected Poems

A bilingual edition, edited by Charles Tomlinson

A dazzling and mercurial writer equally at home with French Surrealism, American poetry, German Romanticism and Marxist polemic, Paz is clearly established as one of Latin America's greatest poets.

Gunter Grass
Selected Poems

Translated by Michael Hamburger and Christopher Middleton

A bilingual selection of his poetry 'exposing the false identities of modern man, the fragmentation of his world, his puzzlement, his littleness and his curious paradoxical courage in recognizing absurdity and facing it'.